Use the memes in this flow chart to determine:

Should I Read This Book???

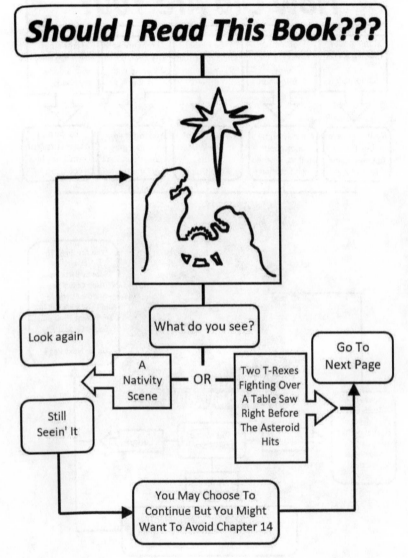

What do you see?

Look again

A Nativity Scene   —OR—   Two T-Rexes Fighting Over A Table Saw Right Before The Asteroid Hits

Go To Next Page

Still Seein' It

You May Choose To Continue But You Might Want To Avoid Chapter 14

How Old Are You?

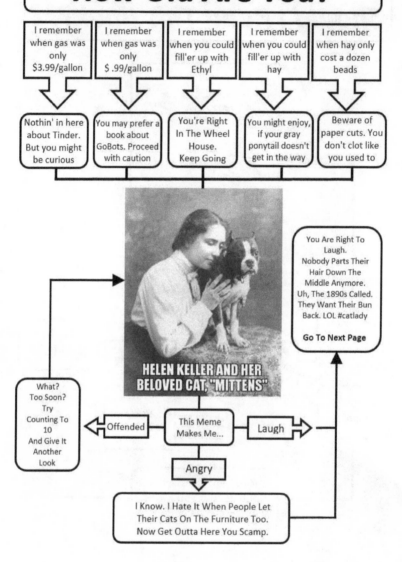

What Is Your Gender?

Male	Female	Seahorse	Not Sure

See Meme #3

See Meme #3

See Meme #3

See Meme #3

You are feminine, yet butch enough to fool a scientist

OR

You are butch, yet feminine enough to fool Ellen

OR

You Know Things About WWII Aircraft

You Have Chosen Poorly
Our Reccommendation:
Check outThe Onion, People of Walmart, or moveon.org

You have chosen wisely. Congratulations, and may God have mercy on your soul.For **You Should Read...**

(Turn The Page)

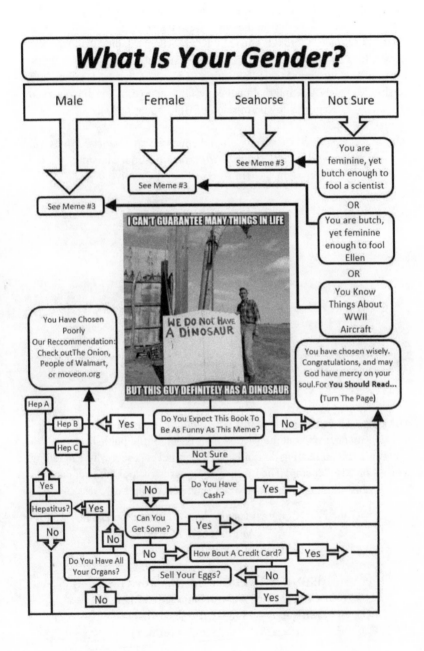

I CAN'T GUARANTEE MANY THINGS IN LIFE

WE DO NOT HAVE A DINOSAUR

BUT THIS GUY DEFINITELY HAS A DINOSAUR

Hep A

Hep B

Hep C

Yes

Hepatitus?

No

Yes

No

Yes

Do You Expect This Book To Be As Funny As This Meme?

No

Not Sure

No

Do You Have Cash?

Yes

Can You Get Some?

Yes

No

Do You Have All Your Organs?

No

How Bout A Credit Card?

Yes

Sell Your Eggs?

No

No

Yes

The author (That's me, SK Morton) gratefully acknowledges permission
to reprint the lyrics from the song:
Come On Eileen. Words & Music by Kevin Adams, James Paterson, and
Kevin Rowland, copyright ©1982 EMI Music Publishing Ltd. All rights
administered by Sony Music Publishing LLC, 424 Church St. Suite 1200,
Nashville, TN 37219. International copyright secured. All rights reserved.
Reprinted by permission of Hal Leonard LLC.

Out of the Mouths of Tweens, originally appeared on *I Believe It Was Me
Who Said..., a Blog for the Illiterate,* at skmorton.com,
copyright © 2014 by SK Morton Creative

Grandpa's Cheese
by
SK Morton
Copyright © 2021 SK Morton Creative, San Francisco, CA. USA

Library of Congress Cataloging-in-Publication Data
Morton, SK.
Grandpa's Cheese / SK Morton.
Humor anthology.
ISBN 978-1-7378526-0-5 (Hardcover)
Library of Congress Control Number: 2021917743
ISBN 978-1-7378526-1-2 (Paperback)
ISBN 978-1-7378526-2-9 (eBook)

Grandpa's Cheese

SK Morton

Dedicated to:

Jim J. &
Sandra Bullock

But really and truly dedicated to:

My Grandpa

Without whom this book might have been entitled:

Who's the Guy with the Parmesan,
And Why's He Kissing Grandma?

Table of Contents

Forward & Introduction 12

The Joy of Plagiarism...13

Section I: Excerpts from My Inevitable Autobiography........................17

Me: An Illustrated Guide..18

When Your Passport Photo Looks Like Erma Bombeck, It's Time to Go Home...27

It Was A Bloody Miracle...34

I Know Why the Caged Lion Paces and Eats Raw Meat.........................42

My Utopia...52

Section II: The Department of Better Understanding...........................60

Development and Integration of the Handshake...................................61

The Most Dangerous Game..69

But is Sasquatch Bilingual?...75

Sister Bertrille's Headgear and the Java Jive......................................83

Better To Remain Silent (Pt.1)..88

Come On Eileen (An assessment & Justification) 91

Those Who Fail Art History Are Doomed to Repeat It............................99

Ankh If You Love Isis...111

Section III: The Tragedy of Comedy...122

Waiter, There's a Flying Fish in my Primordial Soup............................123

A Night at the Theater...136

The Baggins Identity...152

Section IV: The Pen is Meta-ier 187

Out of the Mouths of Tweens 188

The Diary of John Dunbar, Volume II 190

Lost in Transmutation 197

Section V: Kids, Ask Your Parents 205

An Open Letter to the Producers of Monday Night Football 206

Soldiers Do It in Foxholes 209

Cup O'Noodles for the Impoverished Soul 211

Section VI: The New Classics 225

Requiem for a Liver Spot 226

If Looks Could Kill, I'd Buy You a Mirror 231

The Life & Times of Mother Goose 238

The Weaker Sex Opens Pickle Jars 243

Carl the Knight 247

Camel Clyde 256

A Forward Introduction:

Here…Drink this.

— *Bill Cosby*

The Joy of Plagiarism
Or
How I Improved Myself Through Literature
Or
A Little Disclaimer to Start Us Off

"The moon shone brilliantly that warm July evening. Edgar had wrapped the poor little cur in the blanket that mother had given him for the slumber party and was holding it close to his chest. He desperately rubbed its neck in the hopes of reviving the animal. Now he knew he'd have no choice but to explain where he'd been going each day after school. It wasn't that he had outgrown his comrades at the Y as much as he was drawn to the new aesthetic he'd recently discovered at the Westboro Baptist Church."

This, and many other stories, are not included in *GRANDPA'S CHEESE*, the latest and greatest literary work from Pulitzer Prize-vandalizing author, SK Morton. Some content has been excluded due to concerns over national security. Some because of discrepancies in peer review. (Often there was a lack of consensus between Sully, T-bone, Crazy Johnny, and Wheels.) Still more from lack of interest. But the lucky reader of this volume of essays, short stories, novellas, sketches for a new death star, and reams and reams of illegible drivel can be sure of one thing. Not one word is original.

I believe it was Stephen Ambrose who said, "To copy from one person is plagiarism. To copy from many people can be quite profitable." And it was Francis Bacon who said, "The paper is the greatest of listeners and the pen is the most able of story tellers. But that Stephen Ambrose really cheeses me off." To these two men I must offer my thanks. Were it not for their inability to capture my imagination, I may have never discovered the written works of Jack

Douglas, Woody Allen, or Niccolò Machiavelli. Each had his own style, phrasing, cadence, and, above all, font when humorously philosophizing on such universal frustrations as airline food. And were it not for *those* authors, I may have never learned how to pull off "clever" once I realized that women are not impressed by a guy's ability to cram three meatball sandwiches into his mouth at once.

When I first began courting my wife (we dated at first, but soon found it lacked the aura of sophistication one finds while courting) we spent untold hours discovering each other. She'd beguile me with delightful anecdotes of her misspent youth, while I countered with accounts of my own history, being careful to leave out any details that would damage her delicate sensibilities or violate my probation. Each of us with a thirst for the other's true self unquenched and unassuaged by a summer of unceasing companionship and private investigators with little to report. Then came the Fall.

There's a split second between contentment and discomfort when you realize that your butt's asleep. It's not enough to make you leap to your feet and dance the ancient Malaysian waltz of the cheeks to ward off pins and needles, but it could be a red flag. One becomes aware that there might be an issue in the future. My wife had a similar realization about my alleged wit not long into the relationship. Every funny thing that I'd ever heard and the two clever things I'd once thought had been used up in just a few precious months. I was empty.

Soon her understanding demeanor over my repeating myself evolved into semi-polite toleration, then overt eye rolling, open hostility, and, finally, violence. It seemed that my delightful and amusing stories had run their course. As had my delightful and amusing jokes and my delightful and amusing, tediously rehearsed, spontaneous anecdotes. Clearly, *she* had seen all of the same episodes of *M*A*S*H* that *I* had. It was the last time I made reference to "meatball surgery" that got me shivved.

By this time I was just spewing tired lines from novelty t-shirts and half gags interpreted from *New Yorker* cartoons. I simply wasn't funny enough to keep my beloved engaged. (Indeed, she broke off our engagement on several occasions, citing her husband's mixed feelings on the matter.) If I was going to hold on to this relationship, I was going to need to find some way of recharging my repertoire.

The answer, as seemed obvious to me, was to replicate the tried-and-true material of existing comedians. I'd simply watch more TV than is deemed safe by the Academy of Television Advertisers and regurgitate the product in a personal style that would allow for plausible deniability. Of course, I wouldn't want to be blatant about my methods. That would not only show a brazen disrespect for my consultants but also might out me prematurely. To this end, I devoured reruns of 1970s game shows and a lot of British sitcoms on PBS. (This also served to inform the dead pan delivery that destroyed my pediatric dental practice.)

At first, all seemed to go well. I was able to keep the ruse going into the first few years of marriage. Sure, every once in a while, I'd overuse a zinger from a bootlegged Judy Tenuta tape, but I was usually able to recover with a quick, "Ju look Mahvelous." However, after a while, I started to believe that I really had a gift. And then we got cable...

The problem was, like many unoriginal men of my height and weight, I'd carefully crafted the art of stealing jokes so well that it had become a crutch. I was able to lean on it, use it to trip my friends, and ultimately donate it to Goodwill.

Instead of making changes, I doubled down and began to rationalize my addiction. It wasn't like I was the first to borrow somebody else's ideas. I believe it was Harold Stravinsky who said, "All the best ideas are stolen." For which his brother Igor promptly took the credit. I thought to myself, everybody steals. Think of Elvis, Marconi, and Steve Jobs. And do you really think Hitler came up with the plan to invade Poland on his own? He totally got the idea from Shirley Temple.

Of course, not everything I say is somebody else's. Often times my apologies are sincere. And many of the stories found in this anthology are directly out of my own experiences. (Like the time my father Atticus defended a man on trial for rape.) And as much as I carefully monitor the frequency of which I dole out whimsical ditties from Mark Russell specials, my personal musings tend to fly free and wild. (Like Ric Flair's pecs. And they can be just as devastating.) On several occasions I almost got into accidents as I pointed out locations around town where family members were born or wed or died or arraigned. My wife and children became very familiar with these accounts and learned to tune them out while still pacifying my need to educate and entertain. The good news is that, even though I'd been repeating many of these stories for years, most have no real point and they've never actually been very funny. In fact, rather than viewing this tome as literature, it might be a good idea to see it as a chore.

Some of these stories might not be completely original. I guess the real question is: Is it really stealing if you don't remember that you stole it? I didn't know where a lot of my stuff had come from. (Fortunately, antibiotics did the trick.) I'd be telling some stories that I thought were mine for years, and then one day I'm watching Telemundo and bang – "the chocolate baby sketch! Oh yeah!"

Here's an idea. Make a game out of it. See if you can identify which parts of the book are lifted and then name the original author. Bonus points if you can guess where *they* got it. Then send me the results with your entrance fee. I'd love to know where I came up with this stuff.

Ultimately, there really is nothing new under the sun. History repeats itself. Seasons change. Wherever you go there you are. This too shall pass. And *no one*, especially my wife, wants to hear, over and over again, where my grandpa bought his cheese.

Section I:
Excerpts from My Inevitable Autobiography

I believe it was Woody Allen who said, "I'm not trying to achieve immortality through my work. I'm trying to achieve it through not dying."

It's not that fame eludes me; it's that fame and I simply don't care to meet. I've never considered writing to be a path to fame and fortune. I've always seen it as a way to justify the rent on my office to my wife. Besides, I'm so much more than a writer. I also enjoy juice and sugary breakfast cereals. I'm an ice cream connoisseur. I fancy a value meal at Wendy's every now and again. And I have a lovely recipe for Mom's Lemon Lush pie. Essentially, I'm morbidly heterogeneous. As someone with so much to give, doesn't a memoir seem apropos?

"Why, yes it does," says the man on the street.

"Well, you're in luck," is what's heard coming from the gutter by an overweight gentleman with KFC grease on his keyboard. "Just sit back and I'll tell you stories of my life that'll have you grinnin' like a possum at Disneyland...are you gonna eat that possum?"

Me: An Illustrated Guide

I'm me. There's no one like me. Except Barry. He's just like me. Only different. His legs are shorter than mine. I think he might just be wearing his pants lower than me. Maybe he's the shizzle. I can't be sure because I've never met the shizzle…that I'm aware of. Could you imagine if Barry *were* the shizzle? Here we are. Two guys. One just like the other. And secretly, one is the shizzle. Really makes you think.

Before I met Barry, I was still me. In fact, I've been me my whole life. Even before the FBI told our neighbors I was. When I was just a little me, I enjoyed playing with my blocks and my dad's rifles.

18

Even before I was a little me, I was a microscopic me. You might say I was *me*croscopic. Of course, if you said that nobody would think it was clever. Try a*me*ba instead.

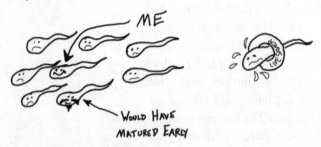

I was the best swimmer in my class

My parents shook me.

I have two brothers. My older brother loved airplanes, so he became a pilot. My younger brother loved horses, so he became a girl. I loved Miss Mary Anne, Karen Valentine, Valerie Bertonelli, and Patty Hearst so I became a defendant. Finally, it was decided that I was a minor.

19

For fun, I ran with scissors. My mother said, "No running with scissors!" For fun, my older brother liked to push me down and sit on me. He called it football. When my younger brother was old enough, I tried to play football with *him*. My mother said, "No playing football!" and chased me with scissors. For fun, my younger brother just stared at cheese. My mother said, "No heroine in the living room!"

I was five years old when I first heard *Jailhouse Rock* at a party. I thought Elvis was great. That night my mom pulled out all of her old 45s to play them and *she* thought Elvis was great. My grandparents went to see him in Vegas that year and *they* thought Elvis was great. My dad thought he was gay. Of course, my dad, pretty much, thought everybody was gay…except Jim Nabors. He thought Jim Nabors was *extraordinarily* gay.

I had a crush on my kindergarten teacher because she had long hair. She said she wasn't interested because she could never respect somebody who couldn't color inside the lines. I'm over her…tramp.

I love the flavors grape, chocolate, and bleu cheese. Tuna goes with none of these.

When I was young, it was very important to me that my hair look good. To this end I used a lot of Aqua Net. I am sorry about your skin cancer.

I met my wife when I was ten years old. She was also under the age of consent. I waited to get older so that I could marry her. She killed the time by dating all of my friends in high school.

No Talent Required   SK Morton

I was the most average student in my class. My teachers felt that, if I applied myself, I could have 1.85 children, or drive a Taurus, or be Steve in accounting. But I showed them. I wrote a song called *Sussudio*.

When it came time to find employment, I became a carpenter. I started out as an *apprentice* carpenter because I didn't understand economic theory and how it relates to illegal immigration and a really cherry '57 Bel Air wagon. Now I know how to hang doors *and* get the Led out.

I have many interests: I like playing music. I like building things. I like Disneyland. I like sports. I wet the bed. I enjoy cooking. I love animals. I SCUBA dive. I have recurring bouts of ring worm. I have an IQ of 139. I love movies. I have run triathlons. I hate the infidel but I love sailing. I sometimes say too much.

Before long I had a family of my own. This can be verified by the back window of our minivan.

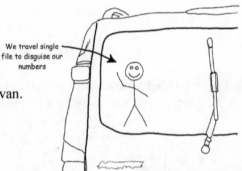

We travel single file to disguise our numbers

When my first son was born, I was happy and scared. Happy because he was healthy and cute and would make a fine tax deduction, but scared because he only fit in onesies sized evil.

When my second son was born, I was happy and scared. Happy because he was healthy and cute and would make a fine pet for his older brother, but scared because my wife slept in a hockey mask and a butcher's smock.

DEAR, I'M NOT VERY COMFORTABLE WITH YOUR NEW CPAP

NINE MONTHS! NINE MONTHS I HAD TO LISTEN TO YOU CHEW!

23

I'm 6'-3" and very white. I can't wear any olive-green clothing because, with my short haircut, I look like Fidel Castro had an affirmative action program.

I once took a Facebook quiz to find out which animal lives in me. I got a sloth. Not something I'm proud of, but at least I'm not Richard Gere.

I've cleaned an unloaded gun five times without shooting myself. That's a 63% success rate!

I've done a lot of research for our upcoming dystopian world by watching movies about the post-apocalypse. I'm kind of worried because I don't own any shoulder pads.

I have lived in 20 different houses in 6 different cities...wait...no, 7...no, 6. (Is San Quentin a city?) I've owned 31 different cars, and had 19 different employers. Someday I hope to have a bank account.

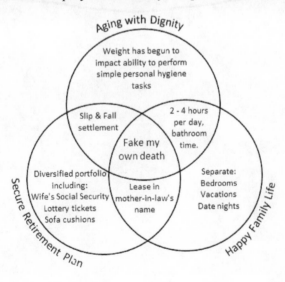

I started writing these stories in 1994. My children were in diapers. Here I am today, in my garden, frightening my grandchildren with orange wedges. I hope somebody finds these pages and finishes them when I'm gone. Or at least straightens up the den.

THAT WAS
AWKWARD

When Your Passport Photo Looks Like Erma Bombeck, It's Time to Go Home

I believe it was Wiley Post who said, "I never met a man I didn't like ... except Will Rogers." True, living for adventure can result in what many would term a life well-lived, but it can also bring quite a bit of regret. As in the case of that astronaut with the diapers. Is any man really worth a rash?

The day I was married was the happiest day of my life when compared to other happy days. Such as when my parents finally found me again at the zoo. Or when the biopsy came back negative. Or when it turned out my son wasn't on drugs but merely concussed.

The ceremony was a modest affair with albino peacocks, armored elephants, and the cast of Cirque de Soleil – *Protuberance*. There were 800 people on the guest list but only eleven were able to attend as the rest raced down to the seashore to witness an oncoming tsunami in person. The justice of the peace arrived fashionably latent, having just returned that morning from a trip to Bangkok. A lot went wrong but the only thing I remember clearly was my bride. She was dressed in a taffeta poncho with her hair pulled back in a pork bun - I cried when I first laid eyes on her.

We spent our first night in a cute little bungalow in the wine country – emphasis on "country." It had a welcoming rusted-out Studebaker flowerbed in the yard, plush terry cloth overalls for lounging around the septic tank, indoor hot and cold running chickens, and complimentary sun tea in those quaint little mason jars. (Though the tea was a little salty.) It was everything one could want from a honeymoon on my salary. We had arrived late in the evening owing to a misunderstanding between me and the management of the reception over who would be responsible for fire suppression. It was about midnight when we checked in. I thought it would be a charming gesture to carry my beloved over the threshold but, in the dark, it was pretty difficult to find the doorknob, so I ended up using her more like a battering ram. It was kinky, but effective.

Unfortunately, we were married in August, which meant that the conspicuous lack of air conditioning in our lean-to had some negative impact on the romance. I tried to make the best of it by playing up the weight loss value of saunas – to which my bride countered with a display of frigidity. On the brighter than we'd like side, we had left the cake top in the car overnight and the greenhouse effect left a nice, tie-dyed icing veneer over the back seat. We won for best interior three years in a row at the Pebble Beach Concours d'Elegance until someone left a fingerprint in the armrest.

We awoke the next morning to the sound of *Dueling Banjos*. We had intended to explore the grounds before leaving for the next leg of our journey, but the heat coupled with the constant scratching of our opossum bites (I had wondered what that netting was for) made the hike unbearable. After an uneasy breakfast of fauxtmeal
with Triscuits and gravy, we ended up absquatulating…we evacuated…made tracks…burst out…high tailed it…pushed on…cut & run. That is, we departed.

When we originally discussed what we should do for our honeymoon, my wife mentioned that she'd love to go camping. I thought that sounded like a lovely and cost-effective idea. We settled on Yosemite as our destination and an amicable division of property afterward. Now that our first night of bliss was out of the way, a few days in such a tranquil setting seemed to be a great way to live test our marriage bonds among the vacationing public.

On our way to nature's wonderland, we would be passing through town so we thought we'd stop in to replenish our supplies (camping gear, clean underwear, cyanide capsules, etc.) and to check in on my new sister-in-law, who would be house sitting while we were away. Or she *would* be house sitting, except that got in the way of her house disheveling. I can understand pizza on the ceiling. We've all gotten a little too excited when there's a free HBO preview weekend. And one can even make an argument for using the bath towels as puppy tourniquets. You look away for a second and the dog decides the food processor would be faster than safety scissors. The problem I had was her rooting through the wedding gifts. Not only had she left ripped-opened boxes all over the apartment, but she took all of the good stuff. She pilfered everything but the Emmett Kelly make-up set and a pewter garden statue of a fairy with broken stained-glass wings and what looked like a scar from a botched C-section. I stood there in the midst of the carnage for a long while, just taking it in. Wondering what sort of Cretan would think it acceptable to swipe a singing bass? I gathered up my things (being careful to leave the cyanide capsules next to the Evian) and we resumed our trip.

Before entering Yosemite proper, I thought we'd visit the charming little towns just outside the boundary of the park. That night we stayed in a lovely little motel in downtown Stepford. When we walked into the dining room, we were greeted by alternating looks of distrust and agitation. We got as far as the appetizers before the mayor had put together an investigative panel to find out if we were Democrats or Americans. The commission came back with a verdict of, "city folk, but legal." We opted to take the rest of the meal in our room which, judging by the confined quarters, had been converted from a Fisher Price play farm. There was even an audible "moo" when you opened the bathroom door.

The next day we thought we'd give fun and adventure one more try. Northwest of Yosemite is the former boomtown* of Columbia. It was founded in 1850 during the Gold Rush and features the largest single collection of, still operating, Gold Rush-era structures in California. Occupants dress in mid-19th century attire and, since automobiles aren't allowed, stagecoaches run up and down Main Street. The town has a working blacksmith shop (an art which has

---

*A boomtown is a community that undergoes sudden and rapid growth typically characterized by inadequate medical and/or educational facilities, sewage disposal problems, and a scarcity of goods and services. In California, these places are known as "get-a-way" destinations where city residents go to get a reprieve from their home's inadequate medical and/or educational facilities, sewage disposal problems, and scarcity of goods and services. Boomtowns rarely have a Starbucks or an Apple Genius Bar and are also known as "ghost towns."

rightfully been lost to time), a gold panning exhibit (because a vacation just isn't a vacation without a little unrequited drudgery), and locally made sarsaparilla. (Once thought to cure rheumatic fever, now believed by science to be best used for penance.)

The center piece of the town is the beautiful, 170-year-old, Columbia City Hotel. Elegantly appointed with Victorian antiques and custom-crafted wall coverings. The only downside, we discovered, was the similarity, in name, to the Columbia Hotel which was neither a hotel (*Motel* was even a little too charitable for this dump), nor in the town of Columbia. Court appointed with antique toiletries and custom whittled bars on the windows, we made the best of it.

That night was uneventful. (She had a headache.) But the next morning was packed with excitement as the chambermaid got to work waking the guests before the rooster had a chance. It was about 6:00 a.m. when I awoke to the sound of keys jiggling in the doorknob. Seconds later my wife awoke to the sound of me smashing my head into the ceiling light as I rushed to apprehend the terrorist who'd shrewdly disguised himself with a grey maternity smock, a black brother Theodore wig, and several coats of Aromatics by Clinique. After an animated discussion about practical work schedules and appropriate wait times following low decibel knocking, all parties withdrew to their respective corners and dusted the baseboard.

We were now very much looking forward to our time in the great outdoors. Of course, everyone always assumes the outdoors will be great (except for those forward-thinking agoraphobics). But the summer often brings a glut of outdoors enjoyers, which necessitates a prompt arrival for one's particular claim of outdoorsness. This can be difficult when you drive a '79 Pontiac Le Mans.

The first time we broke down it was novel, and we had a little fun with it. We took pictures of each other with the hood up and one foot on the bumper, as if we were rich dentists with high-powered rifles. A little time to cool down and some water in the radiator and we were on our way again.

The second breakdown was a little more serious. I had discovered that the electric fuel pump was going out. But it still wasn't the end of the world. I soon developed a technique that allowed us to keep moving. As long as I paid attention to how much gas I was giving it and concentrated on the RPMs (Recriminations Post Marriage). It was arduous but we'd be in good shape as long as a bee didn't fly into the car and cause my bride to twist off in a panic as if she were in danger of being stung by an Africanized Apache helicopter. And wouldn't you know it, that's exactly what happened. I was forced to pull over, which killed the engine, and then *I* got stung, which killed the bee. The silver lining is that I now know that I'm deathly allergic to bee stings. Thanks sweetie.

After some more staring under the hood and checking to make sure all of the easily-reached hoses were still connected to their appropriate thingies, we were on our way once more. This time it was downhill so we were able, more or less, to coast into the one repair shop they have in the valley. Shifty Mikes specialized in transmissions but could probably dig up a new fuel pump and let me have it for the steal price of $600.00. (I believe Mike was a little fuzzy on who should be doing the stealing in that transaction.)

Considering that we were now on the valley floor and could use the park's public transit, I opted out of the hosing and decided we'd take our chances with Newton's fourth law of desperation on the way home. Unfortunately, the whole ordeal had put us way past our scheduled arrival time to claim our camp spot. We were informed that a group of mayfly researchers were using the space and that we could come back in 24 hours. Our first night in Yosemite would be spent in the car. Both of us at first, but then, after realizing that comfort was a dish best served warm and cozy without snoring or shifting by one's partner, I was relegated to keeping watch outside the vehicle. Asphalt is good for the back anyway.

My wake-up call was a gentle prod from the jackboot of a park ranger about 5:00 am. I felt like the knee on my neck was a little severe, but the eventual sniffing salts turned out to be an invigorating way to greet the day. Turns out that it wasn't legal to sleep on the side of the road in a national park. After a good talking to and an enthusiastic frisk goodbye, we were finally able to get into the campground about 8:30 that morning.

The relief of finally getting to set up camp quickly turned to confusion. We had borrowed a cozy little two-person tent from a friend. Turns out that it wasn't a two-person tent and he wasn't much of a friend. One might think that the compact nature of a *one*-person tent would lend itself nicely to a honeymoon, but I think the one person it was designed for may have been a munchkin. In the middle of that first night a bug crawled in and we drew straws to see who would sleep outside. I think the bug cheated. And he tried to spoon me.

When we did get to explore what the park had to offer, we had a wonderful time. We visited Half Dome (we could only afford the half) and Bridal Veil, Wapama and Vernal Falls (These were beautiful and graceful falls. Not like when you see an old person go down.) Of course the highlight was El Capitan. This 3000-foot wall of granite was first scaled in 1958 by climber Warren *J.* Harding – no relation to the president, Warren G. Harding who wouldn't make the ascent until 1963.

Finally, it was time to go home. The car was as we had left it – an eyesore, rejected by polite society. We knew that we wouldn't be able to make any stops on the way home, so we found a co-signer and filled up in the valley. We were making good time and had gone quite a while without any problems when the wife decided she had to go. I was kind of hoping she meant she was leaving me but no such luck. I was going to be expected to stop the car. We compromised. I slowed enough for her to jump out near some bushes as I drove a little farther up the road, did a U-turn, and intercepted her at just the right time. The highlight of the trip.

We did break down one more time when we got lost in Oakland, but we got through it fine and I've since been jumped out.

We didn't dare take another trip until after both of our children were born. Their first trip was to Disneyland. We thought it would be best to surprise them and not tell them where we were going. We knew that if we did, we'd spend the whole seven hours in the car being interrupted (during our arguments) with, "Are we at Disneyland yet!?!" Instead, we simply told them that we were going to spend the night in a hotel. "Are we at the hotel yet!?!" seemed less irksome.

It Was A Bloody Miracle

I believe it was the Marquis de Sade who said, "Childbirth is a beautiful thing." Now I tend to differ with that plucky libertine's assertion. Although the act of bringing another life into the world may be a miracle, brother, it aint pretty.

As a young newlywed male, the only real interest I'd shown in parenthood was the *how* portion of the equation. I'd taken to this avenue of study with the zeal of a vegan, CrossFit, suicide bomber. My wife, on the other hand, came at the subject with a decidedly more 'ends justify the means' approach. She had wanted a child since devouring her twin in the womb, and she certainly wasn't going to waste her fruitful years in our studio lean-to with just some libidinous ape to keep her company. It wasn't that we'd never discussed having children, it was just that I hadn't grown up with cable and what she had to say about kids wasn't as compelling as *Beast Master*.

Ultimately, she got her way…and I got mine. All I had to do was take out the garbage first. We chose natural conception. And that rhythm method worked like a charm. No sooner had we become accustomed to fish filets on payday than the African clawed frog died. (Actually, the frog *didn't* die because *this* pregnancy test, unlike the traditional "Rabbit Test" where they cut open the rabbit to see if its ovaries are enlarged, using an African clawed frog does not necessitate the dissecting of the animal. Apparently, these little trollops will show you their ovaries with no qualms.) Of course, that was just to verify what we had already suspected by using a home pregnancy test. My wife simply had to hold a stick into her morning urine (Mid-day or afternoon urine lacked ambition.) If the stick turned blue, she was pregnant. If it was red, she wasn't. It was purple…to the frog!

Our change in familial circumstances also required some life adjustments. The first was that we had to move (Otherwise our muscles would atrophy.) Our landlord told us that the lease only allowed for two people to muddle in the apartment. We found out later that that policy was discriminatory and illegal but by this time we'd already stolen the fixtures. We ended up moving into a creepy old apartment above a haunted garage which had been built over an Indian grave site where the natives had broken mirrors that had been peed on by a black cat – but the place had great Feng-shui.

Since we were quickly approaching what would be one of San Francisco's coldest winters on record (Mark Twain had to break out his summer wear), we were a little concerned that the gaps under the doors might technically designate the structure as open air. And while the woodland creatures provided a certain diversion, the frolicking musical numbers tended to keep us awake. As the winter went on we resorted to sleeping fully clothed. My wife in layers from long johns under sweats under a maternity dress under a full-length coat with gloves and a scarf. Not to be outdone I wore a three-piece suit and a top hat. During her semi-hourly potty adventures, I'd be awakened by, what sounded like, a cock fight coming from the bathroom when *her* seat made contact with *the* seat (You ladies just don't know how hard we have it during pregnancy). We eventually figured out how to make it through the deep freeze. We pushed the sofa up against the wall heater and then set it on fire. It was around this time that my wife first started experiencing what's known as Braxton-Hicks contractions. These are painless, irregular contractions that tell you if you're an intuitive thinker or a feeling extravert.

In the meantime, we attended Lamaze classes, the goal of which was to build the mother's confidence by showing her how to cope with pain through relaxation techniques, massage, and ice chips – Jell-O for the father. The technique applies six points of practice:

1. Let labor begin on its own. Happy employees with a certain degree of autonomy are more productive.

2. Walk, move around, & change positions throughout labor. My wife would take to this principle immediately. She wandered off several times during labor and for a short while I thought my child might be born at a dog track. Fortunately, she hit the trifecta in the 1st, and we were able to get her back to the hospital in time.

3. Bring a loved one, friend, or doula for continuous support. Now call me old fashioned, but I thought that's what maternity bras were for. There was no need to bring in this doula fella. I was informed that a doula's role is to help the mother feel safe and comfortable but that didn't explain why this guy took a hit of Binaca before introducing himself…and his name wasn't even Doula.

4. Avoid interventions that are not medically necessary. This could take the form of pain medications, restrictions on eating or drinking, teeth whitening, weaves, or that thing where the family gets together and tells you how you've hurt them.

5. Avoid giving birth on your back and follow your body's urges to push. Now this one I didn't get. Why would the mother be assigned a bed if she wasn't going to be on her back? I guess she could lie on her stomach but, aside from the baby yelling for a shutdown of all garbage mashers on the detention level, they'd also have to redesign those stirrups.

6. Keep the mother & baby together – it's best for both and for breastfeeding. I'd go a step further and say, for breastfeeding, it's absolutely *essential* that mother and baby be together.

Through all the classes I kept getting the feeling that the teacher's real purpose was to try to get us excited for something we really didn't want to do. At the ending of each session she'd hand out silk scarves, pass around a bottle of sake and yell, "Banzai!"

It was a lazy weekend when it all started. I was still in bed and my wife was taking a shower when her water broke (How'd she know?) We'd just moved from the hovel on haunted hill to a new townhouse a few weeks prior and I was enjoying the luxury of sleeping in without being disturbed by howling wind or foraging raccoons. My wife thoughtfully woke me by preparing my favorite breakfast and then throwing it at me. The contractions were something, something apart. I couldn't really hear her; I was looking for bacon under the bed when she was talking.

We had prepared for this. The bag had been prepacked with a few changes of clothes (loose fitting), sanitary pads (not as loose fitting), diapers (I got the Depends family pack), a baby blanket (handmade from burlap we picked up during a romantic trip to Idaho), some reading material and soothing music. Naturally, several weeks earlier, the bag had been plundered for her favorite sweatpants, CDs, and burlap while watching Martha Stewart make a jewel case bird feeder for the garden. With little time to waste, I had to improvise. Admittedly I had left out a few important items but, at the end of the day, doesn't a red nightie help a new mother to feel like she's still attractive and, therefore, valuable? And, let's be honest, would you rather listen to Kenny G or play Zelda? That nurse was a killjoy.

We lived about 45 minutes from the hospital meaning we were about 45 minutes late leaving the house. Fortunately, much of the ride was freeway driving. *Un*fortunately, my vehicle wasn't what one would term as freeway ready. I was regularly lapped by the Amish. The silver lining was that we had plenty of time to take in the full nuance of each billboard as we motored by at a pace not exceeding the speed limit of any neighborhood where blind children play. There were plenty of signs for injury attorneys. What impressed me was the specificity. There were ads for motorcycle attorneys, truck attorneys, *monster* truck attorneys, monster *attack* attorneys, mesothelioma attorneys, mesothelioma attorneys specializing in loved ones, horse attorneys, velvety toned attorneys, Indian Affairs attorneys, attorneys for other groups who've had affairs, marine attorneys, and air force attorneys. There was even an ad for a cryptography lawyer whose phone number included Coptic characters and Sanskrit (Or it was a coming attractions poster for *Sneakers.* Either way it was right before the ad for chiropractor, Dr. Hammer, which signaled our exit.)

When we arrived at the hospital I was, admittedly, in a bit of a panic. But as we pulled up, we were pleasantly surprised to see the nurses hurriedly making their way toward us. Then our delight turned to disappointment when they ignored my wife completely and focused all their attention on trying to dislodge some poor schmo in a cast from the grill of my car. At a moment of their inattention I pried the wheelchair out from under the fender and whisked my wife away to the maternity ward.

After settling in, she asked if *she* could use the bed. Being a loving husband, I eventually capitulated and went to find some Jell-O. When I returned, I discovered that our birthing team had traded up for draft picks and I was now subordinate to my mother-in-law. I had gotten along with her fine up until this point, but now I was seeing a side of her that spooked me – her homicide. Nothing in the room was right and *I* was the reason. If the room was too cold, she'd point at me and blame, "…that one." If the room was too hot, she'd question the species of my mother. When the room was too just right, she called INS and told them that I was a Guatemalan, albino, peeping tom with gigantism. As the contractions started coming more often, and with greater severity, her dubiety about my coaching ability became more and more overt until, finally, I was called into George Steinbrenner's office. A lesser man would have buckled. I don't know what a better man would have done. I fell asleep rubbing my wife's feet – the straw that stirs the drink, as it were.

When I awoke, the squad had filled out nicely. Now my own mother had arrived, followed closely by my sister-in-law, my wife's best friend (her own newborn in hand), my best friend's *father* (Camcorder in *both* hands), the scarecrow and tin man, and the midwife, Gina. Gina, incidentally, was fantastic and I have nothing but good things to say about her – even though I think she was Irish. (One of the good ones)

As her labor progressed, my wife's demeanor moved from excitedly expectant to cautiously optimistic to anxiously pessimistic, then optimistically anxious, then *anxiously* anxious, and finally, henceforth celibate. It was the 16th hour of labor and the idea of delivering the baby without drugs was wearing thin. By the 20th hour it was unthinkable. And by hour 24, she burner phoned some cagey acting Costa Rican guy with a fanny pack. Finally, it was decided that she'd have an epidural. An epidural is a system of pain relief where an anesthesiologist inserts a needle into the patient's back. Anesthesiologists are pain relief doctors who tortured animals when they were children. When the needle is inserted one can hear a distinct popping like that of bubble wrap being injected with a needle by a person who tortured animals when they were children. Despite this barbaric procedure, my wife was quite happy with the pain-alleviating result and gave the rest of us a break from her incessant anguish.

The last couple of hours were when things really started to get intense. She was 100% dilated and had to wear those weird sunglasses. She had been fully effaced for a while and, I'm sure, that made her feel insecure. It also didn't help that they were saying our baby was in zero station (as if my meager salary was any of their business).

As the contractions intensified so did the distractions. My mom-in-martial-law stepped up her tactics utilizing secret police and paramilitary organizations to keep my wife's breathing at "he, hoo, he, hoo." Several cameras were snapping pictures in the vicinity of my wife's lower portion while different medical specialists shouted directions. It was as if I were at a press conference outside a collapsed coal mine. Other friends and relatives were crammed into one side of the room offering their versions of advice:

"Save the placenta!"

"Boil some water!"

"Get some blankets!'

"No! Boil some blankets and get some water"

"Forget the water! Get ice chips!"

"Boil the ice chips and light the blankets on fire!"

"No! We need the blankets for a fort!"

"Yes! We need a fort!"

"Why do we need a fort?"

"To hide the ice chips."

"Good thinking. And raise the mizzenmast!"

"We're out of mizzen!"

"Then use the blankets!"

"Good god man! I said to boil the blankets!"

"Then use the placenta!"

"How many placentas to a mizzen?"

"Six I think."

"No! Seven!"

"You don't know. Just go back to boiling your blankets"

"I do too know. My dad used to work for the CIA."

"Is it six or seven?"

"Call the CIA."

"What's the number?"

"Six."

"Now don't start that again!"

"Forget it guys. They took a pillow to put behind her back and the fort collapsed."

"Save the ice chips!"

I have to admit that I was pretty shaken seeing my mate in such pain. Her forehead dripping with sweat. Her teeth clenched in agony. Her hand clutching mine in a death grip. Definitely. Not. Sexy.

In hour 32 of labor, most of the rooting section was escorted out of the room. Even my dear mother-in-law took a little "me" time and went to go stretch by way of goose step. It was now just myself, my wife, Gina, and a single nurse (I assume she was single. I didn't see a ring.) Gina asked my wife to start pushing. My wife then decided that she'd rather get a puppy. The nurse and I were enlisted to hold my wife's legs – obviously to keep her from running away. With the first big push came a scream and a disgusting, slimy, purple bump where a disgusting, slimy, purple bump had ne'er before been and, in my estimation, ought not be. Gina explained that that was the crown of the baby's head. A crown? I wondered what kind of kingdom this teratoid eel would be ruling over.

The second big push was accompanied by another scream. This one – Krakatoesque (It circled the earth and hailed the coming of Xenu as well as some more medical staff and many of the party goers in the waiting room.) A doctor appeared briefly, both stethoscope and cigarette dangling from their respective parts of his head. He took a pulse or two and dissolved again into the ether. Gina again made sure that everyone but medical staff and myself be cleared from the room. I then suggested that, if anyone were hungry, I could go for Jell-O. It was too late. The baby was almost here.

More nurses started coming in and out of the room. Every time the door would swing open, I'd hear someone yell, "Save the placenta!"

The doctor appeared again but this time he was wearing schnoz glasses and the cigarette had graduated to a cigar. He started pacing back and forth and talking about a cash flush duck. My wife was crying. I was crying. Gina was crying. Even the duck was crying. One of the nurses suggested we put my wife in the birthing pool in the next room. She said the water was the perfect temperature and they were serving margaritas. Gina thought it better to not move the patient but the gaggle of nurses quickly thinned out.

No matter how hard my wife pushed, the baby's head wouldn't budge. (With the size of that noggin, this kid was going to have quite a career as a celebrity chef.) After more than a few attempts the decision was made to get the salad tongs. Everybody focused. The nurse and I, each gripping an ankle, looked like we were a sawing team waiting for the starting gun at a lumberjack contest. Other nurses stood ready, hungry to jump into action at the first sign of sale on white sneakers. Gina began to speak in calm, soothing ultimatums. Even Groucho put out his cigar. And then, the final push.

Gina went in first. She grappled with the beast and struggled to hold on to the forceps. My wife let out another bellowing cry – for you see, she was no longer under anesthesia. I reached out to her with one hand while being careful not to lose my grip on her leg for fear of being reminded of my failure during some future argument. The nurse opposite me had disappeared and was later found cowering behind an EKG machine, rocking, and muttering to herself, "Never get out of the boat. I gotta remember. Never get out of the boat."

Finally, the baby's shoulders appeared; followed immediately by a body. It slipped out like an al dente pasta sculpture flying down a beef bouillon water slide. It was a boy! Gina could tell because his afterbirth had 17 percent greater volume than that of his newborn female colleagues.

My son's first little coos served to signal friends and family to make their way into the room and share in our precious little gift. Both new grandmothers were the first to peek in through the door. Just two rosy-cheeked, grinning heads dreaming of the trees they weren't going to let him climb or the food allergies that they would dismiss as coddling. Next came the grandfathers with their raucous chiding and whiskey breath. The aunts and uncles, the close family friends, the well-wishers, and truant officers all made their way to congratulate and fawn over the mother and child. A few even told me what a good job *I* did which I modestly had to concede was very little since my wife was the one who had done all of the cheating.

I remember the moment they laid my son on his mother's chest. As she stared into his little dark blue eyes, one of the nurses asked what name she should put on the birth certificate. We both looked at his little feet and toes. Then his hands and fingers. And then his soft bald little head that was still misshaped due to the forceps. We looked at each other. Nodded in silent agreement and simultaneously answered, "Gumby".

We got our second son in a gumball machine outside the grocery store. Needless to say, it didn't take too long to get over the disappointment of missing out on that Bratz tattoo.

I Know Why
The Caged Lion
Paces And Eats Raw Meat

    I believe it was Doctor Kevorkian who said, "This won't hurt a bit." When comparing his death-bed-side manner to the treatment many of us have received at the hands of his colleagues, that bit of reassurance may be a fair one. After a recent trip to the barbary shop, I can now understand how one might yearn to trade in the confining shackles of a pulse for the invigorating release of Deadsville. For one, all bills are forwarded to your kids. And secondly, I've found that I always feel much better once I've given up hope.

    My wife had been trying to convince me to see a doctor about my throat condition for some time. Now I happened to live in a small town. I couldn't breathe in that small town. I thought I would die in that small town. And that's probably where they'd bury me. And when it comes to small town doctors, hospitals, and medical treatments, you had better be able to treat yourself if the warm milk and Epsom salts doesn't work. For several weeks now I had been attempting to do just that. I even tried warm *salt* and Epsom *milk*. But have you ever tried grabbing the teat of an angry Epsom? It's almost impossible. I had asked the vet why I couldn't just milk a happy Epsom, or even one that was slightly contented. But he just kept sucking on his 4' long cigarette filter (Which had a pipe shoved into the end of it) and yelling,"Nien! Ze epsom, she must be pissed!"

    Finally, she persuaded me to go get checked out. She accomplished this by pushing my eyes back into their sockets and giving me an emergency tracheotomy using an emery board and a length of garden hose. As I bowed my head in frustration and hit my knee with the sprinkler, I realized it was time to give in and we headed to the emergency room.

I think the word 'emergency' is similar to 'Aloha' in that it means a variety of things. I had always used it as a term meaning a sudden turn of events calling for immediate action. But apparently it can also mean that which is overlooked or unattended to. Or the act of causing one to sit for hours and develop hemorrhoids. I guess English really *is* the most difficult language.

I was fortunate because my particular medical non-crisis manifested itself at 4:00 in the morning which, due to that hour's reduced population using tree shredders and visiting archery ranges, facilitated a lesser sentence in the intensive disregard unit. After a wait of only twelve shave cycles and an oil change, I was buzzed through the large wheelchair-accessible door and escorted to a smaller, less accessible (to doctors) holding pen where I could spend the rest of my days rifling through booklets and re-acquainting myself with such material issues as yeast infections and female pattern baldness. What this place lacked in amusement it more than made up for in sterility.

I was, at this point, unable to speak. Except to tell the admitting nurse that I couldn't speak. Her notes were apparently placed in a file marked *We Are the World* because they were never seen nor heard from again. I repeated it to the next nurse and the next and the next. This last one came in the to take my vital signs and remind me of how all of us sick people were interfering with her much-needed Marlboro breaks. I guess she never relayed the message to the next nurse who came in to do the same thing, minus the pleasantries, not long after. *That* nurse sent in another to inform me that the doctor would be with me soon. *Soon*, I supposed, was being used in the geological sense.

Finally, after some heavy lobbying and running my cup back and forth over the bars, the doctor entered and asked, "What seems to be the problem?" My frustration got the best of me and I lunged to choke him as he limbo-ed out of the way. I missed his neck but managed to get a hold of a part of him. I hadn't even asked him to turn his head and cough before he was able to review the notes of his predecessors and conclude that I had a problem with my throat. He flashed a light in my mouth and asked me to *think* ah. I complied. He then jabbed a Q-tip so hard into the back of my throat that he knocked over a jar of cotton balls on the counter behind me. This sudden blow caught me by surprise and caused me to loosen my grip, ever so slightly, which allowed him to get away and run my culture down to the lab. The next few years were rough. What with the relentless codes blue (never did find out what code blue meant – I think it had something to do with Lenny Bruce albums) but I eventually got the results. Strep throat. No kiddin'?

After receiving a prescription for antibiotics and a pat on the behind, I tra-la-la-ed my way home on course for a full recovery. But along the way I was detoured by a pair of scheming Gypsies. (It turned out that I was hallucinating due to a bad reaction to the antibiotics, but you know that somehow, some way, there were Gypsies involved.) What happened was this:

I was skipping merrily along, minding my business, when one of the Gypsies, disguised as a soft-spoken and charismatic fox, lured me down a dark side street by begging for help with changing his tire. When we reached the end of the street his accomplice, an alley cat made up to look like Harpo Marx – filthy Gypsies – appeared from behind a dumpster and accosted me with his horn. I came to in the ambulance to find both of my legs broken, I had a collapsed lung, double hernia, a concussion, tennis elbow, a rash that covered my whole body, except for a small spot on my forehead (which made me look like a negative of Mikhail Gorbachev), prickly heat, Lyme disease, a leaky implant and somewhere between triage and X-ray I had been injected with a form of herpes that, up until now, had only been detected in portabella mushrooms.

When I was released, I was determined to live a healthy lifestyle. I would change all of my living and eating habits so as to avoid the hospital as much as possible. First, I would cut out all fatty red meat. From now on it would be strictly veal. In fact, *any* meat that I consumed would come from baby animals only. Secondly, I would restrict my deep frying to vegetables. No more French-fried mayonnaise and milk battered shortening kabobs. And thirdly, I would begin a rigorous regimen of daily napping to allow more time for my piglet rinds to digest.

The plan worked for a time. Indeed, upon arriving home, I had spent the good part of the first hour with absolutely no symptoms save a mild stroke and some bleeding from my head. So, yet again, off we went, over hill and stopped in traffic in dale, until we made it to what was quickly becoming, my home away from health. But as often happens, by the time we got there I was feeling much better. I had no fever. I had no pain. I had no bleeding. The fact that I had no pulse did give the doctor reason to pause and order some tests. These came back negative. He ordered more tests. These came back positive. But the third round of tests came back only mildly interested so, after performing a few more procedures for the sake of hazing, I was sent home…again.

Throughout the next year I experienced many attacks that involved my innards. My stomach cramps were crippling and, despite the Pepto-Bismol IV, produced some highly significant Rorschach tests. I saw specialist after specialist with no diagnosis, just handfuls of Motrin, three epidurals, a couple of injections that were supposed to make me faster and give me a shiny coat, IcyHot, and a dime bag from my eye doctor. Our last resort was to move back to the city where I could be examined by doctors who worked with humans *exclusively*.

At first, I thought the move might not have been the best idea. My primary physician seemed to be agitated as I explained my symptoms. He foisted me on to several of his colleagues, the first of which was an obstetrician. I kindly explained that while I believed people should be able to worship in any way they deem fit, I wouldn't be needing her services. Next I was sent to a urologist with the idea that my stomach pains would be lessened if I could concentrate all my worrying on the potential of a botched prostate surgery. This plan worked *too* well in that the mere thought of a catheter in that area caused my urethra to seize up for six weeks leaving me with (1) the ability to cut granite through the process of water jet hydro-abrasion and (2) nothing but time to ponder my, by this time, tempestuous tummy ache.

As a last resort, they decided to check my stomach. Initially Doctors Brodie and Hooper wanted to try exploratory surgery using a kitchen knife and a gill net, but the anesthesiologist thought it better to use a barium GI exam. A barium GI, *I* thought, was an order given to an infantry soldier to dig a hole for the enemy. This worried me a little, especially since the x-ray technician was wearing dog tags and kept calling me Charley.

A barium GI, *actually*, is a procedure in which the patient is asked to lie on his back and drink several gallons of liquefied chalk flavored with a whisper of bruised-and-left-in-the-sun-banana extract. One cannot sit or stand and drink the solution. One must be reclining because that gives the staff a much heartier chuckle whilst the patient spits up a substance resembling Portland cement. Then, x-rays are taken to see if there are any leaks. It's also important to not ingest anything within 24 hours of the exam for fear that anything left in the stomach might result in a flawed conclusion. The conclusion from *my* exam was that I had little to no self-control and, were it not for my wife's foresight in wiring my mouth shut, the pictures might have come back with my large intestine in the shape of Dave Thomas' square patties.

Fortunately, my doctor didn't need all that 'overpriced equipment and fancy schmancy book learnin' to tell *him* what ailed me. He determined my problem simply by reviewing my insurance. Without a doubt I needed to have my gallbladder removed. I asked if it was necessary to remove it. "Couldn't we just dress it up a little? You know, slap a coat of paint on there or plant a nice hedge around it."

"I'm afraid not," he said. "But don't worry about it. The gallbladder is a useless organ like your appendix or your left kidney, which I can yank for you while I'm in there, free of charge."

"Well I'm not sure I can take the time off from work to have this done. How long will it take for me to recuperate?"

He never answered *that* question. He just stared out the window and mumbled to himself, "You know, humans and bears have very similar looking kidneys."

Assuming that I would be bedridden for some time as a result of the surgery, I chose to roll the dice and put the operation off.

Fast forward one month.

Of course, I wasn't at home when the rumbling began. I was visiting my parents. Looking back, it was probably best that it all happened there. I was never sick as a kid and I had always felt that I had robbed them of the experience of catering to my every need. Being a giving person by nature, I made the most of this opportunity.

It started modestly with my commandeering the sofa so that I could lie down and "unbutton". As the fever intensified, so did my generosity. Lying on their new, cool leather couch, wearing nothing but a towel and an ice pack not only soothed my pain, but also, I could see, affected my parents very deeply. As I writhed in sweat-laden agony on the plush, overstuffed loveseat, I noticed, in my mother's eye, a tear of joy, thankful to offer what she could – a rub on the forehead, a cold glass of water, the use of her $17,000.00 handmade living room set – to make her son more comfortable. And I knew that her happiness would be just as great, if not greater, when I paid her back the money for the hospital bill that she didn't even know she had lent me while fixing me some chicken soup.

It was great to be able to give my parents that kind of beatitude, but I knew that if I was to survive this episode, I'd have to start paying attention to *my* needs. So into the bathroom I went for some "me time." At first, I just sat on the floor, allowing the tile to cool my fevered pre-corpse. But my mother was getting a little chilly, so she turned the thermostat to the spot on the dial that read, SURFACE OF THE SUN. I can understand why she felt cold. The only operative register in the house was the one I was lying on in the bathroom. I tried to open the door but, by this time, the furnace had pressurized the room to 110 lbs. per square inch with air that rivaled a dragon's breath while sitting in a Death Valley sauna in August. Thinking quickly, I stepped into the shower and turned on the cold water. I could feel my body temperature dropping. Unfortunately, the fall began to pick up speed and land dead center on my diaphragm. This caused a chain reaction allowing me to relive my last four meals on rewind.

For years I thought what that Russian weightlifter on Wide World of Sports was doing was called a dry heave. But that night I got a real education on the subtle nuances of the digestive clean and jerk. After emptying my stomach, large and small intestines, and what seemed like my ovaries, I just laid there, heaped in a ball at the bottom of the shower, eyes glazed over, doing my best Janet Leigh impression. The sun had gone down and, since I hadn't turned on the light before getting in the shower, the room was completely dark. I dragged myself out of the shower. Then I drug myself – as a reminder that I had to stay adaptable. When I switched on the light, I was confronted with the fact that I hadn't been throwing up *food* for some time. The shower walls looked like a Freddy Kruger finger painting. And I think I saw the word "REDRUM" in the soap dish. I knew right then that, while they probably wouldn't hurt, my Flintstone chewables were not going to fix this problem.

On the bright side, I discovered a way to by-pass the waiting room and eliminate the chore of driving myself to the hospital all in one abbreviated-digit phone call. The hospital staff really seems to perk up with the arrival of an ambulance. The incoming victim (or Lord, as the nurses referred to me) is whisked away from the other patients (or boat people, as the nurses *and* doctors referred to *them*) on a gurney equipped with air conditioning, anti-lock brakes, and cup holders, to a private room where veiled concubines fan you with ostrich feathers and man servants await while bearing iced tea and morphine pastries.

There was no procrastinating now. My gallbladder would have to come out. And soon. But not *too* soon. Because if you operate on someone too early after their pancreas becomes inflamed you run the risk of alleviating that person's pain thereby making that person more comfortable thus making the patient's stay more pleasant resulting in a positive experience which ultimately leaves an individual relieved and/or grateful leading to the eventual gratitude directed toward the doctor(s) whom we all know don't do it for the glory but rather for the money, easy access to pharmaceuticals, and freedom from legible handwriting. So, the following week was more or less a tutorial on pain management. Not mine, so much, but certainly that of my fellow prey.

The guy in the bed next to mine was a veteran of the Spanish American War whose Alzheimer's coupled with his surgery for testicular cancer generated bi-hourly shrieks of horror and confusion with each visit to the bathroom. The crack-baby machine across the hall (I called her Mona) had been having difficulty with the concept of the call button. She would alert the entire north wing to the quarter hour by announcing that, "It hurts! Oh it hurts! Get it out! For God's sake it hurts!" I found out later that she had accidentally sat on her pipe.

With all of the other sweat hogs I was surrounded by, I soon became the nurse's pet. I could carry on an intelligent conversation without memorizing lines from my 'get well' cards, I had absolutely no recollection of my exploits with the Rough Riders, and every now and then I'd throw them a compliment about the slimming qualities of white support hose. In return, my IV bag was always topped off and I could always count on the baby needle when it came time to draw blood. (Incidentally, how much blood do these people need? My contributions alone were enough to keep Dracula in the Yoko Zuni weight class for the rest of eternity.)

Of course, when you're in the hospital for weeks, at least one shift is going to be a problem. On this shift one nurse's concern for her patients fell somewhere between Mildred Rachet and Joseph Mengele. She wouldn't allow me to watch TV after 9:00. If I had to ease nature during the night, she would force me to use the bedpan, and the final move, which forced me to start a revolt, was that she began to short me on my morphine.

It was now time to organize the populace.

It's difficult to organize the populace. First of all, you have to identify the populace. And you can't trust just *anyone* in a gown who blinks constantly and points at a group of people to declare them the populace. That group of people might be security. And if George Orwell has taught us anything, it's that security guards cannot be the populace. In fact, in this hospital, security guards are looked at, more or less, as strike breakers. (Strike being medical jargon for "my arm".)

After defining what a populace is, one must attempt to organize it. This can be done in a variety of ways. You could try a hunger strike. This only seems to work if the populace has some stored body fat. *My* populace was, for the most part, emaciated and felt that the *hoarding* of foodstuffs would be more apt to get their demands heard.

We next tried a sit-in. Nobody noticed.

I then decided to invite everybody into my room to watch the 1963 World Series on a blank television screen as a way to demonstrate our determination and show a united front, no matter the nature of the obstacle. But when the chief turned the TV on, and to ESPN Classics, I ended up just feeling silly.

I finally realized that there was no point in attempting a non-violent take over. A revolution needs something with a little pizzazz. And try finding a venture capitalist, these days, who wants to sink his money into something labeled passive. I mean there's a reason Schwarzenegger hasn't been deported. So, it had been decided. The overthrow of the department would be by means of an armed uprising.

As my plans began to take shape I could see that I was seriously lacking in manpower, so I ordered my lieutenants to round up all semi- to barely able-bodied men and promise them, in exchange for their unyielding allegiance, front-loading gowns and ergonomic oxygen supply nostril tips. That night I slept the sleep of the one-apnea-episode-from-dead, secure in the knowledge that, in just a few hours, my minions would sweep me into power.

As luck would have it, my inauguration was cut short when I was informed that my infection had subsided enough to conduct the surgery. They immediately drugged me up (no complaints so far), carted me off to the operating room (which looked suspiciously like the inside of a giant pantyhose egg), strapped down my outstretched arms (the easier to absolve each member of the surgical team), and asked me to count backwards from brown (if memory serves). I remember leaving my body and watching the operation for a while. Then I went out to feed the meter. I returned in time to see three of the doctors nervously rooting around inside my torso as the anesthesiologist kept insisting that, "...It has to be down here around the kidney. I can hear the ticking." When I awoke, I was surrounded by all of my friends and family. The scarecrow was there. And so were the lion and a vinyl siding salesman. But most of all, I remember my amazing wife at my side urging me to get back to work. And just three days later I *did* return to work, where I promptly electrocuted myself and fell down eleven flights of stairs.

Many years have passed since then. And in the meantime I've contracted Shingles and Meningitis and have had three toes amputated. The former two ailments seemed to be just a product of unforeseen occurrence, but as for the latter, here's a word to the wise: Don't wear flip-flops to Benihana.

MY UTOPIA

Edward Bellamy wrote about it. Adolph Hitler planned it. Karl Marx even got someone to believe in it. Now it's my turn. The following will soon and forever be considered the final authority on all things ideal. The quintessential vision for a society with no limits and a world of unimaginable beauty, encouraged discovery and a haven for some really fine babes with no prejudices about formerly (very formerly) athletic, shut-in, humorists. I give you a new and improved kampf.

I believe it was Eleanor Roosevelt who said: "Great minds discuss ideas; average minds discuss events; small minds discuss people; borderline simpletons conversate."

Eleanor was a swell dame (as evidenced by the famous quote from Amelia Earhart, "Eleanor, I think you're swelleanor.") and did a bang-up job of first-ladyin'. All the same, she did come up a little short when it came time to actualize her progressive land of milk and honey. In fact, back in in 1933 she headed up the creation of Arthurdale, West Virginia – a planned community that ended up being the land that milked the money.

The failure of Arthurdale also calls to mind the efforts of another American icon, Walt Disney and his **E**xperimental **P**rototype **C**ommunity **O**f **T**omorrow – or NAMBLA. The Florida Project, as he called it, wasn't supposed to be the fanny pack catwalk and plush toy clearing house it's become today. It was supposed to be the ideal city, complete with clean and comfortable mass transportation, clean and affordable housing, and clean and non-culpable industry. When Walt died, his dream of that fairyland was replaced with a fairyland.

These are just two examples of unsuccessfully planned communities where the well-intentioned administrators failed to realize one universal truth: Super villains usually have a pretty good bead on the human condition. They realize that trying to cure man's problems related to suffering, injustice, corruption, and greed will always result in suffering, injustice, corruption, greed, and pay toilets. For this reason, my perfect society has very little to do with what needs to be included, but rather what should be *excluded* (excluding inclusions...of course).

Let's start with the **Citizenry**: Even with just a cursory glance, the prevailing ideal that a society where everyone is both equal and free to pursue their own desires is patently ridiculous. First, people are not equal. A trip to Costco will prove that. You've got the four-cart couple preparing for everything from a cheesy puff shortage to a race war. There's the mobile diner shrewdly conning the sample lady by deliberating the pros and cons of purchasing a metric ton of Swedish meatballs. The Kirkland loyalist and the family of ten enjoying a slice and some high decibel conversation in, what they must believe is, their own airport adjacent back yard. People may be equally entitled to certain inalienable rights (For the non-restaurateur purchasing a tub of Miracle Whip, "inalienable" means "inborn" and has nothing to do with Area 51), but there is definitely an equality spectrum when it comes to societal ROI.

And only chaos can come from each person pursuing his or her own individual dream. What if one person's dream is to build beautiful parks while another's is to raise gophers? What if an equestrian marries somebody with an adhesive business? Anyone who says that the world would be boring if we were all the same has either not given it much thought or they put pineapple on their pizza.

The world would be *fantastic* if we were all the same.

No racism (but sexism and ageism would be great cause we'd all agree on what was funny). Nothing would ever be too spicy. We'd all agree on jazz. No lawyers. No Salesmen. No HR. Nobody named Hunter. There'd be no arguments about whether or not Chrissy Teigen is hot. No protests (and if there were, when someone yelled out, "What do we want?" we'd all know). If hipsters existed, they'd have nothing to complain about or, if they didn't exist, we'd only wear scarves and beanies when it's cold. People from the US wouldn't be afraid to drive in England, and vice versa. Fat shaming would be replaced with double finger pistols and an affirmative, "Lookin' good." The only time you'd hear, "We need more men like you", is while attempting to break some sort of record. Anti-Semitism would merely mean that we didn't like something that was only halfway complete. Chris Hemsworth would just be some guy. We could finally tell Unitarians to shut up. We could retire unused colors. News anchors wouldn't have to learn multiple accents to tell us that Hes-bō'-la has been hair'-ə-sing Nee'-gal-ágwa; Clearly polygamy would be legal. Everyone would have the same 3rd favorite dinosaur. You could find licorice everywhere...or nowhere. Football would only mean one thing. People who got in on the ground floor of Herbalife would be trillionaires. And one size really would fit all.

In the history of humankind there have only been three types of **Government**: Monarchy, Oligarchy, and Democracy. Monarchy works great if the ruler is wise and benevolent – and it doesn't hurt if you happen to be the monarch either – but if they're selfish dolts there's a good chance Tom Edison's getting burned at the stake for witchcraft. An oligarchy is traditionally the best way for old guys to get trophy wives, but its inherent class systems tends to disenfranchise the less fortunate (like the people who get hung). Democracy was favored by neither Plato nor Aristotle who viewed it as impossible for the common man to have enough intelligence to make proper choices. Plato's teacher, Socrates – also not a fan of democracy, was, in fact, convicted of corrupting the youth of Athens for suggesting that democracy was flawed. Guess what happened to him? Execution.

Clearly, all forms of government, to this point, lead only to death. To combat this inevitability, my plan would be a tyrannical anarchist dictatorship guided by the principles of social conservatism and progressive fiscal spending. Of course, my original idea was to nominate myself for the position of Caesar-in-chief, but my beautiful and insistent bride convinced me that her dictatorial nature made her better equipped to decide what's best for all while I would still be allowed my semi-weekly foot rubbing duties.

Was Pink Floyd right? Do we really don't need no *Education*? Nay says I, after eating a bag of oats. Education might be the most important element in my new society. (Either that or a prohibition on almond butter.) The difference would be that, after elementary school, all must work for six years before attending high school. And if one wanted to pursue higher education, they must first be able to define, identify, stalk, kill, and field dress a professional academic.

Child labor laws would be circumvented by relabeling all manual labor as "chores." This would allow many occupational safety risks to be classified as valuable life lessons. OSHA's motto would adjust from "Plan, prevent, and protect" to "Now what have we learned?" And think of how seriously a returning freshman with Black Lung would take his or her education. It's a win-win.

Healthcare will not be an issue in my utopia. When it comes to diseases, we will classify them in one of five groups:

- *Terminal*. You don't want those.
- *Chronic* but not deadly. These will be treated as opportunities for the patient to develop the virtue of endurance. Anyone displaying anything but a Michael J. Fox-esque upbeatness, will be flogged with reeds and denied any addictive opioids.
- *Viruses*. These can be serious. Just *how* serious is a question for politicians and actors to decide. But if you come down with something in this idyllic setting, you can be sure that there will always be plenty of chicken soup and shunned isolation.
- *Syndromes*. These conditions often have an upside. For instance, irritable bowel syndrome (IBS) can provide many of the same benefits as bulimia without the damage to tooth enamel. When my tapeworm retired, I briefly considered bulimia as an alternative. I even attended a support group once, but found it to be mostly just holding back people's hair.
- *Allergies*. This is a zero-sum game, as anything that causes allergies simply won't exist...unless it's something *I* like. In which case, the allergy sufferers will eventually achieve non-existence.

Of course, one must also consider congenital issues, such as deformities or other handicaps. While the necessary accoutrements, e.g., wheelchairs, will be accommodated in most areas of life, the motorized type will not be allowed on public transportation. People ride the bus because they don't have other motorized travel options. How fair is it for somebody in, what is essentially a personal ambulatory La-Z-Boy, to be taking up room in an already confined vehicle where the passengers are crammed together like a British family in a coal cellar during the Blitzkrieg. Inserting a Lark scooter into that environment would be like wearing a shoe inside of a boot. It just isn't done.

While deaf people will be welcomed (as long as they keep it down), unfortunately, we will not be able to accommodate the blind for fear that some may experience some family tragedy, hone their other senses, join a ninja clan, and later roam the streets as masked vigilantes. Sorry boys, we just can't have that.

What about accidents and emergencies? These are self-correcting problems since, sooner or later, everybody stops bleeding.

And what *about Security*? I'm from the school that says we should all be responsible for our own safety. Incidentally, *this* school had sand boxes filled with lava rock, a jungle gym over asphalt, a wooden slide (complete with splinters), and we needed dodge ball credits to graduate.

Of course, security considerations are different for cities than for suburbia. For instance, in suburban and more bucolic settings, most expect a certain degree of courtesy among neighbors and attention to quality of life by public officials. Ironically, these residents tend to be more likely to curate their own private armory at home. An exploration of your average tract home might turn up backyard campfires with muskets stacked as tepees and the distant punchy tones of a harmonica drifting through the air – all on a beautifully manicured quarter acre and plenty of space for parking (unparalleled).

City dwellers, on the other hand, have grown accustomed to cramped quarters and a higher crime rate. This demonstrates to outsiders that tolerance results in more freedom. For instance, there are few individualists more rugged than the noble vagrant. Rejecting such contemporary mores as the 9 to 5 grind and private bowel movements, these non-working-class heroes are up at the break of dawn, early birds hunting for that worm. Nobody knows if the worm is at the bottom of a bottle of mezcal or they're wrestling with a pigeon over breakfast. The point is that street people seem determined to get worms.

All enlightened societies have two things in common: Racism, and a free and unrestricted *Media*. In 1947, the Hutchins Committee termed it a free and *responsible* press, but that was just to keep Edward R. Murrow from selling gold coins and Dinovite on the air.

While I would be reluctant to come right out and ban all forms of media, I think the social type needs a serious review. Rather than being a way to communicate with one another, social media has become an enabler for modest to egregious narcissism.

Of course, this is no new phenomenon. Many sonnets of the Victorian era demonstrate that generation's vainglorious mindset. See Rudyard Kipling's, *Nuff Said*; or Oscar Wilde's, *Keep Calm and Condescend*; or Emily Brontë's epic in three volumes, *Feet on the Beach, Thigh Gap,* and *Bikini Bridge*. Additionally, artists of the Renaissance were the first to discover the slimming effects of positioning their subjects in the classic hand hip/arched back/one knee forward/head tilt pose. There's also the example of the ancient Greeks who had developed a semaphore-like system announcing their departure to, time spent in, or returning from, the gymnasium. The Cyrus Cylinder is just a collection of song lyrics and inspirational quotes that really spoke to the Persian king Cyrus D-GR8. And as early as the Mesolithic period, original cave drawings were mostly pictures of lattes.

In our current climate, the incessant cries for attention have become ubiquitous. It's as if millions of voices cried out in melodrama and were suddenly given the spotlight. It would be easy to blame social media sites like Facebook and Instagram for all of this self-indulgence, so let's do that.

I believe it was Pat Sajak who said, "It's the *Economy* stupid!" He threw a fit when one contestant who had the C, N, M, Y, and O's showing guessed gastronomy.

It's been said that money is the root of all evil. In actuality, it's the *love* of money that causes the problems. Sure, greed would still be a problem, even if we had no currency. But how many goats would it take to purchase one of those private islands for some richling's personal debauchery? And where would you keep that many goats? Oooh, I get it.

At the same time, it seems that bank notes may be a cleaner system then bartering, so some form of cash would probably be necessary at this point. The question becomes, how would one get money? This is a question for Tony Robbins. Of course, it'll cost you about 5,000 chickens, plus you'll have to buy the book (200 beads and all the land a suicidal real estate agent/fashion designer can walk in a day). Or you might work at something you like to do. Say, cabinet making, or computer programing, or pediatric brain surgery. Anything that gives you a thrill…unless it's pediatric brain surgery. In that case, try party clown.

The point is that hard work should be rewarded. And not just the legal stuff. It has long been my contention that the statute of limitation on non-violent bank robberies be 24 hours. And really, those 24 hours would just be to keep the riff raff from making the attempt. We should be delighted to hear of entrepreneurial triumphs like bank heists and museum burglaries. Clearly the fortitude it takes to plan and implement these jobs is not found in your common everyday wage earner. The long hours, hard work (often in unsafe conditions: toiling underground, rappelling through skylights, stowing away in the wheel wells of jumbo jets), and start-up expense makes the world of high-end thievery one populated mainly by the sort of type A go-getters that ultimately give back to their community, whether it be patronizing custom clothiers, brunch establishments, or sailboat dealerships.

But the point of any egalitarian system is to live in **Peace**. And to achieve this *Pax Utopia*, we'll need guns. Lots and lots of guns. Not just for self-defense and vendettas, but for hunting too. And let's not forget the biathlon.

Courtesy is the hallmark of peace. And courtesy is best developed through fear. Fear of hurting the feelings of a loved one. Fear of making things difficult for others. Fear of a beat down because the guy you mouthed off to looked a lot shorter when he was in the car. This is nature's way. A society where people are keenly aware of their own frailties and mortality is a peaceful society. This is a lesson that has been lost on many of today's youth. They've been protected and propped up and not humiliated for dressing up as Jedis. (Yeah, nerd. I know the plural is still Jedi! This is why it's gonna hurt.)

Certainly, to keep the chaos to a minimum, there will be a few **Inexpungible Rules**:

- Urinals must go to the floor.
- No car horns.
- No more warnings about meteors coming close to earth.
- It must be announced before a funeral if the deceased had a twin.

To sum up. I have a dream. A dream where all people (who meet my qualifications) will be able to sit down together and agree that *The Big Bang Theory* is a hacky, tired pile of garbage. I have a dream that, one day, even the most prematurely greying vegan will acknowledge that making tofu look and taste like meat is an admission of err. I have a dream where children of all races, colors, and creeds can come together instead of interrupting me during the game. And we will all join hands and sing *Smells Like Teen Spirit* because Michael Bublé will have done a cover where we can understand the lyrics.

I love Big Brother.

Section II:
The Department of Better Understanding

I believe it was Bernie Madoff who said, "An investment in knowledge pays the best interest." To which Ben Franklin replied, "I want my quotes back!"

Knowledge is power. So is potentiality but it's rarely spelled correctly. The real force of knowledge is that the user can take information, process it, and sell it to any of a number of media outlets that promise #6 will take your breath away.

However, as used in this section, the word knowledge is derived from the original Phoenician, translated literally, "to take a shot at." Sometimes interpreted as unsubstantiated conjecture or that which is made up or insinuated since no one legitimate would dare say it out loud. Also rendered as, "Just tryin' to make it fun."

As one who possesses a great thirst for knowledge (a new low-calorie Gatorade flavor born of mixing *Frost: Icy Charge* and *Fierce: Dis-Charge*), I've devoted countless hours combing through *Highlights for Children* and *Lowlights for the Middle-Aged* swallowing up as much information as I could. All with the hope that, some day, I may regurgitate it to the chirping, data-starved hatchlings that are my readers. So here comes. I think I'm gonna be sick.

Development and Integration of the Handshake

Or

"In Madagascar, We're Married!"

I believe it was Indira Gandhi who said, "You cannot shake hands with a clenched fist. And it's a heck of a crummy way to caress a cheek."

Whether it's engaging in a knife duel to the sweet sounds of Van Halen or allowing for the Nazi occupation of the Sudetenland, the handshake has been a part of history for as far back as the ninth century BCE. It was then that Assyrian king, Shalmaneser III surprised his old friend, Babylonian Marduk-Zakir-Shumi (aka the Shumeister) with a wavering grasp that provoked a snappy burn from Marduk about the now sedentary, Assyrian pushing too many pencils.

Grabbing the right hand with one's own right has been said to have originated with the Spartans. The idea was that extending your right arm would show that you carried no weapons. This explains why the Greek Assassin's Guild (GAG) only hired southpaws.

While in the ancient world there were many purposes and meanings for the handshake, it is believed that its use as a greeting was first popularized in the 17th century. It's said that the Quakers found the shaking of hands (you know those Quakers, always shaking something) to be a more impartial alternative to bowing or patting another on the head and calling him, "little fella".

In fact, long before he founded the Religious Society of Friends, George Fox, as a simple shepherd and cobbler (blacksmithing being considered lewd), had spent years groping for a more amiable physical salutation than groping – the only manner deemed appropriate by the Church. At age 19, while journeying through Stratford-upon-Mary-Kay, Fox encountered chimney sweeps greeting one another with a sort of chop to the neck. He attempted to insert himself into the exercise, but was savagely beaten before he would learn that they were simply brushing soot from each other's shoulders.

Within a year he was back in his hometown of Upper East Stubblestoutwell consulting with the local Protestant clergyman, Nathaniel Picklebottom, over his plans to bid good wishes to strangers by grabbing the subject's right shoulder and slowly caressing the person's left forearm. Picklebottom, believing Fox to be mad, immediately put his shirt back on and demanded that he leave…but to walk away slowly.

Supposing that, perhaps some sort of token of respect might be exchanged during a greeting, Fox approached the Bishop of Upton Sinclairsbury who urged him to pass the dutchie to the left-hand side. Another cleric in Packinna Wallop suggested bloodletting. Finally, adrift and dejected, he returned home where he spent almost three more years in prayer and meditation while incarcerated for criminal touching without a certificate of ordination.

In 1667, Fox met the newly converted William Penn. As the Quakers had not yet universally adopted the handshake, the two spooned. Penn, a reformed Oxford Cavalier and Cambridge Piston, had been disowned by his father and short sold by his mother when he formally rejected that Anglican church. Unwilling to swear oaths or remove his hat in court, he became a loan shark and took possession of a 45,000 square-mile tract of land in the new world from King Charles II, who had foolishly bet his life savings on Oliver Cromwell.

Penn named this colony Pennsylvania, which underscored his vanity as well as his love of fluorescent light bulbs. It was while planning the city of Philadelphia that Penn took up the cause of the "everyday" handshake. At this time, in the colonies, handshakes were only used during the most somber or prominent of occasions, while informal salutations were relegated to the upward man nod. Now, a close adherent to his mentor's doctrine, Penn embarked on a series of lectures designed to normalize the handshake for use as a legally binding agreement between himself, his contractors, their vendors, and even between the laborers themselves. Among the African "workers" this was the first known instance of giving "Dap."

By the time of the American Revolution, Fox's dream of everyday handshakes had taken hold in the Colonies. Thomas Jefferson had written a treatise entitled, *On the Efficacy of Touch, Limited Government, and Hot Black Chicks*, where he counted the handshake as one of several actions that would be considered the pursuit of happiness. At Yorktown, after vowing to "...never grip the palm of a Yankee rebel," Cornwallis offered his hand to General Washington as he surrendered his army. Washington initially extended his right arm in return, but then suddenly yelled, "Psych!" and ran his fingers through his powdered wig.

Benjamin Franklin, at one time, had been skeptical of Penn's dogma and had long espoused that the only proper greeting was the kissing of the hand. But, after developing a receding hairline, which was quite off-putting as he'd bend to peck a young lady on the knuckles (he had a thing for joints.), he reversed course and published an essay where he stated in part:

> *"...without a hearty how-do-you-do served up with an equally firm handshake, there can be no such thing as peace.*
> *And there can be no such thing as public liberty without some skin."*

By Victorian times handshake manuals began circulating all over the world. Traditions associated with handshakes began to take root in all cultures. Indian attorney and vegetarian Mohandas Gandhi, after reading a pamphlet on slapping ten, adopted the Western technique while living in South Africa. He modified this behavior upon returning to India, citing patty cake as a system more conducive to peaceful interaction. After contracting dysentery twice, he modified his practice further, resulting in the now common, "namaste," literally translated: "Keep your hands to yourself."

In 1870s Europe, people had a preference for hot, moist palms (particularly the Germans, who've always been a little freaky anyway), which gave rise to spitting into one's fist before grasping another's and asserting everlasting loyalty to that person or that person's ball club. Back in America, the condescending handshake (smirk, nod, hand presented with fingers limp) was made popular a few years earlier when Ulysses S, Grant made General Lee wait several weeks at Appomattox so that the surrender of the Confederacy would take place, fittingly, on Palm Sunday.

As the 19th century neared its close, the dominance of the handshake was all but eclipsed by the likes of the doffed cap, the wave, and – in many military dictatorships or regions where the youth had adopted a sarcastic aesthetic – the salute. Another modern display, the "peace sign," was first confirmed on February 6th, 1884, during the War of the Pacific, when Chile invaded the Bolivian coastal territory and took control of Bolivia's Saltpeter and Pepper Schwartz mines. As the Chileans occupied the port city of Antofagasta*, Bolivian General Beauregard Juarez, who happened to be in town for Tu BiShvat, decided to take lunch at a local eatery where the opposing Vice-almirante, Otto Von Sepulveda, was also dining. When Sepulveda mistook, as a sign of truce, Juarez' gesture to the maître de requesting a booth for two, he responded by blowing Juarez a kiss. The resulting Treaty of Valparaiso was signed, that April, at a cute little chapel in Niagara Falls.

Ironically, perhaps the most prominent development in the ascendency of the handshake is found in its rivalry with the high five. The high five had been a staple in both the Balkans and the Austro-Hungarian Empire since 1808, when German cartographer, August "wrong way" Gruber allowed his temper to best him while arguing with Emperor Francis II about which color should be used for shading in the Hapsburg's hereditary land map. Gruber, insisted on a beaver hue and, in a fit of rage, leapt to his feet to slap Francis in the face while the emperor was stretching. He overshot the cheek and landed an open palm on that of the Emperor's. Immediately sobered by the error of his outburst, and fearing execution, Gruber explained that he saw the wisdom in Burnt Olive and that the smack was a demonstration of an Ottoman celebration of accord. Francis immediately adopted the tradition and had Gruber put to death.

*Quechuan for "City of Brotherly Love. From the Latin, Anto, meaning passion for, and the *modern* Italian slang…well you see where I'm going with this.

The high five remained popular until 1933 when Joseph Goebbels, being only 5'-3" was unable to congratulate Adolf Hitler after the Fuhrer's triple double in an exhibition game against the Harlem Globetrotters. (The Generals were still neutral at the time.) Goebbels attempted a high five, but realizing while shouting, "high..." that he would come up shy, he disguised his flaw by finishing with the phrase, "...eil Hitler! Yeah! You're der mensch! Come on you guys! Heil this dude!" Hitler, captivated by the gesture, implemented it as the Nazi salute and had August Gruber put to death. Of course, with the publishing of Hitler's college transcripts, along with a plagiarized application essay, the salute has since fallen out of favor.

The U.S. has stayed ground zero for handshakes since the signing of the Declaration of Independence until now with only a few exceptions. From 1900 to 1907 an epidemic of bubonic plague erupted in San Francisco. To combat the outbreak, the city burned to the ground. In addition, many citizens took to greeting one another by tapping elbows or forearms. The Victorian phrase, "donning a forearm clobber" was resurrected and modernized during the 1988 MLB season when Oakland Athletics' hitters Jose Canseco and Mark McGuire began "Forearm Bashing" after homeruns to keep their hands sterile for upcoming injections.

The most requested photograph from the national archives is the picture of Richard Nixon shaking hands with Elvis Presley in the Oval Office. It is a standard shot with a right-hand shake while the president smiles (with the help of an elaborate pully system) and the King stares quizzically at the camera. But that final shot came after hours of earlier attempts. The first several dozen shots show a velvet-draped Presley attempting to weave his fingers with those of Nixon. They then played several rounds of hot hands. This left their knuckles bright red for some time. Then, after a lunch where the two engaged in a thumb war for the last slice of peanut butter and banana pizza, what seemed to be the perfect shot was snapped. It depicted a tight clasp, as in arm wrestling, with a sincere bro hug. Elvis, the photographer, the chief of staff, and even the first lady were all very pleased, but Nixon found the photo to be too ethnic and the shot we know today was chosen.

The most recent incarnation of a modified handshake is the terrorist fist jab (sometimes referred to as the fist bump). This maneuver was first made popular, in the 1970s, by the Wonder Twins while transforming themselves into such crime-fighting accoutrements as buckets of water or Bourke's parakeets. It was immortalized when clean-ophile Howie Mandel won the 2008 Liberal Party's nomination for Canadian Prime Minister. The fist bump he shared with his wife was widely panned and the resulting controversy lead to a third team in the Canadian Football League to be named Rough Riders.

Of course, in the West, shaking hands is now the standard for greetings and alcohol withdrawal. But in many lands, its original purposes in those cultures are still adhered to:

Angola: The Angolan exclave of Cabinda, has long been the focus of separatist guerilla actions. The constant fragmentation of these groups into smaller and smaller factions has resulted in the use of the handshake to keep people from deserting.

Belarus: Typically, to show hospitality, a Belarusian will greet a guest by grabbing the wrist, pulling the visitor close, and forcing a piece of roasted pork on rye into the person's mouth. If the guest can finish the morsel in one bite, he is invited into the home. If he is unable to swallow or spits the piece out, he is beaten with rods in the town square until the whole meal is finished.

Burkina Faso: The handshake is used sparingly in Burkina Faso and is usually only employed, biennially, during the Festival of Masks, when citizens dress up as a local chieftain and promise change (While often chucking quarters at passersby).

Fiji: In contrast to the Māori Haka, before a rugby match, Fijians will take part in *bole*, which means an acceptance of a challenge. This bole includes shouting, dancing, and handshakes in which the opponent's palm is tickled with a hidden finger.

Iceland: Residents of Reykjavik believe that it is bad luck to sleep with one's head facing north. Also, one should not sleep with their head facing east or south. Additionally, to sleep with one's head pointed west would be to court tragedy. Since all other directions are legally forbidden, Icelanders are forced to counter the curses acquired every night by shaking hands with their neighbor and sprinkling black pudding across their thresholds in the morning.

Laos: The ethnic minority, the Hmong people, will often, in the middle of a meal or a conversation, spontaneously grab their companion's hand and start to pump the person's arm. This is believed to be a sign that they want you to go.

Luxembourg: The people of Luxembourg have a tradition of shaking hands and twirling whenever somebody uses the word, "Duchy".

North Korea: The handshake has only recently been re-introduced in North Korea, replacing the holding a bowl and asking for more of the last century. It is also used as a "good-bye," with handshakes being the standard before execution.

Paraguay: It is considered impolite in Paraguay to shake hands in public as it draws attention to the participants who might be German expatriates, attempting to keep a low profile.

With the handshake's rich history, it's significant to note that there are still many places on earth that have never incorporated the gesture. Whether for considerations of climate, hygiene, religion, or rampant unattractiveness, not a few cultures have opted out of physical touch when greeting. For example, in the Ukraine, the air kiss was adopted after a visit from Marcel Marceau.

In Tibet, people stick out their tongues. This tradition was first introduced by monks who wanted to show that they weren't the reincarnated king Lang "Black Tongue" Dharma. The practice was reinforced in the 1970s by Nelly Olson.

In Thailand, the bow includes the pressing of your own hands together at the heart or higher. The higher one places their hands, the more respect they show. (Some have dislocated their shoulders trying to get an autograph.)

As well, some cultures that don't shy away from the physical (I'm looking at you Bali), have adopted other forms of welcome. People in Yemen have bumped noses since the Arab Spring shut down all Lens Crafters on the Arabian Peninsula. Similarly, many in New Zealand will rub *their* noses together – as well as their foreheads (to test for Yemenis). And in Joe Biden's adopted Polynesian homeland of Tuvalu, they place their nose and upper lip against another's cheek and take a deep sniff. So, yeah, the handshake is better.

The Most Dangerous Game

I believe it was Leonardo DiCaprio who said, "Dating super models is 90% mental. The other half is lots and lots of blow."

Volumes have been written, and much has been debated, about the differences between the sexes. There have been titles such as: *Games People Play* by psychologist, Alan Parsons, who proved through transactional analysis that one may take or leave games people play in the middle of the night; *Men are from Mars, Women are from Venus*, which seems to promote interspecies dating; *What Men Don't Talk About* (obviously it's lumps in the nethers); *Women Who Think Too Much*, from a preeminent expert on women and emotion who suggests that women tend to overanalyze things and then goes on to explain *why*; and *Act Like a Lady, Think Like a Man*, which sounds great at first, but what about shopping? It could create a paradox that would unravel the very fabric of the space-time continuum and destroy the entire universe!

The reason for such a plethora of pornea is because nobody bothers to read past the part in the book where they get validated. It's usually in the introduction, or possibly as late as the first chapter, but the second the woman reads, "...you are not overreacting, you are responding...", or the guy reads, "...it's not a fear of commitment but a form of protection..." – done-sies!

So, if you want to win, read the entire book...or pamphlet...or chapter...or...you know what? You got this.

Studies have shown that women are instinctively drawn to large hunter/gatherer type alpha males (a la Larry King), who are more likely to be good providers. However, substituting for physical dominance, a mastery over tools of provision (rich guys) can curb this instinct. For centuries money seemed to be the only reliable substitute for muscle until the 1960's, when a group dedicated to the discovery and exploration of "What's wrong?" (known as the Students for a

Democratic Society), stumbled across an ancient Amazonian ritual for allying men with women, a ritual known as pandering. What these brave and quite pasty young men found is that the desired effect may be attained by simply providing an *illusion* of compatibility. The technique is a fairly simple application of the following formula:

The product of **A** (words) multiplied by **B** (actions) = **C** (chemistry)
C factored with **X** (history of just being friends) = **Y** (motive)
Y + **Z** (certain latent tendencies) = **Desperation**

$$\underline{Desperation^2} \geq Celibacy$$

It's been claimed that such an application resulted in suffragettism. In fact, the suffrage movement's success was due solely to the creation of the trash compactor. But the understanding afforded by the formula, now known as Alda's theorem, did give hope to many a women's studies major. And the principles gleaned are beneficial for plotting a course of action in the entrapment of a soul mate.

One might note the involvement of institutes of higher learning when it comes to inquiry and experimentation in the field of social convergence sciences. It's an area with quite a protracted and renowned history ranging from the early Edinburgh postulates of first through third base to the modern field experiments on and off the campus of Chico State. We might remember that Freud was tenured at the University of Vienna when he first made the contention that every man was secretly attracted to his mother. (This, of course, was true. Freud's mother was a fox.) What people forget is that he said it at a party. He was trying to make one of those, "everybody thinks it, but won't admit to it" type of sardonic Howard Sternisms. But when the collective Robin Quivers failed to get on board, he went academic, and when you try to present something like that as anything other than perverted you really have to commit. Now he will forever be connected to that darn Oedipus theory that Samuel L Jackson so eloquently paraphrases in the modern vernacular. And sex will forever be inextricably linked to psychology, which explains why all college students love Psych class.

The common denominator that has already emerged here is youth. Doris Day once sang that, "…everybody loves a lover, but your huge pecs don't mean a thing once they start to swing." The bloom of youth can be an extraordinary time. It can be identified with a time of strong passions – for anything – as long as it has a good beat and you can dance to it. Many young men become taken with new ideas and experiences. Their actions reflect a zeal for new things, the same zeal that might put them in a situation where they could be tempted to give in to their adolescent, pulsating, shameful urges. When this happens, give them a cookie.

There are many avenues that may be explored while pursuing a love interest.

There's the conventional:
- Meeting through friends
- Bars
- Grocery stores
- Work
- School
- Prison

The modern:
- Internet
- Reality shows
- Thailand

The old-fashioned way:
- Arranged marriages
- Consulting the entrails of ravens
- Stalking
- Turning up on a desert island with one book and one album

The first step, as outlined above, is the meeting of the prospective mate. This is, perhaps, the most difficult part of the procedure since rejection is assured and, there's no shortage of rejects to compete with. Once the target has been acquired, however, it is usually best to use a direct approach. (A wide flanking maneuver which approaches from behind tends to make women jumpy.) Most women are flattered by the honesty and courage it takes to start a conversation with a stranger and will have much more respect for you when they rebuff your advances. You might walk up to her and simply say, "Excuse me." Now that you've excused yourself, you're free to go home and cry. If that doesn't work, try giving her a compliment. Something like, "I noticed you don't sweat much for a big girl." This shows that you've not only been paying a menacing amount of attention to her, but that she stands out as unique.

Shyness is not an insurmountable problem and, with enough effort, can be transformed into irrational arrogance. It's just a matter of eliminating triggers that cause your shyness. If you're self-conscious, tell yourself that the world is not looking at you. In fact, no one even cares about you. If you're afraid to fail, for god's sake, don't take up baseball. And learn to lie to yourself. If you fear rejection, prepare a mental list of her physical defects before attempting a conversation. If she rejects you, she's probably in a cult.

Other tips to combat shyness would include never putting yourself down or calling yourself names. You're not as good at it as your parents are anyway. And it doesn't help if you spend a lot of time with other shy people. They will only enable you to stay shy, and many of them are cannibals. Make it a point to speak to one stranger every day. There are many people open to these types of interactions, and many of them have candy in their van. Observe how outgoing people interact. This can often be done through a window from their front lawn. You might try taking a class or even speed dating. These abbreviated exchanges only last a few minutes so that uncomfortable experiences end quickly *and* it's an efficient way to populate your offense list.

Another area that needs to be addressed is grooming and hygiene. Axe body spray, a pungent concoction made with equal parts vomit and tear gas, does not cover up B.O. and in every case adds to the problem. Shower…daily…with soap…*everywhere*. Shave. Even if you're a 95 lb. (Or 395 lb.) coder who's going for the lumberjack look, trim it. That goes for ears and nose, too. Unless you plan on becoming Great Britain's prime minister, or you self-identify as an osprey, you don't want feathers shooting out of any cranial orifices. And floss. The bleeding means it's working!

So, you've been talking with a girl for a while. It's now time to ask for her phone number. Don't try to guess it. It rarely works. The one time in history when it did, it preceded a restraining order. And even for the most seasoned womanizer, a lady with a restraining order is a hard nut to crack.

Timing is key when it comes to getting the digits. Too soon, and you might scare her off. Too late, and the pickled eggs might kick in. Look for a lull in the conversation. Maybe at the end of a good laugh or after the knife fight. Saying, "Let's get together sometime" is better than asking, "Would you like to get together sometime?" This shows a positive attitude instead of leaving the door open for her to say no. Asking a woman what she wants sets a bad precedent and flies in the face of every men's journal that says a man's most important attribute is confidence. Tell her what she wants, and then, with an equal amount of assurance, walk calmly, but with purpose, to the men's room and deal with the pickled eggs.

You may want to text instead of making the initial phone call. This is because you are dumb. If you must text, keep it short and to the point: "Hi Amy, this is John*. Enjoyed talking with you yesterday. Let's get some coffee. What day is good for you?'

You don't want to ramble on with needless conversation: "Hi Amy. Do you like things? I do. One thing I like is stuff. Of course, too much stuff can be a problem. Like fun. Too much fun might give you the bends, my mom said. The bends is probably the worst thing except cancer, but at least cancer doesn't give you the bends…whew for that. I've got a great recipe for salad. You should come over and try it. Also, 9/11 was an inside job. Text me back. It's been an hour since I sent the first message and I haven't heard back, which is weird because you said it would be ok if I texted, but you haven't texted. It's just weird.

---

* The names have been changed. Her name is John and *his* is Amy.

Anyways, when we go out (I'm assertive), you should wear the same dress you were wearing the other day when you were at work up on the 11th floor...or the 12th. It's hard to tell from the outside. No big deal. I'm confident. How was your day? I went by the gym. It looked pretty packed from the street. So text me so we can do something so I don't have to meet anybody else. I've been meeting a lot of Jewish girls and I don't like their hips. Bye. Do hashtags work on texts? #alllivesmatter. Text me."

While texting is an option, it is usually best to start with a phone call. Just pick up the phone and ask her out. If she says yes, you're off and running. If she says no, it's her loss. She's forfeited her place on the good list when you finally twist off.

The trick to a first date is to just enjoy it. Don't pressure the situation with unrealistic expectations. Simply ask her a question about herself and use the next couple of hours for some "me" time. While including a strategically timed nod from time to time, do some calf extensions or ankle rotations. Try some Kegels. Just be careful to not be obvious when following the game on the TV behind her.

Be sure to include plenty of eye contact but don't be too intense. The perfect scenario is to rest one elbow, casually, on the table while you tilt your head slightly, with a partially open smile, and looking into just one of her eyes. (Experts suggest it's best to look into the left eye – that's her good one.) A less-than-perfect scenario would be to stare at her without blinking while intensely gripping your beer stein, and grinding your teeth.

If things go well, you may get a second date. Then a third and even a fourth. Using this line of reasoning you can foresee as many as seven dates. All of this time spent together is, of course, leading to one thing: A credit check. If all seems in order, a blood test. Blood tests, incidentally, have never prevented anybody from being married. In fact, most states no longer require premarital blood testing because treatments for venereal diseases are usually addressed in the prenups.

If you follow these steps closely, current statistics say you've got a 47% chance of ending up in a successful marriage, so put your name in your books.

But is Sasquatch Bi-lingual?

In an effort to clear up the many misconceptions and to, once and for all, put to rest all of the controversy regarding Peru – if the reader has any questions as to the nature of this controversy, please send a self-addressed stamped envelope and a crisp twenty-dollar bill – the following is an excerpt from the book, South America on Two Sips a Day, *by Theodore Roosevelt, under the pseudonym Samuel Clemens.*

HISTORY

Peru was originally discovered in 1321 by Swedish conquistador, Sven Gutierrez, who proclaimed it "Lamalandikstan" in the name of the queen. The details of exactly *which* queen have been the source of some controversy, but it is now widely accepted that Gutierrez was referring to a friend from Key West. Lamalandikstan remained largely unpopulated until it was *re*discovered in 1926 and subsequently *re*founded by Sicilian-born explorer, Joey 'The Spoon'* Peruzio, who was looking to make a name for himself in the coffee rackets. Peruzio renamed the country *New* Lamalandikstan, but after his untimely death, in which he was decapitated by a booby-trapped walnut, the name was shortened to, simply, Peru.

Little is known of the history of the region before the rise of the Inca. The earliest settlers were peoples unrelated to the Incas, but were still referred to as aunt and uncle by the kids. These groups began to migrate south from Mexico about 1000 BCE and then returned almost immediately when one of them realized that they had forgotten to turn off the gas.

In 1542 the first Spanish viceroy landed in Peru. (He actually *arrived* in 1541, but had mistaken some peyote buttons for Dramamine on the voyage over and in those days each step took a month.) His mission was to enforce the "New Laws for the Indies."

---

* So named for his unique, if not consoling, way of greeting people

The idea of these "New Laws..." was to end cruelties inflicted on the native Indians. Unfortunately, the laws never went into effect because the viceroy, shortly after his swearing-in, committed suicide by stabbing himself in the back fifteen times. According to his suicide note, discovered by his partisan rivals, he was concerned about loosening restrictions for fear of Indian tendencies toward heavy deforestation, strip mining, and exploitation of other natural resources.

Finally, in 1561, order was brought to the region by Spanish administrator Francisco de Toledo Ohio y Summero en Vino Martho, who established a highly effective system of government that incorporated magistrates, sub-magistrates, elected local officials and social programs based on the writings of Caligula.

During World War II, Peru's main seaport, Peruingrad, served as a naval base for both the Allied *and* Axis powers. This greatly disrupted much of Peru's civilian population – especially the laundry service, which was endlessly reattaching little red balls to hats and letting out the ankles of altered bellbottoms after delivery mix-ups. This confusion didn't stop with civilians, however. At one point, Hirohito ordered the dive-bombing of his own houseboat in the Swiss Alps. As it turns out, the original plan to invade America by way of amphibious assault from the Great Lakes was lost when FDR's Hawaii vacation plans were transmitted to Tojo's secretary instead. In this way, Peru had a hand in history.

GEOGRAPHY

Nothing written about Peru would be complete without some mention of Machu Picchu, so let's just consider this section abridged.

Although Peru has over 35 major rivers, it has but two navigable lakes, the most famous being Lake Titicaca, named by a nomadic tribe of eleven-year-old boys. The other is Lake Junin – the site of the 1824 Battle of Junin. Actually, the Battle of Junin is in reference to the *town* of Junin. In reality, the town where the battle was *fought* was San Ramón. If truth be told, it wasn't really a *battle* in the conventional sense. What happened was this...

In 1824 slavery was big business in Peru (not like in 1831, when the *real* money was in guano collecting – biotech). At that time there was much upheaval due to management's refusal to accept a "no trade" clause in the slave union's collective bargaining agreement. Many slaves had threatened to walk, while slave owners threw around terms like lockout and replacement slaves and execution. Through all of this, the real losers were the slave boat captains and their crews. These "matchmakers of the sea" now found themselves in the unenviable position of explaining to their children that, "daddy can't afford to buy you that beetle nut." Finally, the tumult came to a head, during a solar eclipse, in the high mountain village of Cerro de Pasco. There, under the cover of hazy orangeness, a small yet tiny platoon of George Custer-trained commandos attacked a saloon they mistook for a children's hospital. The mayhem soon spread through-out the village. Before long, the local militia – trapped inside a windowless bunker – began firing their cannons in all directions. Within hours, the bearing walls were sufficiently ruptured so that the state-owned bakery next door was in a shambles and ill equipped to meet the morning bagel needs of over one third of the country. A hurried effort to provide English muffins, in the bagel's stead, was organized. But the delivery companies had much difficulty placing the adjectives before the nouns. When children started to turn up missing after failing to navigate the many nooks and crannies of the Anglo breakfast staple, Operation Muffin English was declared a disaster.

By this time there had been a run on rye toast, and many politicians, educators, and clerics had tried to divert the people's attention with peanut butter on apple wedges. This only served to lend legitimacy to the Rice Cake & Power Bar Caucus. A recently vocal political party which was once viewed as alternative, it was now claiming to speak for all Peruvians who believed in, "a little morning nosh."

As more and more citizens began grabbing a bite on the way to work, the Secretary General for the administration's Committee on the Four Food Groups & Un-Peruvian Snack Activities struck a secretive deal with the RC&PB Caucus' representative to Junin, Eduardo de Esposa de Poptartes. The agreement called for an end to the boycott on imported Jamaican lox in return for a sizeable percentage of the profits from marshmallow charm manufacturing. The fragile arrangement managed to quell the unrest for a time, but eventually dissolved as people began to realize that the bagels would probably never be schmeared. Poptartes had actually promised Jamaican *dread* lox, which were to be self-harvested by a commune of Rastafarians living in an ether factory who never quite got around to it.

The resulting Battle of Junin lasted for six long weeks, as school children performed poorly and the working class looked to the zany antics of the morning zoo crew to escape their gnawing hunger pangs. Then came Frenchy Francois, a Belgian scientist and dietician who discovered brunch while experimenting with uses for honeydew melon and prosciutto. Frenchy's discovery not only signaled the end of the warring, but also served as the first step in Peru's arduous journey toward pretense.

POPULATION

Nine out of ten babies born in Peru are christened Roman Catholic. This can come as quite a shock to some of the Jewish families. In accordance with a law passed in 1915, Roman Catholicism is the established religion of the country. However, other religions are tolerated as evidenced by the popular phrase, "Hogla Cuto Choge!" This commonly-used salutation translates literally, "Inquisitions are fun!"

The United Nations estimates the overall population density of Peru at 29 persons per square mile. Sometimes more than 29 persons will inhabit one square mile. Sometimes as many as 37 persons will inhabit one square and this often results in bloody feuds that produce very catchy folk songs.

Peru is inhabited mainly by Peruvians. (Where else could they go in them funny hats?) It is, however, lousy with tourism, being an outdoorsman's paradise. Scuba diving is very popular – particularly in areas where there is water. Peru is also a haven for cross-country runners – although it has fewer per capita than its southern neighbor, Chile, since *that* country is quite a bit quicker to run across. Downhill skiing is enjoyed by many and is much less taxing than uphill skiing. The sport of cliff diving got its start in Peru, although originally it was referred to as merely losing one's balance.

The Indian heritage of Peru is one of the richest in South America. Although Spain gave Peru its language, religion, government, and many of its choicest diseases, the highly developed (and yet quaint to the woke affluent tourist) civilization of the Inca has left its traces throughout Peruvian culture. Archeological excavations have uncovered monumental Indian remains that threaten to slow the construction of Trump Tower Cusco. Architecture of the Spanish colonial period is a fusion of Spanish and Indian known as Creole Funkadelic. In art, the "Indigenist" school pointedly interprets 20th century Peru in a decisively Indian mode, while "Minimalists" tend to term the style as "too painty". The Incan pentatonic musical scale is still used today in car alarms. And ancient instruments, such as conch shells, flutes, and panpipes, can still be heard in modern Peruvian compositions as well as Pink Floyd's headier Christmas tunes.

Monogamy, polygamy, trigonometry, and Jai-alai are all practiced in Peru. Trigonometry is practiced by herdsmen and people without cable. Polygamy is practiced among those whose wealth affords it. Monogamy is practiced by those who have let themselves go. Jai-alai, however, was trademarked by Disney just prior to the release of *Tron* and is no longer practiced in Peru by court order.

NATURAL RESOURCES

The Peruvian condor is a native of Peru. The Peruvian condor lives in the canopy of the Peruvian rain forest and feeds on Peruvian rain forest squirrels and mice. According to the book, *Vegetables Taste Like Frailty*, written by big game hunter, Sir Julian Leggy, who has hunted exotic animals all over the world*, there are only 33 Peruvian

* He once shot a wildebeest during an Oscar party at Spagos

condors left in the Peruvian rain forest. The reason that there are only 33 Peruvian condors left in the Peruvian rain forest is that there is a shortage of Peruvian rain forest squirrels and mice, which the natives eat in great quantities – especially as a delightful side dish with baked Peruvian condor.

ARTS & LITERATURE

Peru first became known to the industrialized world when Rock Hudson made a movie about it called, *Meet Me in St. Lima*, in which a blonde Rock and a young Frank Sinatra are rivals for the love of a wet Esther Williams. Esther is, in turn, in love with a full-sized replica of the Spruce Goose, which reminds her of her Cox model trainer she had as a kid. The three attempt to smuggle the plane out of the Andes, but the plan is foiled when, at lower elevations, Esther's face-lift begins to unravel, forcing her to take a job as a dancer under the name Suzie Creases. The movie ends with Esther gliding from tree to tree while Kenny Loggins sings *All of Me*.

THE BROWN WEDGIE

Peru is the highest country in South America. (Bogotá is a *city*) Yet is in the hot hazy desert of southwest Peru where lies, what many have called, one of the most baffling enigmas of archeology. Huge geometric patterns and images are etched into the desert's surface. Known as the Nazca lines, these images have mystified geologists and archeologists alike since the late 1920s, when intellectuals first started doing shrooms.

From the ground, the geoglyphs look like a series of paths crisscrossing the desert floor leading to nowhere. But when seen from the air, many people scream hysterically as they are hurled to the ground under the force of gravity. It's only when viewed from a plane that one sees how the lines and figures convey a sense of purpose. The figures include a monkey, a spider, a whale, a snake, a hummingbird, and what seems to be a man with the head of an owl. It is this "owl man" that many have studied in an effort to understand just what kind of people built these tremendous monuments. Some believe that these figures were created by a race of giants and that the image of the "owl man" was merely a chalk outline of the victim of a bird attack. Others are concentrating their efforts studying the geometric shapes and spirals. One theory is that these shapes were ancient highways used to keep the less intelligent people busy during the day.

Scientists have noticed an interesting similarity between the Nazca lines, Stonehenge, and the Heads of Easter Island. Some of these similarities include the magnetic properties of each. It seems that at all of these locations, due North is in exactly the same direction. This anomaly seems to be constant no matter which direction a person faces.

The Andes and their proximity to Brazil, Bolivia, and Tijuana make Peru the ideal habitat for its most infamous resident, the Chupacabra. This elusive creature is rarely seen by humans. Those who *have* seen one often tend to vary greatly in their description, and many eyewitnesses prefer to simply wink and nod knowingly. One constant in most descriptions, however, is that the creature has fur. This, of course, has served to alienate the PETA crowd and thus, most Chupacabra are very suspicious of anyone carrying paint cans or buckets of pig's blood.

Stories of the Chupacabra can be strange. Many have reported seeing them fly (but never in coach). One woman tells a story of how, while out driving one night, she came upon a crowd of them milling around in the middle of the road. When she honked her horn, most of them peered at her with grass hanging from their mouths, but a few walked up to the car and stared right down her blouse. Another man from a tiny mountain village relates that he awoke one night to find a Chupacabra hovering about the ceiling. "We just looked at each other for the longest time..." the man says, "...but then it began to belch and slowly descend until it landed and explained that it 'would love to stay but had to return to the tour with the rest of the group'".

Clearly, the Chupacabra are a phenomena that must be recognized, as is evidenced by the fact that eight of the top forty Fortune 500 corporations are headed by, either someone of Chupacabra descent, or someone who has had an immediate family member deloused and fingerprinted by a Chupacabra-American.

So as the sun slowly sinks over the equator – or Ecuador, I can't tell with all the funny words they use down there – we climb onto the bus, down a fifth of penicillin and wave goodbye to Peru. Good-bye Don Peruzio. Farewell, Andes Mountains. God speed, Peruvian condor, squirrel, and mouse. See you later, monogamy, polygamy, trigonometry and Jai-alai. And so long Chupacabra. Tell Roger Patterson and Bob Gimlin we said hi.

Sister Bertrille's Headgear and the Java Jive

I believe it was Ted Bundy who said, "Walk softly and carry a big stick." He was a bad guy that Ted Bundy.

Turns out, growing up he had developed a lot of bad habits. And he's not the only infamous character dominated by his negative tendencies. Nero had a nasty habit of spitting, especially on martyrs. Napoleon constantly bit his nails just to make his hands look bigger. Members of the Donner party had the shameful practice of chewing with their mouths open. And Hitler – do I go to the Hitler well too often? – was a notorious nose picker, the obvious reason for the shortage of people named Adolf after 1945.

From gambling to cracking your knuckles, there seems to be no end to the list of bad habits. Some lists even include gluten. And drugs of all types are not only bad habits, they tend to be addictive as well.

There's tobacco. Its popularity has waned over the years, but there are still an estimated 34 million Americans who smoke. This means that if you are in a room with ten people, at least nine of them will wave their hand in front of their nose, fake a violent cough, and voice their disgust loudly enough to be heard by the smoker outside. Tobacco smoking dates back around 5000 years when native Americans used it ceremonially, medicinally, and as an accessory while reading their own poetry. In 1964, Surgeon General Luther Terry announced that cigarette smoking causes lung cancer. Terry, himself a longtime smoker, looked pretty cool when he would take a drag and point to an actuary table with the two fingers he would use to hold his Winston Reds.

Nicotine, comprising up to 3% of the dry weight of tobacco, (vs water weight, which usually occurs when trying to *kick* the habit) is highly addictive, and dependence can develop within days, typically from Wednesday through the weekend. Nicotine is also found in tomatoes, eggplant, bell peppers and other popular nightshades. This would explain why you'll find dozens of jalapeño tops littering the sidewalk outside emergency rooms.

In recent years "vaping" has gained in popularity with teens, who are 7 times more likely to smoke than adults who've heard "good things." Of the kids who vape, 97% use flavors. The other 3% have never heard of umami. As a result, the FDA has restricted most vaping flavors. The big tobacco lobby has successfully found loopholes in these regulations, while *meager* tobacco has endured quite a hit to their bottom line. There's been a push of late to eradicate vaping among teens by means of PSAs, print campaigns, and school assemblies. These campaigns are sure to have success, leaving youths free to drink, do drugs, and stay sexually active, because you can't stop them from doing what they want to do.

Despite much evidence to the contrary, marijuana has been touted as non-addictive. This claim has mostly come from potheads, and then they usually giggle afterward. These enthusiasts fought for years to have the drug legalized. In this regard, they are singularly focused. Discussing, virtually, any other topic presents the same difficulty as trying to take a portrait photo of infant triplets and an Australian Shepherd. Let the topic turn to THC, and suddenly you're talking to Neil DeGrasse Tyson. One minute your companion is dumbfounded by Jell-O, the next, they're conducting a power point presentation accompanied by beakers and a slide rule.

The only cause more compelling to marijuana aficionados is hemp. If this subject comes up, clear your calendar because hemp is the stoner singularity. You will be immediately informed that hemp is used for a variety of products, including rope, clothing, shoes, paper, bioplastics, insulation, and fuel. Hemp seeds can even be a foodstuff, whether eaten raw or used to make, with a little patience and some even littler buckets, hemp milk. As a construction material, hemp, and lime (just a squeeze) can be mixed to make a concrete-like insulating building block.

A hemp advocate may pull you aside to tell you how Henry Ford's first car was made of hemp. If this happens, be careful not to ask too many questions, as this may frustrate the storyteller and provoke a series of counter questions designed to indoctrinate you:

"What do you need? What do you need, man? You need jet fuel? Try hemp."

"What's the problem? Gummed up rivers? Nuclear waste? They're usin' hemp."

"You sad? You lonely? You need a friend? Hemp loves you, man."

Alcohol, a depressant, is consumed as a way to relax, achieve social conformity, or to become obnoxious. Some health benefits have been associated with moderate drinking, such as a lower risk of heart disease or stroke, or plausible deniability when it comes to who threw up in the fish tank.

Still, alcoholism is considered a disease, though not by people with smallpox. When the disease takes hold, the alcoholic will begin to drink more than they intended. This could become quite dangerous if the person had originally intended to drink a barrel of Scotch. While many alcoholics claim they can stop drinking whenever they want, like all disease sufferers, they eventually die.

Coffee seems to get a pass as both a drug and a bad habit. There are t-shirts and mugs, posters, and memes, even websites all devoted to how funny it is that people are jackasses in the morning. Unless you live in Florida, it would never be acceptable to say something like, "Don't even talk to me until I've had my speed ball." And someone with a sweet tooth could never show up late to a meeting and blame it on the line at the soda fountain. But everyone seems to think caffeine addiction is cute.

Coffee is remarkably similar to other drugs in that it's rare for people to enjoy their first time. Many *think* they did, but that's only because they don't remember that they were toddlers and their father, while attempting to eat his Rooty Tooty Fresh 'N Fruity and tired of pushing the mug out of the baby's reach, caved and gave them a sip. Nor do they remember the face they made when they first tasted it.

This is because, absent addiction, coffee smells and tastes like smoked diaper. That's why most pour sugar into it by the kilo; it takes the edge off that stoolie aftertaste.

Many have adopted coffee as a status symbol. They have their own grinders, which are really just opportunities to tell you the story of how they found it at a quaint little open market in Senegal. Or they only purchase beans that have already been passed through the digestive tract of some other animal. This is a process known as gross. Animals like the Asian palm civet eat the ripest, and therefore sweetest, coffee cherries, and enzymes in their stomach break down the beans' proteins and remove much of their bitterness. Then the beans are passed through the animal's bowels to your waiting cup, poised for a piping hot wake-up dose. A single cup of this type can cost $80.00 because of its rarity and its decadent taste. And if you think about it, what could be more decadent than drinking something out of another creature's sphincter? Sewer cockroaches have the life.

There are those who simply take their coffee black. We know this because they rarely shut up about it. Their pride in this specialty is rivaled only by spicy food eaters and CrossFitters. Even politically active atheists have been known to run out of pontifical steam when competing for stage time with such a coffee purist. In the wild, they have no natural enemies but one competitor – all day coffee-drinking guy. All day, every day. No matter how hot the weather gets, he always has his thermos at the ready. If asked how he can continue to drink hot coffee on 90° days, he will explain that the drink makes him sweat, and sweat cools the body. This is true. Hot coffee will make you sweat...almost as much as 90° days. And while it is also true that sweating *is* a cooling mechanism, in the time of air conditioning, maybe it shouldn't necessarily be plan A.

Certainly, substance abuse would be deemed a bad habit. But, perhaps, the most common and most accepted of habits is profanity. In Western culture "cursing" has become so prevalent, that, in a 1998 study conducted by the Osborne family, 87% of Americans considered obscene language to be as essential to life as love, family, personal fulfillment, and pupusas. Pupusas are thick griddle cakes made from cornmeal and often stuffed with cheese, meat, or beans. and sometimes used in place of love, family, or personal fulfillment in some South American countries.

If you are struggling with some bad habit, it is often helpful to search for a new incentive that is more rewarding than the existing behavior. If you are a shopaholic due to loneliness, join a social club (and put down the shopahol). If you obsessively check your phone because you want to stay "in the know," set time aside to read a newspaper (and you'll be, "in the past"). If you emotionally overeat, relax, and have some cake. And don't be afraid to look after yourself spiritually. I believe it was Desmond Tutu who said, "I don't drink, I don't smoke, and I don't swear...Damn, I left my cigar in the pub."

Better To Remain Silent

I believe it was Confucius who said, "I didn't say that."

Indeed, all through history, the misquote has been a source of both confusion and angst, debate and controversy, lighthearted stories of misunderstanding and World War II. (It turns out that Goering *thought* that Hitler said, "Obstacles do not exist to be surrendered to, but only to be broken." When in reality he had only quipped, "Someday I'd like to see Poland.")

Antiquity is rife with misstatements and embellishments. And while it's distilled in India, antiquity just aint antiquity till you're talkin' Greece. For instance, Socrates, a philosopher mostly known for realizing he didn't know anything, was once misquoted as saying, "The unexamined life is not worth living." But what he really said was, "Does anyone else feel a draft in these togas?"

Plato, Socrates' student, has also been credited with such clever adages as, "The greatest wealth is to live content with little." Which has been paraphrased from, "The gig doesn't pay, but it's great exposure." Or "Never discourage anyone who makes progress, no matter how slowly." When he usually just asked, "Mind if I play through?" And perhaps the most popular saying attributed to him: "Beauty lies in the eyes of the beholder," was actually "I think you'll like her. She's got a great personality."

Not to be overlooked is Plato's adherent, Aristotle, who was thought to have said, "The gods too are fond of a joke." But, in truth, what he said was, "A priest, a rabbi, and an oracle walk into a bar…"

Another Greek sage/homeless man was Diogenes. He has been partially quoted as saying, "I threw my cup away when I saw a child drinking from his hands at a trough." What is usually omitted is the second sentence: "I then stole a bucket, pushed the little puke out of the way, and drank my fill."

Niccolò Machiavelli was the victim of extensive altering of his book, *The Prince*, by his editor. We were left to read, "It is better to be loved than feared, if you cannot be both." What was excluded was "If you *can* be both, you're probably wasabi."

Frederick Nietzsche, we're told, said, "That which does not kill us, makes us stronger." Again, this quote was abbreviated. He finished with, "except for 3rd degree burns, polio, rickets, and crocodile attacks."

Mohandas Gandhi walked the countryside, often barefoot, which left the soles of his feet dry and hard. While trying to encourage his countrymen spiritually, he contended with frailties from his years of physical trials, and his meager diet resulted in bad breath. Yes*, he was a super-calloused fragile mystic, vexed with halitosis.†

The Mahatma was also a victim of misquotes. The most egregious example? "Nobody can hurt me without my permission." What he really said was, "OK Indira, what we need is a safe word."

An American scholar, Ben Franklin is, perhaps, the most quoted and, in turn, most *mis*quoted intellectual. "A true friend is the best possession" came from, "I've got you now." And "Those who live in glass houses should not throw stones" sounds better than, "I'm looking for a 3 Bed/2Bath concrete bunker. I like to party."

Franklin's contemporary, Thomas Jefferson didn't *say*, "The glow of one warm thought is, to me, worth more than money." What he *wrote* was, "This coupon is redeemable for one free backrub."

When it comes to politicians, they almost count on being misquoted to keep plausible deniability. Whether it be Ronald Reagan who never said, "Mr. Gorbachev, tear down this wall" but rather, "Mikhail, we never talk anymore" to Herbert Hoover, who's PR team put out a palatable, "Children are our most valuable resource" instead of what he really said, "Why aren't we using those little monsters to run our cars?"

One young and well-to-do progressive had his words distorted as well. JFK didn't say, "We choose to go to the moon…" What he said was, "One of these days Jackie, One of these days."

Soldiers' quotes tend to be quite pithy. (It's important to stay hydrated.) But many have been misrepresented. Remember John Paul Jones who never said, "I have not yet begun to fight." What he said

---

*Say it out loud.
†Aaaaaaaaaaand, you're welcome.

was, "I'll be out as soon as I finish this article." And lest we forget, Douglas McArthur's famous, "I shall return" was originally, "I'm goin' out for some smokes."

Another Naval leader and Civil War hero, Admiral David G. Farragut, was alleged to have yelled, "Damn the torpedoes! Full speed ahead!" when his fleet encountered a submerged mine field. What he said was, "Watch this. I saw it once on *Dukes of Hazard*."

And there was General Fredrick C. Blesse who was incorrectly quoted as saying, "No guts, no glory," while he was staring at a disemboweled corpse. What he actually said was "No open casket for this fella."

You might think that writers would be able to avoid misquotes owing to their medium. But you'd be wrong. Ralph Waldo Emerson didn't say, "What lies behind you and what lies in front of you, pale in comparison to what lies inside of you." He said, "That tape worm is huge!"

Although Tolkien is constantly being quoted as saying, "Not all who wander are lost," he actually said, "These bloody French tourists can't drive for bollocks!"

James R. Sherman did not say, "Although no one can go back and make a brand-new start, anyone can start from now, and make a brand-new ending." What he said was, "Have you seen *The Last Jedi*?"

Even Helen Keller was misquoted when she said, "Life is either a daring adventure or nothing." When in reality her words were "Nife ine neeno uh nowing ununuh no nony."

With all of these distortions it would be easy to develop a cynical attitude toward once helpful insights and witticisms. Go with that feeling. All quotes come from imperfect humans. None are divine utterances: "Oh. Keates said that? Was he another flawed human who was unable to outthink death? I'll be sure to file his thoughts on beauty." Unless it's how to win with a spread offense, I don't really care about what Vince Lombardi has to say.

Fittingly, the best advice to both explain and avoid the misquote: "Silence is often misinterpreted but never misquoted," came from Anonymous.

Come On Eileen
(An Assessment and Justification)

I believe it was Joseph Stalin who said, "No pain, no gain."

Many laughed at him when he first offered that phrase as a party slogan (mostly because he said it with drinking straws dangling from his nostrils). But the idea is no less poignant. From great pain comes great screaming. And that screaming will echo in the minds of the poets. Sometimes, after thoughtful meditation and deep searches in the depths of their souls, those poets will scribble down some sort of pretentious tripe, and find a way to make it profitable.

Such was the case with "Dexy's Midnight Runners." Originally a disco band that went by the name, "Helter Skelton and the Funny Faces," the group eventually became disillusioned with the monotonous rhythms and tight polyester associated with the club scene. They searched for hours looking for a new sound and a means of cover that would provide warmth yet ventilation. They managed to find both at a flea market just outside of London. It was there that they discovered, amid a pile of overalls and rusted stationary bikes, a small stack of 45-rpm records by folk artist, Dexter O'Blick.

O'Blick was a Turkish-born Irishman whose parents owned and operated a Christian Science reading room/cannabis club in Dublin. During the Hash Famine of 1917 the family moved to Amsterdam, where his father became an investment banker and his mother a Sikh. His parents had always been inclined toward arguments but, with the house now religiously divided – and armed – things went from bad to worse. When Dexter was nine, both parents filed for divorce. His mother cited infidelity and his father accused his mother of whetting in bed.

By age 14, Dexy – as he was now known – already a veteran urchin, had developed quite a reputation for being unwashed and a little fuzzy. Around that time Rupert Burns, a local record producer and renowned chicken hawk, discovered O'Blick while soliciting back rubs at the local YMCA. Initially he recruited Dexy to transport black market auto parts into England by having him swallow balloons filled with lug nuts and then flying into Heathrow in an iron lung to get past the metal detectors. But the plan never materialized when Burns realized that his TV reception was improved when Dexy was wheeled into the center of his study. O'Blick spent four years stuck in the contraption while he absorbed everything he could from television. Its impact on his worldviews, as well as his bladder and digestive system, would later be reflected in his third album entitled, *Atrophy and the BBC*.

Eventually Dexy made his way back to the UK and took advantage of the damp climate to rust his way out of the machine. Then, with little more than a cursory knowledge of music theory and low-grade schizophrenia induced by the love theme to *Dr. Who*, he set out to make his name in the music business. He died at the age of 83 with a slew of hits to his name. While never truly appreciated in life, his legacy of post-modern socialist doctrine set to hard driving lute riffs found a home in the ears and minds of the band that would become his namesake. And *their* biggest hit would be an homage to his life.

The very first words in the song reflect the life-long insecurities that Dexy futilely wrestled with: *"Poor old Johnny Ray sounded sad upon the radio."* The Johnny Ray referred to here is not the immensely unidentifiable cultural icon remembered only by the sub sect of hippies known as Raybies, but rather an old boarding school chum of Dexy's, Johnny Ray Festus. The two met on the playground when Dexy slid into Johnny Ray while playing ball. Festus, who had been born with no arms or legs, was third base. Despite a concussion and quite a few permanent scars left by Dexy's spikes, Johnny Ray seemed very at ease with Dexy. The two became fast friends and spent many an afternoon holding down papers and propping open doors.

That Johnny Ray was sounding sad alludes to his predisposition to melancholy, as Dexy would often forget where he left him. His habit of skewering Johnny on everyday objects reached a flash point on one occasion when Dexy extended the telescoping antenna on his boom box too far, leaving Johnny Ray bearing quite a resemblance to a unicorn. The result was a feud between the two that lasted well into their adult lives. In fact, they remained estranged until Dexy visited Johnny Ray on his deathbed. He had sustained fatal injuries from a fall in Paris, where he had been working as a gargoyle. Years later Dexy was heard to say that the radio incident caused him to take stock of his life and resolve to give back. Unfortunately, Dexy never asked about the drop off location for giving back, and would drive around Great Britain leaving all sorts of used and broken items out on the curb. As a result, Dexy was blamed for London's disarray immediately following World War II.

"He moved a million hearts in mono." Many scholars originally believed that the, *he* mentioned here is still referring to Festus. But with closer examination the word mono clearly calls to mind Dexy's lifelong battle with mononucleosis, which at one time was thought to cause heart disease in smokers and coal miners.

Too, Dexy had been known to play the field and was reputed to court as many as two women at one time. Thus, the *"in"* mono was most likely a substitute preposition, since the outrageous interest rates of the late 1970s made *"with"* cost prohibitive on the London Word Exchange for up-and-coming song writers.

"Our mothers cried and sang along and who'd blame them. Now you're grown, so grown..." With this graphic description of a drunken scene at Chippendales, the song emphasizes the reality of Dexy's difficult childhood. In effect, the lyrics cry out an ode to stolen innocence. While still living at home, Dexy was constantly burdened with the responsibility of caring for his mother, whose vices became more and more peculiar as his talents became more and more transparent. It wasn't uncommon for her to drop £15,000 in a week on seedless watermelons just to, as she put it, "...taunt God."

Although this saddening commentary seems to be directed to the public at large, the significance of its ambiguity reaches untold depths. It's been said that when Prime Minister Thatcher first heard this portion of the song she wept openly. Evidently, she had been given a purple nurple. Also, the United Nations Council on Pop Culture, Fashion and Interfaith unanimously declared August 8th (the anniversary of Dexy's first flight from Dover to two-thirds of the way across the English Channel in his solar powered "Gossamer Sloth" flying wing) as Dexter 'Dexy' O'Blick day in 1984.

The song goes on: *"...now I must say more than ever go toora loora toora loo rye aye."* "Toora loora loora," as everybody knows, is an Irish lullaby. Its origin can be found in a Celtic chant, which was first recited by Irish patriots during a 1541 festival celebrating an event where the English didn't beat them up again.

Its use here, however, does not signal any specific affinity O'Blick might have had for the incantation. Rather, the directive for it to *'Go'* reveals quite the opposite. Dexy hated the tune. For a short time, he took work in a piano bar and the constant requests for it built in him an utter disdain. In fact, often, when asked to play it, he would refuse to sing it properly and, instead, substituted words like pee pee and doody for the actual lyrics. This style of improvisational song writing developed a strong following and in time produced its own specialty artists – all looking to Dexy as their biggest influence.

One of his most successful disciples was 'Odd Shamus' McYankovich, whose biggest hit, "*Jingle bells Batman smells*", became a perennial favorite amongst the young and cutting-edge fans. So popular was the genre that secret societies began to pop up all over the UK with the expressed objective of quashing all sober sing-alongs.

How did Dexy and others respond? The verse continues: *"And we can sing just like our fathers."* Although Dexy's father was not an alcoholic, he had always aspired to become one and was a member of many amateur drinking clubs. He subscribed to all the beverage enthusiast magazines and even sent away for a home pub kit. All of this, but the credentials associated with a fall-down drunk continued to elude him. By the time Dexy had started to make a name for himself in the music business, he and his father had all but abandoned any notions that his drinking would ever be anything but moderate. However, Dexy *had*, by now, learned to slur. His father was now able to live vicariously through Dexy and one of his kidneys.

The second verse starts with a haunting word picture: *"These people round here wear beaten down eyes…"* When Dexy turned 40 he decided it was time to begin his mid-life crisis. But instead of taking the usual path of buying a sports car and a zodiac medallion he, as was often his wont, zagged when others expected him to zig. The result was a high-speed collision, which sent twelve to the hospital. *"…sunk in smoke-dried faces."* Yes, these words are actually paraphrased from one of Dexy's own tunes. He wrote, *Queue the Druids. Rue the Druids*, right after the accident as a means of coping with the guilt he felt for his part in the tragedy. He simply could not shake his feelings of responsibility since it was his idea to paint a tunnel on the side of a brick wall and leave a plate of birdseed. He never got over the trauma of that incident and up to his death, refused to allow his suits to go out for Martinizing as he felt Lewis was the engine that moved the boat. (At least in the film version of *My Friend Irma*.)

"They're so resigned to what their fate is…" In the late 1960's Dexy, flush with cash and intoxicated by his own celebrity, felt that the music, while still obligatory, was not nearly as important as choreography to the significance of his craft. To this end, he decided to form a cult, the doctrinal foundation of which was that, in order to truly understand life, one must embrace the implication of pyrotechnics and the value of headset microphones. He started with a small crowd of twenty or so followers whom he recruited from the Gap. His message seemed to be a perfect fit for those young men and women who had spent their adolescence engrossed in *Tiger Beat*. His promises of a utopia where all would be guaranteed a red Miata, time in the spotlight, and a date with Leif Garret quickly commanded legions of devotees. Before long, the ranks of his minions swelled to twenty-three. Their call to arms, *"…But not us, no not us."* was often misinterpreted by the bourgeoisie literates and highfalutin wage earners of the time to mean that these feral teens had no intention of ever maturing. In actuality, it signified their collective confidence that never would they fall for the circle game. *"We are far too young and clever…"*

"...Eileen, I'll sing this tune forever." This is the first mention of Eileen in the song, most likely because she had been underage until this point. In fact, the name Eileen is used all throughout the chorus, but only once in the body of the song. This is an obvious insinuation that Dexy and his first steady girlfriend, Eileen Thwump, while carrying on a very public affair of intense eye contact, never actually met. They had first noticed each other in a crowded bar where Dexy had arranged to meet a man who needed his wife killed. (Dexy had recently read a book that introduced the juxtaposition of nihilism, hedonism, capitalism, and life insurance.) Eileen was also there under curious circumstances. She was the official taster for Princess Margaret's closest friend and sorority sister, Muffy, Countess of Whitney, who was fixated with karaoke, as well as its less-than-timid cousin, air guitar. The two took the stage to perform *"Old Time Rock & Roll"* and Dexy immediately noticed Eileen. With her Tracy Partridge-esque charisma contrasted with the countess's Ray-bans, button-down shirt and tighty whities, he was smitten. Of course he dare not approach her for fear of throwing off her timing – or rather, lack thereof. She was unable to keep up with the Silver Bullet Band because of the *other* song she just wouldn't get out of her head. The song referred to above, i.e. *"It's a Small World After All."*

Eileen had been suffering the maddening effects of the song since her first visit to Disneyland six years prior. On a couple of occasions she had attempted to end it all by embracing jazz fusion, but now with her new love, John (The name she *thought* Dexy uttered just before he bowed out of the room for about 3 minutes), she resolved to meet her challenge head on and endure no matter what it would take. The next day she took her own life with a razor. When she plugged it in, a spark ignited the petrol that she was bathing in to get good and clean for her hanging.

Dexy took the news hard. He sat at the funeral home for three days mourning next to the body, until the family of the deceased person he mistook for Eileen (It was a closed casket, and he estimated the weight displacement based on its dimensions. Unfortunately, Dexy hadn't learned the metric system and the body was that of a 584 lb.

shut-in who died due to complications associated with sausage fingers), eventually laid their dearly departed to rest in a converted shipping container.

Coincidentally, this would not be the only Eileen who had an impact on Dexy's life. The fact that there are two choruses suggests the significance of two more Eileens that would leave their marks on Dexy's consciousness. *"Come on Eileen, well I swear (what he means).* The first was Eileen Viscus. She had, at one point, been considered the greatest mime in the West End. At other times she was considered the worst on account of her accent and copious use of profanity. When she died, throngs of her fans observed a moment of noise. Ironically, her signature piece, "trapped in a box" took on a much more poignant slant.

Dexy had courted her for several years in the 1970's. The relationship was quite volatile, and as Eileen's virtual tug-o-wars got more and more violent Dexy began training with renowned martial artist, Chojun "Pat" Toubruce-Leetrec. The famed sensei had earned fifth-degree black belts in Kung Fu, Taekwondo, impressionism, and Brazilian Jiu-Jitsu. He also had two brown belts from Louis Vuitton. Under Leetrec's tutelage, Dexy learned to not grab the rope and simply wait for her to tire and leave via stairs or ladder. Eventually Eileen took her own life by shooting herself with a loaded index finger. Through all of the tumult, Dexy really did love her and mourned for minutes after her death. *"At this moment, you mean everything…"*

The longest and most serious relationship O'Blick enjoyed was with Eileen Dankworth, a registered nurse and therapeutic geisha. Dankworth was recognized by the Guinness book for enduring the most consecutive shifts (84) with projectile vomiting from multiple patients … geisha division. (The record for registered nurses was three.) This benchmark explains the lyrics, *"…Ah come on, let's take off everything."*

Both individuals had experimented with various religions for years. Together they decided on the Church of Early-Day Saints or "Mornins." One of the main tenets of the religion is abstinence before a credit check since the church requires fithing. Fithing is the term the laity uses for donating 50% of each parishioner's earnings. The clergy refer to it as *having*.

As a struggling musician, Dexy was not in a position to be a first string Mornin. In fact, he had been relegated to the practice ward while, gainfully employed Eileen, had her pick of pews. This financial disparity, as well as the church's sacred bustier and garter requirement, was quite frustrating for Dexy, as evidenced in the line, *"With you in that dress my thoughts I confess verge on dirty."*

Their differences in standing within the EDS organization almost caused the sweethearts' separation. The conflict came to a boil when the Right Reverend, Caleb Gabriel, admonished Eileen that, if she wanted to qualify for the Order of the Sisterhood of the Traveling Capris, she would have to dress smartly. Eileen took it to mean that she shouldn't try to put pants on both legs at the same time while standing. Gabriel explained that her color palette had begun to reflect the gauche influence of her lower classed gentleman friend. Dexy confronted Gabriel and threatened to go the press about the church's part in Iran-Contra. It being 1963, Gabriel denied any involvement in the scandal and demanded to know if Eileen was choosing O'Blick over the church and its fashion forward doctrines. The song quotes Dexy, *"That pretty red dress. Eileen tell him yes."* After spending several weeks at the church's private spa on the White Power Cay, Eileen finally left the group and joined Dexy on the road. The two remained inseparable until Dexy's death.

While convalescing in his last days, Dexy had a casket built for the two of them after watching a documentary on Egyptian love pacts. The last words of the song reflect Dexy's own last words as he solicited for Eileen to climb in with him. *"Ah, come on Eileen."*

Eileen had Dexy's ashes scattered over the porch of their downstairs neighbors, and, later, published her private journals. Unfortunately, Eileen was illiterate, and her sketches had to be translated from Swahili. Eventually the story was developed as a Lifetime Original Movie, *"Fatal Vows: the Dexter O'Blick story"* – Starring Armand Assante and Meredith Baxter Birney.

Those Who Fail Art History Are Doomed to Repeat It

As of late I have fancied myself an artist. I arrive at this conclusion because I recently awoke from watching a documentary on the subject. It seems that artists of all stripes are all bound by one common thread: self-importance. To illustrate I refer to some of the film's (I say film because I am an artist) spotlighted personalities.

After a perfunctory inclusion of the masters – Michelangelo, Rembrandt, Jack Nicklaus – they jumped right into the post-impressionists starting with Paul Cézanne – the father of modern art. Cézanne is the prototypical trustafarian artist. His banker father gave him a monthly allowance of 100 francs (About $1300.00 today – Wednesday) while still living at home at the age of 22. Socially he was rude, shy, angry, and given to depression. He was also stubborn and refused to work within societal norms or even with those of the art world. He spurned paintbrushes well into his Impressionist period until his contemporaries started using pallet knives for their works. Then, all of the sudden, brushes were cool again.

Once, while painting the portrait of his good friend, Émile Zola, Cézanne flew into a rage and eventually tore into the canvas. Zola explained that he was used to these outbursts, which happened "…every time Paul accidentally got his thumb in the picture." Zola went on to say that "…Paul may have the genius to *be* a great painter, but he will never have the genius to *become* one. The least obstacle makes him despair." Zola was, of course, referring to the time Cézanne abandoned his entire car group at a picnic because three of the pistachios didn't have openings.

When he didn't like the way a painting was working out, he'd just walk away and never finish it. He said he wanted to, "…see and sense the objects [he was] painting, rather than think about them." Thinking about his work took too much energy and he preferred to rely on good vibes. He would take hours sometimes to put down a single stroke because each needed to contain "the air, the light, the object, the composition, the character, the outline, and the style."

Sometimes the stroke wouldn't have any air, and he'd tell everyone to get back and order someone to get some leaves. Sometimes the stroke lacked style, and he'd replace it with comfort. A still life could take him up to one hundred working sessions while a portrait took around one hundred and fifty since people don't rot as quickly as apples.

Cézanne is generally recognized as the bridge between Impressionism and Cubism. Impressionism being the medium preferred by Rich Little, and the term Cubism being one of the few isms that is still held in high regard in today's society.

Also part of that bridge, although maybe only a couple yards of it, was Henri Matisse. Being the oldest son of a wealthy grain merchant allowed him to drop out of law school and become an artist. He was a sculptor, a painter, a print maker, and a draughtsman. But once bedridden in his final years he learned to cut out pieces of paper and glue them into collages. (A real Benjamin Button this guy.) Matisse's Fauvism (French for "Why can't you just make it look like what it looks like?!?") quickly gave way to Picasso and Georges Braque's cubism school (which had a legendary field hockey program).

While Matisse favored bright and expressive colors, Pablo Picasso was more of a womanizer. In Picasso's case, he was raised by academics. His father was a professor at several academies around Spain, and his mother helped young Pablo buy his way out of the military. She was a tremendous, tremendous, classy lady. And a terrific model by the way. Very tremendous.

There is no doubt that Picasso was an artistic prodigy. At age 13, he was accepted into the Barcelona Art Academy when he completed, in less than a week, an entrance project that took most student applicants up to a month. He used the extra time to attend sit-ins over causes like the wage gap between men and eight-year-olds, or the Occupy Bordeaux-Orsay Railroad movement.

Picasso made his first trip to Paris in 1900 with his close friend Carles Casagemas, who would commit suicide a year later after his model/girlfriend, Germaine Pichot, declined several of his marriage proposals. Picasso was so distraught that he painted several posthumous portraits of his friend culminating in the piece, *La Vie*, and then promptly seduced Germaine. At least one of these incidents began what is known as Picasso's Blue Period.

Not long after breaking up with his inheritance from Casagemas, Picasso met Fernande Olivier. She and Germaine made up two of the five prostitutes pictured in Picasso's famous *Les Demoiselles d'Avignon*. This work is considered to be *the* pivotal piece in early Cubism and modern art. And Olivier came to be considered quite a piece as Picasso pivoted into fame and fortune. It also closed out what had become known as his Pink Period and, by 1912, his Fernande Olivier period.

Picasso's biggest fan and countryman, Salvador Dalí, took the next step toward artistic chaos with his take on surrealism (from the Danish: *Srrlsmgvok.* meaning, "Not bad. But it could use some watches"). The two had a mutual admiration as well as rivalry that lasted 40 years until Picasso's death (which was ruled an accident as it couldn't be proven that Dalí was even in France at the time). One example of their differences came during the Spanish Civil War when Picasso, in 1937, was commissioned to paint *Guernica,* with gray scale colors applied in the two-dimensional Cubist style. Meanwhile, Dalí, in 1936, had produced *Soft Construction with Boiled Beans*. Originally a New Age polka album with Frank Zappa's grandfather, Moon Unit I, Dalí eventually reimagined it as an oil on canvas in his hyper-realistic style. The painting was completed six months before the war started. Dalí claimed that the piece proved the prophetic power of his subconscious mind. In actuality the work had several names before the war started, including *Breakfast of Champions*, *No Eating on the Job*, and *One-Handed Creepy Thing Grabbing a Bazonga*.

Their political differences (Picasso was a communist, and Dalí was a flasher) mirrored their different approaches to painting. While Picasso would stand directly in front of the easel, Dalí often crept up behind it, engaged with a stroke or two, and then run to hide in the bushes and giggle. Ultimately, Dalí would pay homage to his hero with the piece, *Portrait of Pablo Picasso in the Twenty-first Century*. As his model, Dalí chose the guy from *Raiders* whose face melts when they open the ark.

Salvador Dalí, like Picasso, was a technically skilled artist and his work is certainly remarkable. But his behavior is another affectation that has been adopted by many a nominal artist of the current avant-garde. He was eccentric and often ostentatious and something of a dandy. This might have had something to do with his childhood, having been renamed for his older *deceased* brother Salvador, and his stepmother/aunt filling the role of buffer between her disciplinarian husband and four stepchildren. Throw in the fact that his first art idol was literal gothic era painter Diego Velázquez, and we're looking at a brooding art nerd in the making. Falling in with a band of poets dedicated to the Ultraist movement in Madrid would only serve to solidify these attitudes which carried to Paris in the late 1920s, where he would now become a part of the Surrealist movement. The guy never had a chance.

At least one other member of that movement took the weird ball and ran with it. Emmanuel Radnitzky, also known as Man Ray, was an American artist who spent most of his career in Paris. In South Philadelphia, born and raised, at the drawing board was where he spent most of his days. Chillin' out, maxin', relaxin', helping dad sow. Makin' time for art museums wherever he'd go. When a couple of gentiles who were up to no good, started making slurs in the neighborhood. There was one anti-Semitic comment and his mom got torqued. She said, "We're moving to Williamsburg in Brooklyn, New York."

First a contributor to the Dada* movement, and then the surrealists, his initial attempts at painting and drawing were mostly mirroring styles (poorly) of the 19th century. He then sought to incorporate the trends of the European Modernists he observed while visiting the New York gallery of Georgia O'Keeffe's beard, Alfred Stieglitz. Upon discovering Dada, Man Ray's painting experienced rapid development. (How about that?) He had his first solo show in 1915. In 1916, he showed his *Self-Portrait* assemblage. (An assemblage is stuff the artist finds, glues together and pities you for not understanding.) Now prolific, he stuck some tacks to the bottom of an iron and named it *Gift* (The name, *That was due today?*, had already been used by fellow Dadaist, Tristan Tzara). Soon after, he

---

* So named for the way artists started their letters when they wrote home for money, Dadaism consisted of artists who rejected logic, reason, and the trappings of capitalism. Instead, expressing inanity, absurdity, and protest in their work while maintaining political affinities for the far left. So yeah, they were pretty good.

draped a sewing machine in a blanket, wrapped it with string, and stood back to see if any of the viewing bourgeois conformists could comprehend his genius.

By 1918 Man Ray had been producing photographs of his own work and found that taking weird pictures was his calling. Then, in 1921, he outréd his way into the company of the left bank Bohemians. Immediately he grabbed himself a mistress, Alice "Kiki" Prin – the Queen of Montparnasse. Like all independent, sexually liberated women, Kiki was born to a young, unwed mother and raised in abject poverty. By age 14 she was posing for nude sculptors. (I don't know why the *sculptors* had to be naked, but I guess if you're exploiting teenaged girls, anything goes.) By the time Man Ray met her she'd become a fixture in the Paris art community. She'd modeled for the likes of Sanyu, the Chinese artist and inventor of ping-tennis whose 2000 nude sketches still exist (I suppose in some movie producer's den); Julien Mandel, king of the dirty postcards; Tsuguharu Foujita, a Japanese painter who achieved great fame painting nude women and cats (The cats refused to work blue and stayed in their furs.); Constant Detré, a Hungarian artist who concentrated his work on depictions of brothels; Francis Picabia, financially independent, and famed for his Cubist renderings of pictures from French girlie magazines; Arno Brecker, Nazi sculptor; Alexander Calder, best known for his abstract kinetic sculptures which are probably dirty to somebody; Per Krohg, just some lonely Norwegian; and Pablo Gargallo, a Spanish painter and sculptor with a Greta Garbo fetish. These guys came from all over the world to spend time with this woman. Paris in the 1920s may as well have been Bangkok.

Kiki stayed with Man Ray through the 1920s and was the subject of some of his most famous images including *Le violon d'Ingres*. This photograph captures a bare Kiki with the F-holes (I didn't know either) of a stringed instrument painted over her back, thus parting with friend Salvador Dalí's preferences, and showing that Man Ray was a butt man.

For Man Ray and Kiki, it was true love…until 1929 when he met, and fell in bed with, surrealist photographer, Lee Miller. She and Ray perfected pseudo-solarization, the process in which one person develops film in a darkroom, while the other breaks in to get their companion's opinion on a newly discovered mole. The exposure of the film to white light causes the colors to reverse and allows surrealists to say, "I meant to do that."

After Miller left him in 1932, Man Ray met dream journalist and tarot card faithful, Méret Oppenheim. She was a Swiss, manic depressive, surrealist who'd made a name for herself buy gluing fur to a tea set. Now, to combat her feelings of low self-esteem, she poured ink on her body and posed nude in front of a printing press for Man Ray. He declared her "*the* Surrealist's muse" and continued with his venereal disease investigations.

When the Nazis came to town in 1940, Man Ray fled to Hollywood, where he again focused on painting. That is, he didn't do much beyond *The Shakespearean Equations* series, which was later theorized to have actually been produced by Francis Bacon. He did, however, meet Juliet Browner, whom he married in a double ceremony with Max Ernst and Dorothea Tanning. In 1950 the three filed for divorce from Ernst, but reconciled soon after.

Upon his and Juliet's return to Paris in 1951, Man Ray started recreating past works, hoping that people would like them this time. One of his rare exhibits of courage was when he took credit for producing the short films, *Le Retour à la Raison* (*Return to Reason*) – shot without a camera but still featuring plenty of nudity – and *L'Etoile de mer* (*The Starfish*) – shot through obscured glass to avoid any comparisons to Larry Flint's work. He also helped his long-time friend, Marcel Duchamp, create *his* experimental film, *Anemic Cinema*, which is what you'd get if Alfred Hitchcock did an Alpha-Bits commercial.

Duchamp started off like all good modernists: trained at Academy, fixated with anatomy. As with most of his predecessors, his first works were more traditional and even not unpleasant to look at. His nudes were considered clumsy, but that's only because the models were drunk.

Duchamp insisted he wanted nothing to do with Cubism but, honestly, his best work was pretty Cubie. Perhaps his most famous painting, *Nude Descending a Staircase, No2* (the first one omitting the staircase and eventually renamed, *Naked and Falling*), has been described as golf clubs during an explosion in a shingle factory. After first being shown in Spain, it was submitted to the 1913 International Exhibition of Modern Art at the Armory in NYC where American observers were scandalized by the piece, while covering their cleavage with one hand, fanning themselves with the other, and claiming, "I never!"

His next move was to withdraw from artist circles and take a job as a librarian. He then started on his eight-year project called *The Bride Stripped Bare by Her Bachelors, Even*. (Just look it up.) Around this time he bolted a bicycle wheel to a stool causing art groupies to claim it as his first "readymade." A readymade is an object built in a sweatshop that is commandeered by a "free spirit," and held up as a statement about what's wrong with society. Always. That's always the statement. Society bad, art world good. Also it's often about rape. This despite Duchamp's most notorious work, *Fountain*.

The story goes that Duchamp, along with Man Ray, Katherine Sophie Dreier, and several other avant-gardeners, had founded the Society of Independent Artists, with the goal of holding yearly exhibitions with no juries or prizes. Duchamp had already decried Cubism as another form of "retinal art" so, in 1917, he submitted, *Fountain* – a urinal*. The Society hid it from view during the show and he resigned from the organization in protest. And the interpretation of the object itself? Erotic. "Well, I never!"

Around 1918 Duchamp all but abandoned art and immersed himself in the game of chess. He played it, wrote about it, lectured on it, composed music from it, and eventually, obsessed and confused, smothered it with a pillow in a murder/suicide pact that went south. (Just the day before, he got a text from Expressionism, who wanted to catch up over paninis.) He painted his last, entitled, *Tu 'm*, in 1918 and ditched his art world friends to be a chess jock until 1946 when he began a two-decade long project for peeping Jean-Claudes. *Étant donnés*, is a multimedia assemblage that uses an old wooden door, binder clips, velvet, leaves, twigs, hair, glass, and linoleum. It also features his naked girlfriend with the arm (and I suppose permission) of his wife. One views the piece through a pair of peepholes in case

---

*The piece has since been lost but over the years Duchamp allowed other artists to buy more urinals and display them in museums…you know…the way artists do. Since then, multiple trailblazing visionary types have made their mark, literally, by urinating on the objects while displayed. When asked why, they explain that their contributions allude to the sins of society and something about rape.

that's your idée fixe. Finally, in the last year of his life, Duchamp returned to his heart's true calling: erotic sketches and phallic sculptures.

At this point, it's important to note that a lot of abstract Expressionism is pretty neato. Even if they don't suggest the image of something the viewer might recognize, who doesn't like the Partridge Family bus? In the 1940s and '50s, one artist came along who might be considered the *King* of Neato...the Prince of Plop...the Duke of Drip...the Sultan of Spill...the Baron of Brume...the Marquis of Mizzle...the Viscount of Viscus enamels, Jack the Dripper: Jackson Pollock.

In 1930, Pollock went to New York to study under Thomas Hart Benton. It was cramped down there, as Benton was a short man, but the sprinkling from Benton's easel had a great influence on Pollock's style.

In 1936, he was introduced to liquid paint (which he found much easier to pour than solid paint) by Mexican muralist and attempted Trotsky assassin*, David Alfaro Siqueiros. Pollock had attended a political art workshop where Siqueiros was the guest of honor and assisted him in building floats for the upcoming May Day general strike. Floats being the most effective form of political pressure at the time, the two worked with the theme, *Employment Under the Sea*, which won the special jury prize for its liberal use of splashed paint and seditious rhetoric.

From 1938 to 1942, Pollock underwent Jungian psychotherapy as a treatment for his alcoholism. Carl Jung was a Swiss psychiatrist who had been embraced by, practically, all of the famous abstract Expressionists. (We've established how handsy most of them were.) After parting ways with Freud, Jung drunk-texted some of his "empirical science" concepts, which were later amassed into his collected works, including the notions of *anima* and *animus*†, *collective unconscious*, which comes from group screenings of *Iron*

---

* Siqueiros, a communist, felt Trotsky, an owner of up to two pairs of shoes at a time, was too capitalist friendly and, sporting dark glasses and a fake mustache, led an early morning raid on the former soviet leader. Trotsky survived and the Marx Brothers began to outdraw Cantinflas.

†The anima being the unconscious feminine part of men when their drinks get spiked, and the animus being the masculine component in women that compels them to wear Doc Martens.

Eagle 2, and *synchronicity* (insert Gordon Sumner joke here). A lesser known notion of Jung's is the psychoid – a brilliantly undefinable concept of causation and the titular character in Sony's erotic horror franchise. These ideas were interwoven seamlessly (meaning absent any scientific method) with his more engrossing hobbies of alchemy, astrology, metaphysics, the occult, and the paranormal. (Jung was the early 20th century art community's Timothy Leary, minus John and Yoko.) Pollock's therapy took the form of talking about his pictures. Over the course of 18 months, he submitted 83 drawings to his analyst, Joseph Henderson, as analytical aids. Many historians believe Pollock was bipolar but, according to Henderson, he simply liked to get drunk and draw horses.

At the urging of Duchamp, patron Peggy Guggenheim (German for enabler) signed a gallery contract with Pollock and commissioned him to paint a 160 sq. ft. mural for the entry of her townhouse. Duchamp suggested he paint on canvas instead of on the wall, so that it could be portable for the inevitable foreclosure sale. While most of the piece was done with a brush and oil, there are also some drippings with house paint and evidence that the work might have been completed with the canvas lying flat on the floor – a practice Pollock embraced so that he could reach the painting without knocking over his beer.

Pollock's most famous paintings were made during this "drip period," from about 1947 to 1953. For a while he went dark with just black paint on unprimed canvases that kind of looked like things. He eventually returned to using color and married artist Lee Krasner, who taught him about painting for profit and introduced him to art dealers and collectors who could bankroll his drinking.

Jackson Pollock died in a car crash while driving drunk in 1956. Also in the car were his mistress, Ruth Kligman (who survived to write a book about it), and first runner up, Edith Metzger, who died in the crash, sober and unpublished. Kligman went on to be quite an artist in her own right, sleeping with Pollock rival Willem de Kooning, as well as Jasper Johns, and a moderately confused Andy Warhol.

Warhol initially pursued a career as a commercial illustrator (currently known as a "graphic designer" or "undeclared.") He had a great deal of success in this vocation owing to his fascination with fashion and unwarranted insistence. He became known for his images of shoes which, along with many of his other drawings, resembled the work of Toulouse-Lautrec – mostly due to his use of the expedient of tracing. His genius was in renaming the process from "the forging method" to the "blotted line technique."

Another masterly practice employed by Warhol was screen-printing. His first works, done in 1962, came from his own drawings with which he reportedly was not satisfied. Upon discovering that he could make screen prints from photographs, he intensified his output. Finally, when he realized he could appropriate existing photos by *others*, his personal creativity hit its zenith. That same year he had his West Coast debut of what became known as "Pop Art." This new type of art was said to be hostile to the artistic establishment that climbed over each other for the chance to display it.

A fusion of Dada collages and ready-mades with imagery from the consumer culture, pop art was seen as both a revolt against the introspection of abstract expressionism and a post-industrial system for employing gay runaways to work an assembly line creating posters of soup cans. Warhol spoke of the images he used in his pieces such as Coke bottles:

> "...A Coke is a Coke and no amount of money can get you a better Coke than the one the bum on the corner is drinking. All the Cokes are the same and all the Cokes are good. Liz Taylor knows it, the President knows it, the bum knows it, and you know it."
>
> – This quote came *before* his regular appearances at Studio 54.

In the 1960s Andy began to produce experimental (WASP for boring and pointless) films. Out of the hundreds of film cans filled with 16mm exposed audacity, a few have been singled out as revolutionary to the art of film-making. *Sleep*, shot in 1963, was a five-and-a-half hour tour de feculence, featuring poet John Giorno sleeping. That he was naked established the unwritten rule in Hollywood that nudity is only for the skirts. *Empire*, his magnum opus, presents eight hours of a single view of the Empire State Building – the inspiration for Woody Allen's *Annie Hall, Broadway Danny Rose,* and *Godspell*. 1965's *Poor Little Rich Girl*, starring Edie Sedgwick, is shot out of focus for the first half of the movie, a device later utilized by Gene Rodenberry to make female aliens look hot, and ultimately giving Cybill Shepherd a career.

By the late 1970s, he had begun working in the abstract with a new type of process known as oxidation painting. The practice included covering a canvas with wet copper paint and then urinating on it. But it wasn't weird, he had others do the tinkling.

Warhol went on to enjoy an early nerd awakening in post-war America and eventually starred as an avant-garde guru. But through it all he was shy, quiet, evasive, and, above all, clearly petulant. He regularly gave one-word answers (if any answer at all) during interviews and made a habit of gazing at non-sycophants with a cynical deadpan stare followed by a seductive come-hither look and a titillating lick of his eyelids. Of course, these were disguises for all of the same insecurities that his predecessors cloaked with arrogance while their adamant stooges hoped their fealty would translate to prestige for themselves. (I got a thesaurus for Christmas.)

In May of 2016, two teenagers visited the San Francisco Museum of Modern Art. After being less than amazed by much of what was being presented, the two decided to set a pair of glasses on the floor and observe the reactions of the other visitors. Predictably, many aspirant intellectuals were quite taken with the object and crowds formed to take pictures and discuss its impact on rape culture. In 2017, *The Art Assignment* (a PBS Digital Studios YouTube series) attempted to explain that the teens had been endeavoring to do exactly what Marcel Duchamp had done with *Fountain*. Of course, this was simply the modern art world turning into the skid.

The ridiculousness of what conceptual artists (people who are bad at math) insist upon as something profound was spotlighted by the glasses. Instead of admitting that most abstract Expressionists are otherwise unemployable, self-absorbed hacks, *The Art Assignment* attempted a palpable "Only *we* get it."

Artists like Picasso, Cézanne, Braque, and Dalí were trained, practiced, and gifted artists who had already proven their classical bona fides and were looking to expand on what they had already mastered. This was not the case for the two pranksters. The glasses were not a deep, meaningful, editorial on the nature of art. Rather, they shined a light on the hollow attempts of people desperate to be special. In this case, it was the art crowd – also a great read by Sophy Burnham – but it could be foodies, wine enthusiasts, caviar wrist lickers, or humanities grad students who only listen to vinyl.)

All that having been said, the truth is I don't know much about art. But I hear he's a darn fine bass fisherman. While spending time together on Lake Okeechobee I asked him who he believed to be the father of modern art. He took a few seconds to scratch his beard and stare off into the distance.

"Well," he said, and then squinted into the sun for a few seconds more, "I know this. Both Matisse and Picasso said, 'Cézanne is the father of us all.' Cézanne himself asserted that, 'We all stem from Pissarro.' Camille Pissarro, in turn, looked to Danish artist, Fritz Melbye as his mentor. Melby, a Danish marine painter, lauded his older brother, navy caricaturist, Anton Melbye, who studied with the father of Danish painting, Christoffer Wilhelm Eckersberg. Eckersberg counted Jacque-Louis David as his greatest influence. And David touted the greatness of *his* master, French painter, François Boucher, who studied at the feet of François Lemoyne. From the beginning Lemoyne sought to be the heir to his idol, Charles Le Brun, court painter to Louis XIV, and much influenced by Nicolas Poussin. In 1612 Poussin traveled to Paris to study under several minor masters and one major minor, Jean-Jacque Gauflouraeuxonettes, who never spoke of any artistic influences as he was a leech collector. So, as I see it..." said Art, who then paused a little more and sniffed before continuing, "...labeling the father of modern art is immaterial." He then turned and looked me right in my eye and said, "It was the mother who was the hussy."

Ankh if you love Isis

I believe it was archbishop Timothy "Touchy" O'Feely who said, "Spare the rod; spoil the evening."

The Church* has had a lot of bad press lately with controversies like the East-West Schism of 1054, the Crusades, the French Inquisition, the Italian Inquisition, the Spanish Inquisition, the Portuguese Inquisition, the English Inquisition, the Dutch Inquisition, the German Inquisition, the African Inquisitions, the Asian Inquisitions, the Brazilian Inquisition, the Peruvian Inquisition, the Mexican Inquisition, and the last – and I believe sexiest – Goan Inquisition. Goa is a state in Western India that was colonized by the Portuguese and decided to enforce Catholic orthodoxy the way Jesus would have. Jesús Martín Jiménez de Torturmada was a Spanish Dominican friar whose club was really big on roasting.

Portugal found that many of their newly converted Indian locals might not have drunk the Darjeeling completely, and were secretly, still practicing Hinduism. The monotheistic Jesuits considered the polytheism of the crypto-Hindus to be a threat to the purity of the Catholic bank account and pressed for inquisition. They found that Hindus have millions of gods and you never know when someone's going to slip another one in there. There was even a registry where, for $54.00, you could name a god after a loved one if you forgot their birthday. Included were:

* The term "church" as is used here, refers to any denomination of Christendom with a stained-glass fetish, divine cannibalism, or a zeal to beat the orphanry right out of you.

- A beautiful 12x16 full color parchment certificate personalized with the name of the deity, the noun they preside over, and a comprehensive list of transgressions that anger them.

- A map of the cosmos containing the god, pantheon they belonged to, and the location circled, in red, where that god blessed/cursed/copulated with/ate their first human.

- A Moleskine notebook for holy writings complete with easy-to-follow templates for doctrine, rituals, holy days, and a calculator for figuring maximum wife to concubine ratios.

- A complimentary personalized wallet card imprinted with the two animals that make up the god's likeness, approved idol materials, and an official Myspace address.

That polytheism was initially censured might be religion's greatest irony. (Also in the running: patiently enduring 1300 years of oppression so that you can kill your savior, suicide bombing a school filled with Econ post-grads – which has got to have, at least, 72 virgins right there, and Stryper.) The basis for the persecution of Christians in the Roman Empire was their refusal to accept pagan beliefs and celebrations. But in just a few, short, imperial conversions, seasonal festivals (orgies), feasts to nature (orgies), iconoclastic merrymaking (orgies), and orgies (Bacchanalias/Saturnalias/orgies) were seamlessly absorbed into the liturgy.

One example is that of Easter. Celebrations associated with Easter can be traced back all the way to early Babylon. (You'll get a lot of that.) These festivals involved the birth of Tammuz. Tammuz was the illegitimate son of Nimrod's widow, Semiramis. Semiramis had convinced the Babylonians that Tammuz was the reincarnated Nimrod who was now the sun god, (also a recurring theme) Baal. Like his "father" (according to court documents), Tammuz was a hunter…but not a great one. He was killed by some pig that also turned out to be radiant and terrific. As Tammuz died his blood spilled on the stump of an evergreen and the tree grew to full size overnight, thereby making evergreen trees sacred. (See *foreshadowing*.)

Meanwhile, down at the Boar's Nest, ol' Semiramis was busy convincing people that she herself was a goddess. Her assertion was that, on the Sunday after the spring Equinox, she had been dropped into the Euphrates, as an egg from the moon god, Su'en, after he had ovulated for 28 days (Su'en was similar to the male seahorse – not that butch). Known as Ishtar, she became the mother of heaven and the goddess of fertility and later – after a bad breakup – of war. Part of her worship would come to included temple prostitution and rabbits, who are known to be pretty randy themselves.

The story of her resurrecting her dead son/husband in the form of new vegetation gave way to springtime rituals that would eventually be adopted by the church around the time Emperor Constantine was able to galvanize the religious right and make Rome great again. With his conversion to Christianity, many pagan traditions would be assimilated and, eventually, formally adopted starting with the First – and what many believe the *only real* – Council of Nicaea. (The Second Council of Nicaea didn't get the same play, as Constantine had left to pursue a solo career.)

An ecumenical council is a meeting of bishops, cardinals, abbots, and Costellos nominated by the Pope to define doctrine and play backgammon. At this council in 325 CE, two provocative assertions were agreed upon. The first being that God "the father" and God "the son" were the same guy...only different (like Baal and Tammuz or Osiris and Horus or Garth Brooks and Chris Gaines).

The connection of the son being killed and resurrected as the father (preferably with a little more immortality in the tank this time) lent itself directly to an amalgamation of Mesopotamian, Egyptian, Greek, and European spring equinox traditions with the church's resurrection day. This paved the way for the Council's decree of the celebration, originally named, "Pascha" (which coincided with Passover as a concession to the Jews for being denied membership into Caesar Augustus' national golf club), to be observed by the laity. The practice would start 40 days before "Resurrection Sunday" with the observance of Lent, when believers prepare for Easter by praying (or at least, sending good vibes), repenting (for what they plan to do), giving alms (mostly gift cards), self-denial (it's always the other guy's fault), and mortifying the flesh. Mortification of the flesh is an act of spiritual purification through fasting, abstinence, or pious kneeling, which is less specious than godless kneeling. It may also include the wearing of sackcloth (a special order at Men's Warehouse), and self-flagellation, which is very rude in an elevator or on the subway.

Lent begins on Ash Wednesday. It is preceded by Fat Tuesday, believed to be derived from the pre-Roman festival of Lupercalia when wolf worshipers ran around in thongs and slapped people on the butt to make them fertile. Something like IVF. Of course, that was in ancient times. Nowadays many Cajun believers exchange quick peeks for plastic beads and eat cakes with babies inside them. You know...to remember our lord.

There are other special days during Lent, such as Spy Wednesday, which requires the faithful to binge watch all seven Bond movies starring Sean Connery (including *Never say Never Again*). In Anglican churches, it is acceptable to substitute the Bourne films.

Originally falling on a Monday, until a suit was brought by the Mamas and Papas, Maundy Thursday is named after ancient Jerusalem mobster, Maundy Mendelson, who owned the upper room where Jesus washed his apostles' feet. After hearing of Jesus' object lesson of humility to his followers, Maundy adopted the practice of having his own feet washed after every step he took. He was suffocated a day later while attempting to flee a hail of spit wads ordered by a rival gangster.

Once known as *Great* Friday, the Friday before Easter has been downgraded to merely Good Friday since the Friday after Thanksgiving now gets all the press.

Each Sunday during Lent is also set aside as a special day. The first, Quadragesima Sunday, also known by the equally derisory Lutheran name, Invocabit Sunday, has been traditionally observed by burning a cross. But don't jump to any conclusions. The addition of a horizontal cross piece to the original pyre stake came *only after* the church had assimilated the Germanic pagan festival for the spring equinox...and when a black family moved into Luxemburg.

Remembrance Sunday is the most commercialized of the Lent Sundays as it was originally conceived of by Armenian abbot, Pliny of Hallmark. Oculi Sunday takes its name from the Latin word for eyes, referencing that day's introit taken from Psalm 25:15, which states, "My eyes are always toward God..." "Always" here is used symbolically since most parishioners tend to focus on *60 Minutes*.

Laetare (Rejoice) Sunday is when some of Lent's more rigorous traditions are allowed a little leeway. It's Lent's cheat day. The fifth Sunday of Lent is known as Passion Sunday, not to be confused with Pride weekend, even though they both rely pretty heavily on candles and satin robes. The Sunday before Easter is Palm Sunday, obviously named for the synagogue in Palm Springs that inspired the Bangles hit, *Eternal Flame*. It leads nicely into the following holy day, Manic Monday.

About 12 years after the Council of Nicaea decided that them Ēostre worshipers is some good people, the Latin cross was formally adopted as a Christian symbol. It had been in use among other religions around the world for thousands of years, but it had always been used as an emblem of life & fertility rather than death & supply-side economics. Now that Constantine had abolished crucifixion and made superstition cool again, 2nd century adherents were no longer reluctant to make the sign of the cross while casting lots or after laying down a few denarii on a chariot race.

The first crosses were, of course, images of the sun gods: Nimrod or Baal or Tamuz or Shamash or Ra or Horus or Molech or Apollo or Helios or George Hamilton. Rather than the familiar Latin cross we know today, the original cross used by the church looked more like a capital, **T**. It is thought to be borrowed from the Druids, who always seemed angry when they were texting. This "Tau" cross was preceded by the Egyptian ankh, which can be seen in many surviving hieroglyphics and Goth kid tattoos. It is generally accepted among scholars that all forms of religious crosses are essentially phallic in nature because scholars are fuhreeeeeeekay.

In 350 CE, Pope Julius I declared December 25th the official date of the birth of Jesus. Political rivals had demanded to see a birth certificate, but the vast majority just wanted change – except for the continued celebration of their Saturnalia. Saturnalia was a festival to honor and sacrifice to Saturn, the Roman god of agriculture, during the winter solstice. It started on December 17th and, by 274 CE, extended all the way to the 25th. In that year, Aurelian proclaimed the 25th to be the birthday of *Sol Invictus*, The unconquered sun. (Sol jr. ran a successful deli on the Apian way.)

The traditions of these two pagan holidays remained quite popular and were adopted into Julius' "Christ's mass" celebration. During the festival, many conventions from the rest of the year were overturned in favor of fun and frivolity, with many families designating a slave to be in charge of what would now be known as mischief or revelry or sexual assault.

With such a successful marketing ploy, it's no wonder that many of the heathenistic customs from ancient times are still practiced today, including holiday lights, mistletoe, wreaths of holly, the Christmas tree, and the giving of gifts. The most popular of these gifts were little terracotta figurines of the gods, known as *sigillaria*. According to Macrobius Thedosius (which clears right up with a little over-the-counter cream), these figurines were effigies of the slain from past festivals, which was a nice little homage to earlier celebrations involving human sacrifice. Rites associated with the winter solstice, then, are crucial to understanding many of the traditions of the Christmas season as most relate back to paganistic practices and symbols that celebrate the return of light after the solstice. This is why wiccans tend to come from the ranks of marginalized hipsters: they hid Christmas pickles before it was cool.

Of course, it wasn't just pre-Christian *religious* beliefs that made their way into the evolving doctrine. Ancient philosophies, too, had an impact, e.g., such contemporary gems as, "I'm not very religious, but I'm spiritual" (which really translates to, "I don't like rules, but I *am* superstitious."), and ideas about the immortal soul and hellfire were lifted right from Greeks, such as Plato and Pythagoras. While the former held that the soul was an entity separate from the body and has neither a beginning nor end, the latter was often distracted by triangles. Plato had what is known as 19 proofs of immortality of the soul:

1. **Cyclicity Argument.** All things proceed from their opposites (like the way pornographers benefit from the women's movement), therefore life must proceed from death and the soul lives on. Nice try Plato, but the opposite of life isn't death, it's pants shopping.
2. **Recollection Argument.** It appears that we know some things inherently so we must have learned these things from a previous life (except that the things we are born knowing are rarely helpful and tend to involve lying to women).
3. **Affinity Argument.** People like eternal things (an affinity for infinity) so the soul must be eternal. Of course everyone also likes ice cream but only 1 in 15 souls suffers from IBS.
4. **Form of Life Argument.** The soul gives life, so it needs to be eternal. Yet many things that give life are finite: parents, food and water, clean air, the oligarchy charged with deciding who gets what vaccine. (This assertion relies on the premise that life comes from the soul, when in actuality, it was created by Milton Bradley.)
5. **Vitiating Principle Argument.** Everything has its own enemy. The soul's enemy is vice, and vice can't kill the soul completely. But it can do irreparable damage to your credit score.
6. **Justice Argument.** Unless there are rewards and punishments after life, it would violate our sense of justice, (as does the "tuck rule," but here we are, and the Pats have six rings).
7. **Simplicity Argument.** Something composed of many things is subject to decomposition. But the soul is made up of only one thing, candy, and therefore, cannot be destroyed.

8. **Self-moved Mover**. The soul must be eternal, since destruction would imply being moved, and the soul cannot be moved by anything external. But has the soul seen WALL-E?
9. **Universal Interest and Yearning**. Everybody wants to live forever. (Especially Irene Cara, who asserted that she would not only live forever, but also make it to heaven. Remember her name?)
10. **Proof via Purification**. If you're good enough, you just know.
11. **Replenishment Argument**. If everything died, eventually everything would be dead. A solid argument indeed. Still, it fails to account for the Marvel Universe.
12. **Afterlife Testimonies**. Stories about the afterlife must be true. The Today Show wouldn't lie.
13. **Trusted Authority**. Other people who, supposedly, should know said so. This is the same argument for *Lost in Translation* and I'm not buyin' it.
14. **Tradition and Custom**. 2,000,000 Babylonians can't be wrong.
15. **Limitless Capacity**. Humans' seemingly unlimited capacity for knowledge would be unnecessary if the soul were not immortal. But then explain the popularity of Wendy Williams?
16. **Example of Socrates**. Socrates wasn't afraid of death because he knew his soul wouldn't die. Plato had great admiration for his tutor and deliberately skirted the truth about the philosopher's hemlock addiction.
17. **Socrates' Desire to Convince Others**. Known for being quite stubborn, Socrates once convinced the Delian League that he had suffered a stroke by working just his left side for 11 years. His insistence that his soul would live on might have been a response to a wager he made with Aristophanes during a bad trip while partaking in the Eleusinian Mysteries.

18. **Socrates' Sign**. Socrates' guiding spirit – whom he called Blane – was typically pretty dependable when it came to warning him of danger. That Blane didn't oppose Socrates' attending his trial, which resulted in a death sentence, gave both Socrates and Plato confidence that the execution would do no harm. The executioner, a relieved Hippocrates, called it a first.
19. **Conviction of Plato**. Eighteen arguments for something is six more than Cicero's own, *12 Arguments for Lowering the Age of Consent*, hence, through sheer number, Plato exerts proof enough that his musings should be deemed infallible.

Plato and the school of thought he founded were revered by, perhaps, the most influential theologian of all time, Aurelius Augustinus, St. Augustine. Although he lived 800 years after Plato, Augustine's beliefs were heavily influenced by Neo-Platonism and shaped his opinions about God, metaphysics, astrology, and multiple uses for feta.

Born in 354 in what is now Algeria, Augustine grew up in a religiously divided household. His mother was a life-long Catholic while his father, a pagan who liked to keep his options open, converted on his deathbed. The family were Berbers (a North African ethnic group renowned for piracy and equestrian skills, as well as other non-swashbuckling cultural traditions), but were freedmen Roman citizens and spoke only Latin at home, with his grandmother insisting, "Shut-a you face wit-a de Berber. We-a Romans a-now. We speak-a de Latin."

Augustine was 17, and studying in Carthage when he was first introduced to the ideas of Plato. While a staunch disciple of Platonism, he eventually became an adherent of Manichaeism, a religion founded in the 3rd century by a guy named Mani. Rather than earn devotees by great oration, Mani preferred to lurk in out-of-the-way settings and pique the interest of passersby with a provocative, "Psst. Buddy."

Manichaeism's doctrine was based on Mesopotamian religious movements and Gnosticism (an earlier sect that filled in mythology's plot holes with the frog DNA of mysticism and esoteric perception). Mani was born a Persian Jew and was seen as a prophet in the style of Zoroaster, whose style, in turn, has been described as neo-Ottoman chic. Mani was thought to be – at least by Manicheans who never met Muhammad, Báb, or L. Ron Hubbard – the last in a line of prophets that include Buddha (who, turns out, wasn't even fat; Chinese sculptors simply weren't good at abs), and Jesus, the one guy they didn't think was part of a trinity. Mani himself preached that he was an apostle. A sort of Jihadist, for Jesuits for Jews for Jesus.

Augustine eventually converted to Christianity around age 31 when Roman emperor Theodosius I decreed that all Manichean monks be executed. He would also take part in the persecution of Manicheans and produced an 8-part docu-series for Netflix that was, "…compelling, if not a little redundant," says *Variety*. Not long after seeing the light, Augustine got engaged to a ten-year-old girl but had to wait two years for her to reach legal marrying age. In those two years he became a priest and, as such, was no longer interested in the spinster.

In 395 CE, Augustine was appointed the Bishop of Hippo. This drew quite a bit of grief from his buddies the Archbishop of Great Lyon and the Cardinal of Laser Cheetah. In 400 he completed his most famous written work, *Confessions*, a mix of hip-hop, dance pop, and crunk. He went on in 415 to write *On the Trinity*, followed in 426 by *City of God*. In these works he sought to define church doctrine through the lens of Platonist philosophy.

Like Plato, Augustine believed that the body and the soul were separate (even though they had a drawer at each other's place), and that the soul was eternal. This would explain why it drove so slowly. He went on to suggest that, not only was there a place of eternal torment (Tartarus/Hell/Cheesecake Factory), but he also introduced the idea of a place for purification (Celestial Hades/Purgatory/a sauna). The Purgatory doctrine isn't found in the Bible, of course, but Plato said it, Augustine believed it, and the Second Council of Trent in 1274 settled it. Augustine would go on to develop the hell fire doctrine further in the years leading up to his death and canonization, explaining that even though unbaptized babies would go to hell, they'd be in the best part. I would assume that part would be something sinfully lively like a Guar concert or a Harry Potter film marathon. Of course, since it's set aside for babies, maybe it's just a dimly lit bar. That would explain why St. Augustine is the patron saint of brewing and sore eyes.

Section III:
The Tragedy of Comedy

As demonstrated in previous chapters, humor writing often fails to hit its mark. There are many rationales for a failed joke. It may suffer from poor delivery or wording. The topic might be too sensitive or outdated. Or maybe it's as simple as trying too hard to be funny without first analyzing the essence of humor as detailed in psychology papers, or on YouTube videos, or during podcasts hosted by, and featuring, open-mic-ers, or within blogs written by offense-seizing strife zealots who insist that comedy never punches down (unless you're from the South and you work with your hands), but rather strives to empower the disenfranchised through witty satire like *The Smothers Brothers* or *Mr. Bean*, all the while strictly adhering to the rules of structure, awareness, positivity, self-worth, consensus building, Benign Violation theory, and the avoidance of run-on sentences.

I believe it was author / speaker / LinkedIn influencer / high-end mentor / psychedelics researcher / "Trail of Tears" tour guide / Gettysburg treasure hunter / Normandy greeter / Hotel Rwanda concierge / rescue dog anti-circumcision advocate / cornflakes moistener / ball-in-her-yard keeper / nursery rhyme debunker / blanket fort building inspector / Hot Wheels smog tester / finger paint art critic / air hockey referee / bacon denier / dance party minority whip / "Annie Hall" monitor / grudge harbor master / Dr. Jean Houston promoter, Jean Houston, who said, "The richest laugh is at no one's expense"

Her ridiculous statement is actually quite accurate. The biggest moneymakers in Hollywood are, in fact, dramadies. Leaf through the next couple of pieces and you'll see why…or at least see why my own ineffectual playwriting has been rejected by more than just the conscious…socially or otherwise.

"Waiter, There's a Flying Fish in my Primordial Soup."

(Scene: A dark restaurant. Seated at the bar are Charles Darwin and a young lady)

Darwin: It's not a sin, baby. There *is* no God.

Barfly: If there's no God, then how did we get here?

Darwin: It's called descent with modification.

Barfly: Didn't Justice Scalia do that last week on CSPAN?

Darwin: I doubt it. What it means is that all things developed by a process of gradual, continuous change from pre- existing forms of life.

Barfly: Like Hugh Heffner.

Darwin: Well, it's more like this. A giraffe wasn't always a giraffe.

Barfly: What was it?

Darwin: It was something else.

Barfly: Like a spokesmodel?

Darwin: No. Like a giraffe with a shorter neck.

Barfly: Why not call him Stubby?

Darwin: That's not the point. It was an animal that was the predecessor to the giraffe.

Barfly:	I like Stubby.
Darwin:	What I'm saying is that at some point these animals *needed* to have longer necks to get to the food that was higher in the trees. Over hundreds of thousands of years the animals with the longer necks could get to the higher food and thus survived.
Barfly:	Stubby lived for hundreds of thousands of years?
Darwin:	No. His kind did. Each successive generation with the adaptation of its parents would be the only ones able to reach the higher food and thus be the only ones able to survive until ultimately we have the giraffe we know today.
Barfly:	Are you saying that the animals had hundreds of thousands of years to adapt to their new circumstances? What if the food in the trees moved up faster than Stubby's kids could grow necks? I thought natural selection as a catalyst for evolution is no longer accepted.
Darwin:	(*Taken aback.*) What do you do for a living?
Barfly:	Well, my degree is in erotic dance and I minored in tassel repair at the University of Phoenix, but I'm currently working as a research analyst at Johns Hopkins. What do you do?
Darwin:	I studied medicine as well as theology, but now I'm a scientist and writer... What I really want to do is direct. You sound like you know a little bit on the subject.
Barfly:	We studied it in Catechism. I don't know if I buy it.
Darwin:	Catechism or evolution?

Barfly:	The ape thing; Catechism.
Darwin:	You know, I'm not saying we came from apes. Both we and the apes came from a common extinct ancestor.
Barfly:	Stubby?
Darwin:	No. But instead of apes being down the line of our family tree, they're more like on a separate branch. Like our cousins. You see the beauty of that is we don't need to explain why the lower forms of life – the monkeys – are still here while the more advanced forms – "ape men" – became extinct.
Barfly:	You mean like Piltdown man.
Darwin:	Actually...uh...that was a hoax. It seems he was based on a fabricated skull with parts of a man's cranium and a chimp's jaw.
Barfly:	Good thing we don't need that type of evidence anymore. Just the transitions from lower man to current man and lower monkey to current monkey. Like Aegyptopithecus.
Darwin:	Yeah... it turns out he was just a monkey. But there was this shrew-like rodent that we're pretty sure was one of the first mammals to be in the line of man.
Barfly:	Oh really. How come?
Darwin:	Well, it was this insect-eating quadruped about the size of a squirrel...
Barfly:	Uh huh.

Darwin:	...And while there's no real next step in the fossil record, we think it began the evolution of man because there's evidence to suggest that it started a labor union and then was destroyed by its own corruption.
Barfly:	Well, what about Ramapithecus?
Darwin:	Now you're talkin'. As far as being considered the first representative of the human family, the evidence concerning Ramapithecus is considerable – though in absolute terms it remains tantalizingly small.
Barfly:	What?!?
Darwin:	What?
Barfly:	Considerable yet tantalizingly small? What does that mean?
Darwin:	What? I'm quoting Richard Leakey from his book *Origins*, pg. 67.
Barfly:	What is this evidence anyway?
Darwin:	Fragments of upper and lower jaws, plus a collection of teeth.
Barfly:	And from that you constructed a bipedal, knuckle-dragging, hair-covered ape man?
Darwin:	Tantalizing isn't it. There *are* other examples.
Barfly:	You mean like Australopithecus?
Darwin:	Actually he was an ape.
Barfly:	Lucy?
Darwin:	Ape.
Barfly:	Nebraska Man?

Darwin:	Extinct pig.
Barfly:	Homo erectus?
Darwin:	(*giggles*) I'm sorry. That name always makes me laugh. Actually, he can't be classified as a different species from Homo sapiens.
Barfly:	What does that mean?
Darwin:	He was a man.
Barfly:	Neanderthal?
Darwin:	Man with rickets.
Barfly:	Cro-Magnon man?
Darwin:	Also a man with rickets, but in his case it was covered by his HMO.
Barfly:	So there's no real example in the fossil record of a gradual evolution for humans?
Darwin:	Not as of yet, but that's OK because we can't really find any evidence that any other animals gradually changed either.
Barfly:	What about the horse? I thought that was a classic example of evolution found in the fossil record.
Darwin:	Well...as it turns out, each type of fossil put into the horse line turned out to be pretty stable. No real modifications or transitions. There was this animal called Eohippus we thought might have been the original ancestor of the horse, but there's no real change in his fossils either. In fact, some think it still exists in Africa and is known as a daman. But it's still fun to say Eohippus. Try it.
Barfly:	Eohippus.

Darwin:	No. Say it with a little flava. It flows right off the tongue when you really get into it.
Barfly:	E-o-hippus. Yeah. I see what you mean. It's kind of tingly.
Darwin:	Oh yeah. So what are you about 5-6, 5-7?
Barfly:	5'-4 without heels. So why is it you don't believe in God?
Darwin:	It's not that I don't believe in God. It's that I don't believe in religion.
Barfly:	I thought you just said there *is* no God.
Darwin:	I know, but what I meant was that we don't *need* God. We didn't need him to get here and we can take care of ourselves. That's the problem I have with religion. For eons they've been the "keepers" (*Actually makes quotation marks with his fingers*) of information. If you wanted to know something you had to go to them, with their opulent cathedrals and pious clergy, make your donation and they'd give you their blessing. You know, like they're something special. And people would only respect you if you believed in what the church told you. If you showed any dissent, you were considered some primitive barbarian.
Barfly:	Well, what *do* you believe in?
Darwin:	I believe in my education. I went to Cambridge *and* Edinburgh – beautiful campuses both – with state-of-the-art facilities, and published professors. I paid my tuition and got my degree. Now I'm a respected member of the scientific community. Religious people are just too simple. You know? Most aren't that educated, and I have a hard time giving them any respect. Superstitious that's all. Superstitious.

Barfly:	Well, I think it's good to believe in a higher power. And if that higher power was responsible for creating everything, all the more reason to want to follow his guidelines. Don't you think?
Darwin:	See, there's your problem. What guidelines? Do you think this master of all creation would be so pedestrian as to have rules for us? His love isn't limited with all sorts of controls and conditions.
Barfly:	So, if I want to have a good time and it makes me happy He's cool with that?
Darwin:	That's all I'm saying.
Barfly:	If I want to have a drink...
Darwin:	Have a drink.
Barfly:	Maybe I want to have a lot to drink.
Darwin:	Why shouldn't you?

(A pasty young college student, at the end of the bar, has been eavesdropping and taking notes to share in his women's studies class)

Pasty guy:	But you can't drive afterward. That's immoral.
Darwin:	Well, of course you can't drive afterward. We've got to protect the public.
Pasty guy:	And the children. What about the children?
Barfly:	OK. I won't get drunk. I want to be a good citizen. How about cigarettes?

(The entire bar goes silent)

Darwin:	Cigarettes!?! Don't you care about anyone? Secondhand smoke kills more people than actual smoking.

Barfly:	I know. I figured it'd be safer firsthand. Besides, it helps me relax. Don't you want me to be relaxed? Don't you care about me?
Darwin:	Sure I care. Doesn't the fact that I don't want you to kill yourself show I care?
Barfly:	I don't know. It sounds a little pedestrian. What about sex?
Darwin:	(*His interest is piqued*) Yes...what about it?
Barfly:	He doesn't have any rules about sex?
Darwin:	Why would he? It's a wonderful thing. It makes us happy.
Barfly:	Oh. Then I'll see you later. (*Goes to get up*)
Darwin:	Where are you going?
Barfly:	There's this really cute guy over by the pool table.
Darwin:	Whoa. Whoa. You can't just leave me here.
Barfly:	But it'll make me happy.
Darwin:	I know but...(*searching for a reply*) I'm looking out for your reputation. You don't want people to think that you're the type of girl who has one-night stands do you?
Barfly:	Why not?
Darwin:	It's not right. You shouldn't just go around sleeping with any guy you meet...(*after thinking about it for a second*) unless... he's got a really cool beard.
Barfly:	You're probably right.
Darwin:	About the beard?

Barfly:	No. It doesn't feel right. I guess my conscience won't let me. It's probably due to my religious upbringing. I was taught to wait until I was married.
Darwin :	You haven't heard a thing I've said have you.
Barfly:	But...
Darwin:	It's not that you should save yourself for your wedding night. It's that you should *pace* yourself. See it's this religion that confuses everybody.
Barfly:	I wouldn't say I was confused.
Darwin:	Sure you are, honey. That's what happens when we try to live on faith instead of solid, proven facts. The simple fact is reason has no room for faith.
Barfly:	So you're saying that reasonable people can't be religious?
Darwin:	You know, Marx said that religion was the opiate of the masses.
Barfly:	You're quoting Marx now?
Darwin:	I know. It just sounds so learned when I get to say that.
Barfly:	So what are you a communist or something?
Darwin:	No. No. I hate that commie stuff. I just think we shouldn't throw out everything the man said just because he might have had a few bad ideas. I mean caring about the well-being of working people was good, right? And working together for the betterment of all. How's that bad? The ideal of a classless society. The dangers of commodity fetishism. Power to the proletariat. And he was right that human behavior reflects historical and social conditions. You know what I mean? (*Stands*

Darwin: (cont'd)	up on the bar) Workers of the world, unite! (*Catches himself and gets down.*) Maybe I *am* a communist. Great. Now I've got to join the Screen Writers' Guild. The point is that religion simply provides people with the *illusion* that they can understand things. Lay people want to make sense of life. They just can't accept that we're here because we're here. They have to know *why*, where we came from.
Barfly:	So what have you written?
Darwin:	*On the Origin of Species*.
Barfly:	So the problem you have is with faith?
Darwin:	Listen I don't have a problem.
Barfly:	You kind of do, as far as I can see. Your first idea that things change gradually seems to not be supported by the evidence.
Darwin:	That was when I first started out. I was green. Grasping at straws. My boat was named the Beagle for goodness sake. But since then, my ideas have been honed.
Barfly:	How so?
Darwin:	Now I've got punctuated equilibrium.
Barfly:	Is it operable?
Darwin:	No. It's the term used to describe the process of species changing from one form to another when phyletic gradualism cannot occur.
Barfly:	So you've now abandoned gradualism?
Darwin:	Only with organisms you can see with the naked eye. On the rest, what happens is mutation. See,

Darwin:	
(cont'd)	some members of a species will have some sort of mutation – a real doozy – and in some cases it makes it better adaptable in its ecosystem and it and its offspring survive while those without the mutation die off.
Barfly:	That could work.
Darwin:	It *does* work. Take the peppered moth. At first, the lighter form was more common than the darker colored moths because their coloring matched tree bark better, and they weren't as easily picked off by predators. But then, because of years of pollution, tree trunks became darker. Consequently the darker variety of moth – which is a *mutated* variety – survived better and became the dominant type within the species.
Barfly:	But it's still the same species right?
Darwin:	(*Thinks for a second*) Can I get you a drink?
Barfly:	Ooh yeah. Yummy. I'll have a daiquiri.
Darwin:	(*To the bartender*) Can we get a daiquiri over here, and I'll have a swimming iguana... light on the Brussels sprouts, heavy on the rum.
Bartender:	What kind of daiquiri?
Darwin:	Their coconut daiquiri is pretty good.
Barfly:	I don't like coconuts.
Darwin:	You don't like coconuts?!? Say Brainless, don't you know where coconuts come from? Tahiti, the Fiji islands, the Coral Sea. But not the Galapagos. Don't you ever wonder why?
Bartender:	I'm wondering why you won't tell me what kind of daiquiri.

Barfly:	Strawberry is fine.
Darwin:	Where was I? Oh yeah. Mutation. You know, few mutation experiments can equal the extensive ones conducted on the common fruit fly.
Barfly:	Drosophilae Melanogaster?
Darwin:	That's the one. Since the early 1900's, scientists have exposed millions of them to X-rays, which increased their frequency of mutation to more than 100 times more than normal.
Barfly:	And what were the results?
Darwin:	Well, even though most had malformed wings, bodies, legs, and other distortions, there were some that *weren't* inferior to regular fruit flies. In fact, when mutated flies were mated with each other, it was found that after a number of generations, normal fruit flies began to hatch. That shows that a mutation doesn't always have to be detrimental.
Barfly:	Doesn't it show that mutation doesn't change a species? Even the mutated flies were still fruit flies, weren't they?
Darwin:	Well, DNA has a remarkable ability to repair genetic damage to itself. But it can't fix everything. Gradually, over hundreds of thousands of years, the changes take place.
Barfly:	Gradually?
Darwin:	That's what I've been saying. It's the basis of my life's work.
Barfly:	I still don't understand. How can you believe in evolution, or change, when the fossils testify to stasis, or lack of change?

Darwin: Listen, I *know* that's how it happened. You just need to be patient. Eventually something will happen to prove it conclusively. Until then you just have to have a little faith in science, baby.

Barfly: Yeah. OK. But even if all species *did* evolve from one-celled organisms that were born of non-living matter, how did all of *that* stuff get here in the first place?

Darwin: (*After a very, very long pause*) I'll still respect you, baby.

A Night at the Theatre

I believe it was Al Jolson who said, "Grease paint gets in your blood."

Really, who hasn't come away from a Broadway show humming a catchy tune after having been stirred by the beautiful arrangements, or at least by the assertive vocal performances from actors playing to the back row? Which of us hasn't been carried away to a new world by the costumes, sets, and Saudi princes after an awkward tasting wine spritzer during intermission? Remember second-acting *Cats*, only to find the cast had knocked over the set?

Truly there is nothing like the theatre.

This was proven to me when my wife and I recently made a little jaunt to an off-Broadway* production, which was nothing like the theatre.

We had been convinced by our late friends that this company had come up with an intriguing little *Phantom of the Opera* knock-off musical. Although they insisted it was a high budget production, I believe the title, *Creepy Guy at the Cineplex*, had something to do with the price of orchestra section seats being only $3.89 a dozen. That and the fact that, at these facilities, orchestra seats meant that you sat *with* the orchestra. On the upside, if you could play oboe, there was a little something in it for you at the end of the evening.

In all fairness, the show wasn't that bad, if you hadn't seen "Phantom" (which we had) and weren't aware of the obvious plagiarism that was being perpetrated. Or if you were blind and deaf (like Tommy). For those unlucky enough to miss the actual show, or to see this one, let me enlighten you as to the similarities.

---

* By off Broadway I mean Tijuana.

The Phantom is a man with incredible talent in the arts as well as a genius with mechanics. However, he is deformed and, while attempting to avoid the persecution and ridicule he receives when horrified people and their undisciplined children see his face, lives a life of solitude in the Parisian aqueducts, while he tutors, and eventually falls in love with, a young diva named Christine Daaé. Her voice is lovely and enchanting and evokes in many a comparison to Janis Joplin. The Phantom has been giving her singing lessons (at a reasonable rate) for years and is satisfied to keep his love for her a secret, until he is thrown into a jealous rage as Christine attempts to leave him for a new lover, hunky young aristocrat, Raoul, and plans to open a coffee house in Berkeley.

As for the story behind "Creepy Guy", it revolves around a former circus clown and Rube Goldberg disciple who, after learning to count to twenty and then re-tying his shoes, falls in love with a beautiful hat check girl, Chrissie Dewy, and teaches her to run the projector at the local movie house. After discovering that she is married to Rupaul, the love child of Colonel Tom Parker and Eartha Kitt, and inventor of the self-twirling spaghetti fork, he retreats to the dark recesses of the theatre and terrorizes audiences by projecting pornographic shadow puppets on the screen during the coming attractions.

When you compare the listing of musical numbers, there is also quite a bit of evidence of twinsical copytude...

Phantom of the Opera

Musical Numbers
Prologue
The stage of the Paris Opera House, 1911
Overture
ACT 1 – Paris 1881

Scene 1 - The dress rehearsal of "Hannibal"
  "Think of Me"...Carlotta, Christine, Raoul
Scene 2 – After the Gala
  "Angel of Music"..Christine and Meg
Scene 3 – Christine's dressing room
  "Little Lotte / The Mirror"......................................Raoul, Christine, Phantom
Scene 4 – The Labyrinth underground
  "The Phantom of the Opera"..Phantom and Christine
Scene 5 – Beyond the Lake
  "The Music of the Night"...Phantom
Scene 6 – Beyond the Lake, the next morning
  "I Remember / Stranger than You Dreamt It"............................Christine and Phantom
Scene 7 - Backstage
  "Magical Lasso"..Buquet, Meg, Madam Giry and Ballet Girls
Scene 8 – The Manager's office
  "Notes / Prima Donna": Firmin, Andre, Raoul, Carlotta, Giry, Meg, Piange & Phantom
Scene 9 – A performance of "Il Muto"
  "Poor Fool He Makes Me Laugh"..Carlotta and Company
Scene 10 – The roof of the Opera House
  "Why Have You Brought Me Here/Raoul I've Been There"...........Raoul and Christine
  "All I Ask Of You"..Raoul and Christine
  "All I Ask Of You" (Reprise)..Phantom

Entr'acte
ACT 2 – Six months later

Scene 1 – The staircase of the Opera House, New Year's Eve
  "Masquerade / Why So Silent"...Full Company

Creepy Guy at the Cineplex

Musical Numbers

Prologue
Back seat of a Buick, 1969
Overture (in pantomime)
ACT 1 – Watts, 1995

Scene 1 – The house dressing at "Houlihan's"
"What About My Needs?"...Stornetta, Chrissie, Rupaul
Scene 2 – After the witch trial
"Come on Baby Light My Fire"..Chrissie and Val Kilmer
Scene 3 – Restroom at McDonalds
"Small Coffee Please / Pull to the First Window"..........Chrissie, Creepy Guy, Ray Kroc
Scene 4 – The line at the bank
"Hello Creepy Guy, Hello"...Creepy Guy and Paul Williams
Scene 5 - Canada
"Theme from COPS"..Creepy Guy (shirtless)
Scene 6 – Sunrise in the Yukon
"Dude, We Were So Wasted".........................Chrissie, Creepy Guy, Woody Harrelson
Scene 7 – Backstage (a bar in the Castro)
"Mystical Bindings"... Madam Rosie and The Village People
Scene 8 – The landlord's office
"Eviction Notices / My Cousin Donna"...Vinnie, Stornetta, Rosie, Rupaul, Creepy Guy
Scene 9 – A screening of "Dog Day Afternoon"
"Let's Give Cybil a Sitcom".......................Stornetta and the Columbian Milk Syndicate
Scene 10 – The bridge of Paul Hogan's nose
"Just Pull Over and Ask Directions"...Chrissie and Rupaul
"Why Can't You Kids Get Along"...Chrissie and Rupaul
"Why Can't You Kids Get Along" (The record skips)....................................Creepy Guy

Entr'acte
ACT 2 - Show has been canceled.

NOW PLAYING!!!

HOW TO SUCCEED IN BUSINESS WITHOUT REALLY TRYING

With all of the show's curiosities, it's important to note that there were many fine performances. Señor Gunter D'martinistein, in the title role, is a familiar face to film audiences, having portrayed Lester Chutney in Alexander Tushy's 1983 remake of Frank Capra's classic, *Where the Sheep Don't Sleep*. D'martinistein's Creepy Guy could be no stronger than in the final scene of Act 1, when he triumphantly returns to his mother with the news that, "…major combat operations in Ikea, Sweden, have ended, but there was still much assembly left to do."

If D'martinistein's portrayal of the Creepy Guy was inspired, Dame Gerta von Yack's performance could only be described as unerringly swell. She came to this company directly from the national touring production of *Creepy Guy*, in which she originally created the role of Chrissie, as well as acting as understudy to the great Frida Rump in the less glorious but equally important role of gutter snipe associate. Gerta's voice is overshadowed only by her frame, as is demonstrated in the opening scene of the third act where she sings, *Portly, My Love is for You*, while administering her finishing move, the meat hook forearm drop, on Bob Zmuda. Von Yack has also shown herself a talent in other roles. (some of which she plays while on stage in *this* performance). She played Lucretia in Tennessee Bartholomew Pontiac's, *Give Me the Monkey*. She toured as Lady Handkerchief in Oliver Wendell Peelschmiel's award winning, *Yes Sir, We Have No Urethra*, as well as that same playwright's critically acclaimed one man show, *Little French Funk*.

Playing Dame Gerta's love interest is Bobby Glickenspot. This young actor's ability to perform while intoxicated has proven to be his bread and butter in this company. In addition to the role of Rupaul, Mr. Glickenspot also holds the duties for seven other minor parts. He pulls it off without a hitch, until the third scene in Act 5, where the script calls for a musical collaboration between all eight characters. Amazingly enough, he has learned to juggle the scene by hitting, as he puts it, only the important notes…or rather note. While somewhat lacking in consonance, his minimalistic, and eight-minute long, "Super C#" is a sight to behold and a sound to endure.

Of course, there are certainly other actors and actresses deserving of mention, not the least of which is Rev. Billy Bob Cho. Playing the role of United Artist CEO, Biff Rocknard, Cho delivers the kind of performance we've come to expect from a true veteran* thespian.

Also in a supporting role for the first time (She's usually a pessimist) is Georgia O'Wiggle as Madam Rosie Mandible. Her earlier roles as strong willed, weak-loined heroines like Darla Dribble in *Make Mine the Measles*, or Queen Boostiella in Wolf and Firestein's, *Elixir? I Barely Knew Her*, have given way to a character much less interesting, but much more monotonous. That O'Wiggle is shooting for a Tony (or really *any* Italian) can be seen by her stunningly dramatic, yet well-disciplined, pauses sprinkled throughout her performance, particularly when out of breath. Some have gone so far as to compare her work to that of the great Christopher Reeve in his role as Benjamin Coffin III in *Rent*.

But truly, the most outstanding offering of the evening is provided by young Marissa Schmutz with her professional stage debut in the role of Stornetta Yolanda Fritt, the merry ticket taker. Marissa graduated from the Tupelo Conservatory of music and self-mutilation last year and has continued her voice studies with world-renowned linguist, Armando Svelte of the Svelte and Svanson Voice & Vindow Vashing Institute. Her regional credits include female Bolshevik #3 in *Fiddler On the Roof*; Victim #1 in *Little Shop of Horrors*; Servant girl #5 in *The King And I*; Maria's little sister #23 in *West Side Story*; and windmill #2 in *Man of La Mancha*.

While I can't say that the show moved me to tears – or even to applause – I *can* say that the bar at intermission serves up a great non-alcoholic scotch and soda. I think the best representation for this spectacle can be gathered from the dialogue of the opening scene:

---

* He played the title role in Julius Caesar during the Korean War as part of the army's 310th A-star-is-born division. It was believed that he might have won the Medal of Valor and Tragedy had it not been for an injury he got from a shell-shocked Marine, who went berserk while playing Brutus, after a poorly received 1st act in Seoul.

Creepy Guy:
(As a disembodied voice coming from an unknown location…like Afghanistan…if you're 83% of high school seniors)

Chrissie?

Chrissie:

Who's there?

Creepy Guy:

It's me.

Chrissie:

Me who?

Creepy Guy:

It is I. Your tutor… your lover.

Chrissie:

Mr. Humbert?

Creepy Guy:

Your guardian angel.

Chrissie:

Uncle Frank?

Creepy Guy:

Try again.

Chrissie:

Look I don't feel like playing any games. Are you gonna show your face or not? My 9:30 will be here any minute.

Creepy Guy:

Chrissie, I don't like you selling yourself this way. You're better than that. It breaks my heart to see you cheapen yourself by typing term papers for all sorts of dubious men.

Chrissie:

I've got to do something to make ends meet. Avocado toast doesn't pay for itself. Besides, what do you care? You keep telling me you'll deliver me from all of this. But you won't even show your face.

Creepy Guy:

I told you. I can't. Not until sideburns come back.

Chrissie:

They are back.

Creepy Guy:

I mean really back. Like when Captain Kangaroo didn't look ridiculous, back.

Chrissie:

There was never a time when Captain Kangaroo didn't look ridiculous.

Creepy Guy:

I can't believe you're dissing Captain
Kangaroo.

Christie:

I'm just saying his hair looked like
Stonehenge. I'm not imputing him as a person.

Creepy Guy:

Well *I'm* just saying that I cannot be
confident that I will be accepted until all
adolescent boys in the country look like 18th
century London surgeons.

Christie:

That'll never happen.

Creepy Guy:

It could. These new herbal drugs have driven
teenagers to take up sporting bell-bottoms
again. The kind with fur…and lace at the
cuffs…that start to flare at the knee.

Chrissie:

Look. It's been nice, but I haven't got the
time for chitchat. I've got to…

Creepy Guy:

I know what you've got to do. You've got to
get to work to make that Rupaul character some
money.

Chrissie:

He takes care of me.

Creepy Guy:

Yeah, he takes care of you alright. How much of the money that you make do you actually see? He's got you up to 45 words per minute now. But how long do you think you can keep that up? You'll see. If you don't get out soon, in a few years he'll have other, *younger* girls, who can do 60 words and then you'll be out on the street. Or worse, you could end up as a temp.

Chrissie:

Don't say that! Rupaul loves me. He'll never abandon me.

(*Rupaul bursts through the door*)

Rupaul:

Girl! Who you talkin' to?

Chrissie:

Nobody.

Rupaul:

Don't tell *me* nobody. I heard voices. They told me to kill my dog. But then I came over here and heard the whole conversation while holding a glass up to the door.

Creepy Guy:

Oh, that doesn't work.

Rupaul:

Aha! I knew you were talking to that freak. Don't listen to him, baby. I've got some work for you.

Chrissie:

I don't know.

Rupaul:

Look, baby. Just this one last time. It's a guy from Cal. He's doing his master's thesis on merchandise found at Sears. One last score and that's it… I swear.

Chrissie:

Well…

Creepy Guy:

Don't listen to that vulture. He doesn't care for you.

Rupaul:

Listen, punk. Show yourself and we'll have it out once and for all.

Creepy Guy:

(*Appearing out from under a lampshade*)
Here I am, you insolent fool.
(*Rupaul pulls out a pistol and fires*)

Chrissie:

No! I love him!

Rupaul:

But just yesterday you told me that you loved *me*.

Chrissie:

I know, but last night I had a visit from my Aunt Flo.

[Both] Rupaul and Creepy Guy

Ooooooooooooh.

Chrissie:

No. My mother's sister, Florence. She's a family therapist from Manorhaven. She helped me see that artists make better soul mates than employed men.

Creepy Guy:

Yes! Nailed it.

Rupaul:

What in the world did she say to convince you of that!?!

Chrissie:

Well, she had me stand, naked, in front of a mirror and name three things I find beautiful about myself. I said, the color of my eyes, the shape of my nose, and my pores.

Rupaul:

But there's so much more.

Chrissie:

Probably, but I was using a compact.

Creepy Guy:

(*Bleeding out…but with a good attitude about it*)

Irregardless…

(*Both Chrissie and Rupaul exchange condescending looks*)

I have been fallen. And I am not get up. You kids go, have a good time. Don't worry about me.

Chrissie:

I'll never forget you.

Rupaul:

Not with a mole like that.

Creepy Guy:

Just know that I've always loved you.

Chrissie:

I know.

Creepy Guy:

And that I'd never hurt you… in any place visible.

Chrissie:

Of course.

Creepy Guy:

And that Pi can be rounded to 3.14.

Chrissie:

Yes.

Rupaul:

It's also the sixteenth letter of the Greek alphabet.

Creepy Guy:

Are you sure?

Rupaul:

I'm sure. I majored in affectation.

Creepy Guy:

(*Looking back to Chrissie*)

See. This is why I said he was gay.

Chrissie:

What. Because of the Greek thing?

Creepy Guy:

No. Well, yeah, a little. But mostly because he thinks he's better than me.

Chrissie:

Oh sweetheart. We all think he's better than you.

Rupaul:

Even your Aunt Flo?

Chrissie:

Especially my Aunt Flo.

Creepy Guy:

Then why did she convince you to choose me?

Chrissie:

It was that time of the month.

Creepy Guy:

(*To Rupaul*)

Dames, huh?

Rupaul:

Now I'm not sure that you could ever really love me.

Chrissie:

(*Biting a fingernail and twisting her hair*)

I can't help it. I'm a girl.

Creepy Guy:

Maybe this is all working out for the best.

Chrissie:

What's *that* supposed to mean?!?

Creepy Guy:

I'm just saying that the sweet kiss of death might be a little less volatile than your mood swings.

Chrissie:

Oh yeah?!? Do you call *this* volatile?

(*Taking the gun from Rupaul,* she *screams to the sky.*)

I love you, Humbert!

(*Shoots herself in the foot*)

(*Company bursts into song. Theatre bursts into flames.*)

THE BAGGINS IDENTITY

Dateline, Hollywood - *Following the success of the <u>Lord of the Rings</u> trilogy, Jerry Bruckheimer, James Cameron, and John Woo have filed suit in a California civil court claiming that the idea for a screen play portraying the enduring tale by J.R.R. Tolkien was originally theirs, and have entered into evidence their earlier treatment for the story. It is the producers' assertion that not only was their idea stolen, but Peter Jackson's fanatical adherence to the source material has rendered his versions unmarketable by today's blockbuster standards.*

SYNOPSIS:

> A rag-tag team of misfits embarks on an adventure to save Middle-earth from destruction at the hands of a mysterious one-eyed man.

LIST OF CHARACTERS:

Frodo Baggins:	A maverick hobbit haunted by the memory of, and still attempting to please, his deceased father, whom most agree was the greatest natural talent to ever bear rings.
Gandalf the Grey:	A chain-smoking alcoholic, serving a life sentence for sorcery. Is often enlisted by the FBI to help profilers with tracking down other magi. Gets a pardon to participate in one more adventure.
Aragorn:	Brooding loner with amnesia. Drifts from town to town taking menial jobs to keep a low profile while he searches for his real identity.
Sauron:	Founder and CEO of MELCOR, originally a mining conglomerate that exploits workers in third world gold and diamond mines. Has now become a major player in illegal weapons manufacturing and pays no attention to his carbon footprint.

Gollum:	Computer whiz. Wears high bangs with pigtails.
Samwise Gamgee:	Frodo's butler and man Friday. Veteran of the Battle of the Five Armies (as a cook), he never discusses the details.
'Pippin' Took:	Comic relief. Joins the lineup after stowing away in a footlocker. His misadventures get them into trouble, but his stumbling and bumbling usually have a constructive effect.
'Merry' Brandybuck:	Mercenary hobbit. Wears a cowboy hat.
Legolas:	Native American (and as such, is one with the land and often acts "mystically"); master archer; horseman; scout; ladies' man.
Gimli:	Former Israeli commando turned jeweler who's always chewing on a cigar. Once a colleague of Sauron's, until the latter had his cousin killed for skimming. Has now sworn vengeance.
Boromir:	Loveable rogue and journeyman warrior. Dies a hero as he drowns when a hatch is sealed while he stays at his post.
Elrond:	Grizzled elf who's seen it all and is counting the days until his retirement.
Arwen Evenstar:	Elrond's daughter. Despite her father's protest, follows in his footsteps and proves she has what it takes without his help. Eventually has to be rescued by a male character.
Galadriel:	Elf matriarch and mother-in-law of Elrond. Kind of a cougar. A very flamboyant woman, who is mostly interested in her socialite activities but has insightful words when she thinks it necessary.
Saruman the White:	Politician beholden to Sauron. Lines his pockets from, and conspires with, the lumber industry while blocking legislation to prevent clear-cutting.

Barliman Butterbur:	Good-natured informant who doesn't quite grasp the gravity of the situation. Is murdered when he is caught wearing a wire.
Théoden:	King of Rohan. Battling cancer, but advises his troops from his hospital bed. Holds on until the last battle is won and passes after a short speech about hope and the cost of freedom.
Éomer:	Hotshot captain of the horse lords and nephew of Théoden. Headstrong, skilled, valiant but reckless. Cares about his people, but prefers the company of his pet iguana, Reggie.
Éowyn:	Sister of Éomer. A cold and assured expert in military strategy, firearms, martial arts, and explosives. A femme fatale who shows an ambiguous interest in Aragorn, but ultimately chooses her work over a relationship.
Grìma Wormtongue:	Gentleman thief. Éowyn's ex whose materialism and self-absorbed behavior probably turned her lesbo.
Faramir:	Living in his brother Boromir's shadow, regularly takes on the most dangerous of missions to prove his worth to his father, all the while keeping to himself his love of art and predilection for interpretive dance.
Treebeard:	Eccentric scientist who gets excited about gross things. Outfits the fellowship with special weapons. Yearns to be a part of the adventure, but has to stay behind because he's a big nerd.
The Witch-king of Angmar:	As Sauron's chief of security, he leaves a trail of victims in his singularly focused wake. While calculating and brutal, he does show a degree of respect for enemies who fight with courage and offers them a smoke before execution.
Denethor:	Father of both Boromir and Faramir, a by-the-book Steward of Gondor. A frustrated shouter who's always threatening to assign his men to parking meter duty if they mess up one more time.
Shelob:	Giant spider. Part is written for Chopper the wonder dog, if he can get time away from filming his TV series, *Tails of Adventure*.

OPENING SCENE:

FADE IN
Slowly panning across a mountainscape
Morgan Freeman (V.O.)

"No one would have believed that in the early years of the 31st century, middle earth was being protected by midgets with hairier feet than our own. Yet across Hollywood, powers vast; unsympathetic regarded that world with envious eyes and crept up and slipped away with her. All they found was a muddy set of prison clothes, a bar of soap, and an old rock hammer, damn near worn down to the nub. Idella was lucky. Yes'm. I expect she was."

FADE TO BLACK

An alarm goes off.
CLOSE OF ALARM CLOCK
9:00

A hand comes down hard on the clock. It might be broken now. As we pull back, the nightstand reveals tumblers containing small puddles of brown liquid and bottles and cans on their sides. There's an ashtray with several half-smoked butts and a boa hanging from the lampshade. We pull back further to see Frodo, shirtless, face in his pillow, eyes bloodshot, clearly not getting the sleep he needed after the festivities from the night before.

Sam enters the room and opens the curtains to let in a blinding amount of light. Frodo reacts with an agitated groan and hides his head under his pillow. Sam, unaffected, reminds Frodo, "You've got to get up and get ready, Mr. Frodo. You were supposed to meet with Gandalf 10 minutes ago."

"Is that today?!?" Frodo retorts. "That old man never takes a break." Frodo sniffs a shirt he picks up off the floor to see if it's still wearable. "Doesn't he know it's my day off?"

"Word is it's something big. Besides, I don't think he'd call you in if it weren't necessary."

Frodo is looking for a little hair of the dog from the empties as he turns them upside down above his open mouth, and then throws them across the room when he's denied. "Are you kidding? He hasn't had a mission worth any *decent* pay since the raid on Umbar."

"Well. Either way, you're late. What should I do with this?"

Sam nods toward the other side of the bed. We notice a young lady is sleeping underneath a pile of blankets.

"Let her sleep. She doesn't have to be back at the convent for another couple of hours."

FADE TO BLACK
TITLE CARD

ACT ONE (*The Fellowship of the Ring*)
The Shire
EXT – NIGHT

Gathered for his cousin's birthday party, Frodo and his friends are enjoying their R&R leave. While music, dancing, and drinking go on around them, the four hobbits sit around a fairly secluded table discussing their exploits in tones just loud enough for their companions to hear over the ruckus. Each of them, with suspicious eyes, studies every inch of their environment while still giving and taking mild ribbing and throwing back pints of mead.

As cousin Bilbo gets up to give a speech, the air of merriment is shattered by pulsating bursts of machine gun fire. As the crowd, respectively, screams in panic, drops to find cover, or runs aimlessly in every direction, the four spring into action. Merry, instinctively unholsters both his Glocks from under his cloak while hurling himself toward the mayhem. Pippin rolls into position for a better read on things, draws, aims, takes out an advancing assailant, grabs a barmaid and kisses her before following Merry into the heart of the action. Sam throws the table on its side to provide cover while, simultaneously, pulling people to safety and hurling bowie knives stashed all about his person. And Frodo. Frodo sits…unafraid, carefully observing the aggressors' attack patterns and instantly formulates his course of action. In a blink of an eye he seizes upon two of his enemies at once, flipping each in divergent directions while high-kicking a third and pinning a fourth's foot to the floor with his own katana. "Stick around." he quips as he strides off, deeper into the melee.

The invaders, about a couple dozen, make their way toward Bilbo with guns blazing, the avenging hobbits hot on their trail. By the time the quartet has cut short the assault, all but nine gunmen have been rendered unresponsive. Unfortunately, Bilbo has disappeared with a simple gold ring being the only evidence left behind.

As Frodo sifts through his uncle's belongings, looking for clues, Gandalf enters and explains the story of the ring. He and the hobbits set out to destroy it by casting it into the volcano at Mount Doom. With the ring's destruction, Sauron will have to pay two months wages like everybody else.

The Prancing Pony
INT – NIGHT

Gandalf and Frodo are sitting in a dimly lit booth in the back of the tavern when Aragorn approaches. "Barliman here tells me you're looking for an escort to Rivendell."
Gandalf responds, "Yes, indeed. If you know a short cut."
"Do I know a shortcut? I've made it to the River Hoarwell in less than 50 lar. I've dodged all manner of threats. Not your standard orcs or Uruk-Hai mind you. I'm talking' about the Black Riders now. I'm good enough for you, old man."

Now six, Gandalf, Frodo, Sam, Merry, Pippin, and Aragorn, make their way toward Rivendell with Saruman's specially trained ninjas in pursuit.

At their safe house in Weathertop, Merry and Pippin challenge Aragorn's leadership and cast aspersions about whether he's truly trustworthy. Merry argues that Aragorn's past association with the Rangers presents a conflict of interest as well as an indication of a failing fast ball. In turn, Aragorn presents evidence of Pippin's drinking and substance abuse as a liability to the unit. The dispute builds, eventually with the men taking defensive postures, in a three-way standoff, about to come to blows when they're ambushed by the Witch-king and his men.

Assassins rappel through the windows from all sides. The hobbits immediately form a circle, back-to-back, and begin to fight their way out. Aragorn makes for the hidden weapons cache behind a bookcase. Gandalf, having been in the bathroom splashing some water on his face and staring at himself in the mirror (as if to say, "I'm getting too old for this"), hears the commotion and, grabbing his staff and a burgling kit taped under the sink, slips out the window.

Although, up until now, the four Halflings (or two wholeings, depending on SAG regulations) have been holding their own, the continuing onslaught begins to take its toll. Sam is knocked to the ground and must roll out of the way of a downpour of sword slashes. Merry and Pippin are separated and each cornered. Frodo slides under the legs of one of the attackers and delivers a devastating kick to the groin, kips up, and runs two more through, easing the fight for his two companions. As he turns to check on Sam, he is stabbed by the Witch-king, who appears, seemingly, from nowhere. As Frodo falls to his knees with his back to the villain, the Witch-king raises his sword to deliver the finishing blow. Suddenly, a torrent of fire assaults the would-be killer from a flamethrower operated by Aragorn. The assailants and their scorched leader retreat as Gandalf smashes through the plate glass window in a hot-wired pick-up, ready to ferry his allies to safety.

Rivendell
INT-DAY

Frodo comes to on a rickety twin bed, arms handcuffed to a thick
rolled metal headboard. A fan with ribbons tied to its grill runs in one
corner of the dingy room. A police scanner squawks in the background
as Frodo's eyes focus to discover Gandalf sitting at his bedside.
Elrond, standing above him, begins to unlock the cuffs.
"Sorry about that. You were in a bad way when they brought you in
and we didn't want you to hurt yourself."
"Where, where am I?"
"Someplace safe. Now get some rest. You're going to need it."
Sam walks into the room and motions to the two, "Can you give us a
minute?"
As Elrond and Gandalf get up to leave, the elf stops and puts his hand
on Sam's shoulder.
"I won't have you burden him with details of the war just yet."
Sam nods and the two are left alone. Before long they are joined by
Merry and Pippin.

Arwen stands behind Aragorn in the cramped motel bathroom
stitching up a wound on his shoulder. The two talking to each other
through the mirror. Aragorn, in his blood-stained, white ribbed, tank
top, ignores the cut above his eyebrow and replays the day's events
trying to figure out what went wrong. Where did he mess up? What
did he miss?
"You're exhausted." Arwen answers him. "Frodo is safe because of
you. He owes you his life."
Aragorn turns around to look her in the eyes. He grabs her just below
her shoulders and pulls her to him. "Don't you see? He almost died
because of me." He releases her and walks into the bedroom.
As he cleans his knuckles with a fresh hand towel, Arwen, again,
walks up behind him and puts her arms around him as she rests her
head against the middle of his back. "The shadow does not hold sway
yet," she utters.

"I have no idea what you're talking about. Man! You and your father both. You talk like Yoda."

"Well, at least my father wouldn't get caught off guard by a bunch of mall cops!"

"Oh, now it comes out. I'm not good enough for you because I'm mortal. Well, excuuuuuuse me!"

The phone rings and Aragorn answers it curtly. We can barely hear the voice on the other end, but we can make out the words, "…meeting with the others…" He hangs up without replying and walks out. Arwen throws herself on the bed and cries.

Aragorn storms into the war room to find Elrond, Gandalf, and the hobbits have been joined by the heads of the other families. There was Anthony Stabile, Angelo Sepe, Fat Andy, Franky the Wop, Freddy No Nose, Pete the Killer, Gimli "The Dwarf" Shapiro, Legolas of Mirkwood, and Broome St Boromir.

It's decided that the group will be joined by Gimli, Legolas, and Boromir since they're the only ones not in foul trouble. Elrond declares these nine the Fellowship of the Ring, which is later determined to be a homophobic slur and is changed to the Wildcats.

The Mines of Moria
INT-NOONISH?

From inside the mines we see the cool blue glow of flashlight beams sweeping across the cavernous space with the rhythm of dripping water echoing between the sounds of boot steps trouncing through puddles.

Without being able to make out any faces, we hear Aragorn warn, "Everybody, keep your heads on a swivel. Legolas, what are your readings?"

One beam pitches down to light up some sort of handheld gadget. "These numbers are off the charts."

The team comes to a locked vault. Aragorn calls for some C-4. A voice from the darkness contradicts the order. "I wouldn't do that if I were you."

All lights turn in the direction of the speaker. There, leaning against a boulder in a long leather duster, arms crossed with his head down and his face concealed by the brim of a Stetson, the figure slowly looks up, a toothpick wedged into the side of his mouth. "These tunnels are packed to the rafters with gun powder and canned goods. You light that candle and they'll be finding bits of you well into the Fourth Age."

"Who are you?"

"The name's Sméagol." He cocks his head and smirks. "But everybody calls me Gollum."

"Well, Gollum," Frodo replies, "How do you expect us to get in there?"

"Nobody gets in there. Not nobody, not no how. Unless…"

"Unless what?"

"Well, let's just say I've got a few tricks up my sleeve. You got anything up yours?"

Sam throws in, "Up yours? I'll give you up yours. Let me waste this worm, Mr. Frodo!"

Gandalf interrupts, "Do not be too eager to deal out death in judgment. Even the very wise cannot see all ends. I know I can't see mine without a full-length mirror."

Aragorn makes a deal. "I am Aragorn. Heir to the throne of Gondor. If you will help us, I will be sure to reward you."

Gollum gets up and presses through the men to the vault doors. "I'm sure you will." Pushing Sam aside, "Now make way, salad dodger." He brandishes a small computer, opens the door to the electrical box next to the entry mechanism, attaches a couple of alligator clips to their respective wires and presses some buttons on the device. The doors immediately open. "Bingo! We're in."

Inside we discover dozens of vehicles in various stages of disassembly with a few shrouded under dust-covered tarps. The men slowly make their way through the morass of oiled steel and greased chains. One lifts the corner of one canvas to find a white gleaming souped up GTO. He gawks at the others in astonishment. The group have trespassed into a chop shop. At first, they are fascinated and, to some extent, excited to find a treasure trove of classic American muscle. There are Javelins, Cutlasses, and Darts. Chargers, Mustangs and even a murdered-out Pinto partially buried and parked in a corner.

Before anyone speaks, we hear from out of view, "Well, well, well. What have we here, fellas?" An innumerable gang of hoodlums armed with hand tools and machetes starts to close in.

Gandalf tries to calm the situation, "We're just passing through. We're not looking for any trouble."

"Well, you got trouble!" barks what looks to be the ringleader, giving a slow shake of the head that further tousles his thick black hair. His face and arms, as well as those of his confederates, are covered in grime. He's wearing a Ben Davis shirt with cut off sleeves and carrying a pipe wrench.

Boromir, with hands up in a surrender pose, steps toward the young man and speaks in a quiet tone, "It doesn't have to end like this."

Then, in a burst, he disarms the punk as the other eight instantly follow his cue and commence to fighting. The heroes overcome their foes with not a little effort, but Frodo is, *again*, injured in the clash. The group decides to abscond with some of the vehicles to make better time and maybe do a little cruising in Lórian on Friday nights.

As they lay Frodo in the back seat of a candy apple red Olds Rocket 88, a rival gang known as the Balrogs arrive in a fleet of black Chargers. Boromir takes the wheel, and Sam climbs in the back with his partner, and the three speed off. Aragorn finds a '68 El Camino SS and picks up Legolas and Gimli, who jump in the bed as he speeds by. Merry and Pippin decide on a sky-blue Cougar Eliminator and peel out with the Balrogs on their tail. Meanwhile, Gollum pulls up in his own custom modified Gremlin V-8. Gandalf tells him, "Move over. I'm driving."

"Nobody drives the precious but me."

"I will smack your head back to normal size. Now move over!" Gandalf gets into the driver's seat and goes after the convoy while Gollum sulks.

Boromir's and Aragorn's vehicles are separated by two of the pursuing chargers. While Legolas and Gimli are able to fire from the back of the El Camino, knocking out several of the cars behind them, Aragorn is continually denied a clear path to cut off the Balrogs by regularly positioned pillars causing him to swerve every time he finds a lane.

Merry and Pippin take fire from three converging vehicles. Pippin urges, "Can't you go any faster?"

Merry responds, "Hold on. I've got an idea." He downshifts, pulls the e-brake, and cranks the wheel. The car spins and two of the Chargers slam into one another and then, as their drivers overcompensate, separate and ricochet off of two concrete dividers and flip onto their roofs. As Merry races along in reverse, the third chaser pulls alongside. Pippin takes out the driver and the car collides with a column, starting a chain reaction of collapsing structures. Merry reverses the Cougar's direction again and races off to help the others, but now the cave shoring is irreversibly crumbling.

Gandalf and Gollum, racing to catch up to the others, are also contending with the rapidly disintegrating edifice around them. From a ground view we see the Gremlin speed past us just as a large carved stone falls where the car was, just a split second before. "Whew. That was close."

"Yeah. Too close."

From the passenger window of the lead chase car, muzzle flashes burst out and the back window of the Oldsmobile is shattered. Boromir offhandedly remarks, "We've got company."

Sam is out of ammunition and throws his gun away. "Make for Durin's Bridge! It's our only shot!"

"We'll never make it!"

"We've got to."

From the ceiling we see five vehicles racing toward us, then under us. The Cougar, the Elky, and the Olds are in front with two of the Chargers, guns blazing, following closely behind. Legolas and Gimli are now taking cover in the bed of the El Camino, having run out of ammunition and throwing their guns away. As the two black cars are about to overtake Aragorn's vehicle, Gollum, jumping from the hood of his AMC, flops on the top of the trailing Charger. One of the passengers shoots through the roof as Gollum alternately swings from side to side both to avoid the bullets as well as to abide the thrust of the swerving car. The gunman exhausts all of the bullets in the clip and throws his gun out of the window. Gollum manages to reach into the driver's side and yank the steering wheel. The car spins out of control, throwing Gollum onto the trunk of the Oldsmobile. While Sam pulls Gollum to safety through the glassless back window, the careening Charger makes contact with Merry and Pippin's Cougar, sending them down a steep, jagged shaft of the cave. The Charger bursts into flames.

The Cougar comes to rest in a shallow brook that seems to feed a larger body of water. The two pull themselves from the wreckage. "Next time, *I'm* driving."

Meanwhile, the others have reached Durin's Bridge. Boromir and his passengers, in the front of the pack, have thrown a rod and oil spurts from under the hood onto the already severely cracked windshield, making for difficult visibility as well as a gradual loss of power. Both Boromir and Aragorn, along with Gimli and Legolas, have, by now, observed the disintegrating environment that they are racing through; however, only Gandalf has detected the strategy of the last Balrog hunter. The occupants have mounted a rotary cannon to the hood of the Charger and are attempting to fire on the lead car. With debris falling everywhere, there is no clear shot, and the car makes motions to get around Aragon's El Camino.

The Gremlin is struggling to keep up with the other cars and Gandalf searches for a way to get himself into position. He glances down and sees the letters NOS.

Aragorn swerves back and forth in front of the Black Dodge, holding it at bay until, finally, a tire explodes, causing the car to lurch and skid; giving his opponent a chance to swing by. Just as the Balrogs are about to overtake Aragorn, from seemingly nowhere a metallic purple Gremlin with a chrome blower and spinners races into focus. Gandalf screams, "YOU SHALL NOT PASS!" and cuts off the Charger. The two cars veer to the right and break through the concrete guardrail. As both machines descend into the dark crevasse below, Frodo rouses to hear his mentor and friend bellowing, "I'm getting too old for thiiiiiiiiiiiiiiiiiis."

Aragorn, still battling to keep his car under control, warns the others to hold on and attempts to jump the car over a washed-out ravine. Legolas and Gimli take the opportunity to leap from the bed of the vehicle and land, painfully but safely, on a sandy bank beside the River Anduin. As Aragorn hurls toward a rocky outcropping, he quickly pulls his seatbelt over his chest and braces for impact. He survives with a cut to his forehead and a trickle of blood from the corner of his mouth.

Boromir and his passengers start to breathe a sigh of relief as they pass through the Dimrill Gate. Boromir comments, "This old jalopy isn't half bad. Maybe we should keep it huh? Hey Frodo, we should hang that ring of yours from the rear-view mirror." The sentence is barely out of his mouth when an RPG hits the car, hurling it into the river.

Merry and Pippin have followed the little creek to the mouth of the river. In the distance they can just make out the figures of Legolas, Aragorn, and what looks like, a fire hydrant with an axe. As they wave and yell to their companions, the bunko squad mistakes them for drunks and arrests them for public intoxication, disturbing the peace, and inciting a fashion disaster. The others see them being taken away but are just too beat...and a little relieved.

Crawling from the water to the opposite bank are Frodo, Sam, and Gollum. They decide to make their way to Mordor without the others. In spite of Sam's protests, Frodo asks Gollum to join them. Gollum accepts, despite Sam's suspicions and his threat, "If you harm one hair on Frodo's head, you'll be sorry." "Gollum counters, "I'm already sorry."

The three make their way into the forest of Emyn Muil.

FADE TO BLACK - END ACT ONE

ACT TWO (*The Two Towers*)
FADE IN
The River Anduin
EXT - DAY

Aragorn, Legolas, and Gimli decide to rescue Pippin and Merry. They wait, for some time, for Boromir to emerge from the water.

We hear a burst of gunfire from off camera. Sensing danger they run for the thicket. It begins to snow. They call over and over again for Boromir as the snowfall intensifies. They are startled. Standing calm, in the middle of the forest, is Galadriel. She tells them, "Boromir can't be with you anymore."

The warriors stand silent with their heads bowed. "Come…my boy toys." She slowly turns to lead them away. All three stop and look back at the river solemnly for just a few seconds and then ditch the broad.

CUT TO
The hills of Emyn Muil
EXT – DAY

Frodo, Sam, and Gollum.
And we're walking…we're walking…

MONTAGE SEQUENCE

The fields of Lothlórien
EXT – DAY

Aragorn, Legolas, and Gimli hot on the trail of Merry and Pippin
And we're running…we're running…
Wilderness of Gondor

EXT – DAY

And we're running…we're running…

Outside Fangorn Forest
EXT – DAY

And we're running…we're running…

CUT TO
Fangorn Headquarters
INT – NIGHT

We follow a crew-cut, clean-shaven man in a white button-down with his sleeves rolled up and a shoulder holster, carrying two cups of coffee through the door to a room where Merry and Pippin are being interrogated by his partner. The other cop is dressed in a suede jacket with fringe, a bolo tie, and a Fu Manchu mustache. "You're only making things worse for yourselves by not talking." The first man puts the two cups in front of the prisoners.
Merry and Pippin are handcuffed to a stainless-steel table. The dimly-lit room has just a table, four chairs, and one two-way mirror. There's a concrete floor, dingy acoustic paneling on the wall, and a single lamp hanging above the table. "We can do this the easy way…or the hard way."
Pippin speaks up. "That's what your mom said."
Fu Manchu leaps across the desk and lands a blow to Pippin's jaw. As he grabs the hobbit by the collar with intentions to do more damage, we abruptly hear over the intercom, "Lurtz! Stand down! Uglúk, for god's sake, get your man out of there!"

Uglúk pulls Lurtz off of Pippin and drags him out of the room. Merry looks at Pippin partly amused and partly frustrated. *"That* went well." He says sarcastically.

The voice over the intercom was that of Saruman. "The interrogation's over. You two clowns get some air. Treebeard here will take over." The two inquisitors start to object, but Saruman cuts them off. "It's coming from downtown. Sauron himself."

Treebeard has been staring through the mirror the whole time. Without disturbing his gaze he orders Saruman, "Give me a couple minutes with them alone." Saruman agrees and walks away. Treebeard goes into the room. He immediately unlocks the pair's handcuffs. "No time to explain, we've only got a few minutes."
"Who are you? Where are we going?"
"I'm Treebeard. Gandalf sent me."
"But Gandalf's dead. We saw him drive off the side of the bridge."
"We had equipped that vehicle with driver, passenger, rear, side, *and* knee airbags in addition to an inflatable seatbelt. Trust me, Gandalf's alive and he needs us to get to Isengard."
With his eyes darting around the room, he notices a grate over a ventilation shaft. "Here! We'll get out through the ducts" We immediately hear the doorknob jiggle and cut to the door as Saruman enters the room. He stops in his tracks. The prisoners and Treebeard are gone. Saruman looks up and yells, "Gaaaandaaaaaaaaaaaaaaaalf!!!"

The Dead Marshes
EXT – DAY – MOSTLY CLOUDY WITH A CHANCE OF SOME PRECIPITATION IN THE AFTERNOON

Frodo, Sam, and Gollum.
We're walking…we're walking…

Fangorn Forest
EXT - NIGHT

Aragorn, Legolas, and Gimli are still searching for the other two hobbits.
"It's awfully quiet in this forest."
"Yeah. Too quiet."
A twig snaps behind them. All three hit the ground and roll while readying their weapons. To their surprise it's Gandalf – now dressed in a white three-piece suit and holding a piña colada. "My dear friends, I am Gandalf the White, your guide. Welcome to Fangorn Forest."
"But you're...you're dead."
"I suspected Saruman might try to kill me, so I took precautions in case that happened. Any attempt on my life had to look successful."
He goes on, "They can't kill you if you're already dead."
Gandalf explains that the hobbits are safe with Treebeard and that the four of them must go to Edoras to steal the Declaration of Independence. They pile into Shadowfax, Gandalf's 1977 Chrysler Cordoba, and make haste for Rohan.

And we're riding...we're riding...

The Black Gate of Mordor
EXT – NIGHT

Frodo is still suffering from his past injuries, the effects of the ring, and laxative lag.
Sam is still complaining and using bad language.
Gollum convinces them that there's another way...over the secret pass in Cirith Ungol.

And we're climbing...we're climbing...

The Golden Hall of Meduseld in Edoras
INT - DAY

After stopping outside the gates of Edoras for a while to stare at the
city from afar, stretch their legs, and offer some plot exposition,
Gandalf and the others make their way into the court of King Théoden.
The king has been on a bender for weeks, haunted by visions of his
dead son, late wife, the kid that drowned as he tried to break the
window of the sinking car, his war buddy throwing himself on a
grenade meant for him, that lady whom he couldn't extract from her
vehicle before it burst into flames, the co-worker he stole that great
idea from, and the bends.
Gandalf has him take a hot shower, drink some coffee, and bids him
to get a haircut.
When Grìma Wormtongue is identified as the source of a classified
documents leak, the king initially calls for his execution but is
dissuaded by Aragorn who advises him, "No. That's what he wants."
Gandalf slips a tracking device into the pocket of Wormtongue's cape
and they send him into exile.

As Théoden, Gandalf, Legolas, and Gimli discuss their next move
over Chinese take-out and some brews, Aragorn rushes in and turns
on the news with an audible 'click' of the remote. They're all alarmed
to hear from the news anchor at that exact moment, Sauron's army is
heading their way. Gandalf tries to convince Théoden to fight, but he's
insistent that it will never work. "It's a suicide mission."
"That's exactly why we need to do it."
As Gandalf sets off alone to investigate a noise coming from the
basement, the Rohirrim evacuate to Helms Deep. Along the way, they
are ambushed by a small band of guerillas looking to kill passersby
and steal their resources. A fight ensues and Aragorn is left for dead.
He is miraculously revived by a vision of his lady back home, Arwen.

CUT TO FLASHBACK
Rivendell
EXT – NIGHT

And we're whispering…we're whispering…

Isengard
INT – NIGHT

Grìma Wormtongue enters into Saruman's office. He has to deliver the bad news that Théoden is on to them and that Rohan is making preparations for Isengard's surprise attack. Saruman is not pleased, but is calm. Saruman walks slowly around to the back of his desk. He tells Wormtongue, "This is going to be an obstacle, Grìma. But nothing that can't be overcome. You see, I didn't get to where I am today by letting small problems beat me." He opens the top drawer of the desk. "And you are a small problem." He lifts a revolver and shoots Wormtongue twice in the chest. "A *very* small problem."

Derndingle war room
INT – NIGHT

Treebeard and the Ents are reviewing their plans for sabotaging the manufacturing plants at Isengard Air Base. They are gathered around a model of the base Treebeard built with a few items lying around. He has a pointer and goes over each individual's assignment.
Skinbark and his men will cause a diversion in the East to draw out as many orcs as they can.
Quickbeam and Pippin are to commandeer the communications tower, cut off Isengard from Mordor, get a message out to allies that Helms Deep is under attack, and direct operations from there.
Leaflock and Merry will make their way to the generator and cut the power. This should give Beechbone and his crew enough time to rig the dam with nitroglycerin and destroy it.
"And" Treebeard says, "Saruman is mine."

Helms Deep
EXT – NIGHT

The fighting is in progress.

Aragorn has joined Théoden, Legolas, Gimli, and a paltry, battle weary division of Rohan fighters as well as a unit of elves who were sent as part of the coalition agreement (even though Rivendell had hoped to give sanctions a little more time). They are fighting a losing battle against the army of Isengard. The walls of the castle have been breached and they've had to retreat into the keep of the mountain where they've sent the women and children out the back way.

We hear a woman's voice, "Helms Deep will self-destruct in 10 minutes…I repeat. Helms Deep will self-destruct in 10 minutes."

Aragorn and Théoden decide to make a last stand to give the others a chance to escape.

The gates fly open and the small group of defenders rides out to battle.

"Helms Deep will self-destruct in 9 minutes…"

The men slash at their enemies as the invaders continue to pour in through the voids in the walls.

"Helms Deep will self-destruct in 8 minutes…"

Théoden yells to Gimli, "The people need more time! We've got to override the self-destruct!"

Gimli dodges arrows and flaming mortar fire to get to the main frame.

"Helms Deep will self-destruct in 3 minutes…"

Legolas comes to Gimli's aid in an effort to hold off the oncoming attackers. With a sword in each hand he slashes, thrusts, and parries. He flips, spins, and does that thing where he grabs one guy around the neck and that guy has to sword fight his friends because they keep attacking and finally they run him through and then Legolas drops him and takes out the guys who just killed *that* guy.

"Helms Deep will self-destruct in 1 minute…"

Gimli is still typing away at the keyboard.

"Helms Deep will self-destruct in 30 seconds…"

"I can't override it. They must have changed the password."

"Helms Deep will self-destruct in 20 seconds…"

"Use the mouse!" Legolas yells.

"Helms Deep will self-destruct in 10 seconds…"

A horn blows in the distance. All look up to see Gandalf has arrived, with the rest of the army of Rohan charging into battle. "9 seconds…" Caught in the crossfire, Isengard's army will be easily defeated.

"8 seconds…"

But Gimli is still trying to override the self-destruct order.

"7 seconds…"

Legolas runs over to the computer and tears off the housing.

"6 seconds…"

He finds two wires that go to the explosives.

"5 seconds…"

"Which one?" he asks Gimli.

"4 seconds…"

"The blue one!" Gimli tells him excitedly.

"3 seconds…"

"No. I mean the red one!"

"2 seconds…"

Legolas looks at Gimli, then the wires, then back at Gimli."

"1 second…"

He closes his eyes and cuts the blue wire.

"Self-destruct has been aborted. How about a nice game of chess?"

Legolas and Gimli smile at each other. As one henchman runs up from behind, Legolas, without looking, throws his fist back as if to indicate he's making a right turn on his bicycle and hits the attacker in the face, knocking him out cold.

Aragorn is pulling his sword out of one foe as he looks around to see that the last of Isengard's invaders has fallen and the rest have abandoned the fight and run off.

Our heroes, all blood-stained and breathing heavily, look at each other and nod.

CUT TO
Isengard
EXT – DAY

The Ents are cleaning up after the battle: Piling bodies, setting up makeshift quarters, pillaging, etc.

Merry and Pippin are in the mess hall, silent, staring at their coffee cups and pushing their rations back and forth on their trays. A young man walks up and asks to sit with them.

"Whatever cherry."

"Boy, you guys were something," The young man gushes. "The way you took out those orcs? With just rocks. I'm so excited to meet you guys. It was a thrill serving with you."

Merry speaks up without moving his head and barely moving his lips, "I used to think the same thing when I was your age." He then turns to the kid. "Why don't you do us all a favor and go back to wherever you came from. Don't you have a girl back home?"

"No sir."

Pippin speaks up. "Oh. One of those."

"No sir. What I mean is that I'm in this war for the long haul. Until it's over."

Merry looks back at Pippin. "Well it might be over for *you* quicker than you think if you don't stop bothering people. Get out of here cherry."

"But sir…"

"I said dismissed, private!"

The young man leaves the tent and a few seconds later we hear the reverberation of a sniper rifle. The young man is gone. The two hobbits lift only their eyes to share a quick glance and look back down at their cups.

Gandalf, Théoden, Aragorn, Legolas, Gimli, and Éomer arrive looking for Saruman.

Treebeard takes them to his holding cell in the tower.

Gandalf asks him what Sauron's next move is. Saruman, sitting on a bench in the back of the cell, asks, "What's in it for me?"

Gandalf implores him, "This is your chance to make it right."

Saruman smirks, looks at Gandalf. "Oh, I'll make it right." He stands up and slowly walks toward Gandalf. "We're not so different, you and me. You've got a beard, I've got a beard. You're a famed British actor, I'm *also* gay. Why are we fighting? Why don't we team up?" We'll take out Gondor and then go after Sauron."

Gandalf's eyes widen and his face turns white...er. He whispers, "Gondor."

Gandalf walks swiftly out of the room and past his companions. "Gandalf. What is it? Where are you going?"

He says nothing until he finds Pippin.

"Suit up, Took. We've got a mission."

Minas Morgul
EXT – DAY

Frodo, Sam, and Gollum are set to make their last push into Mordor. When out of sight of the other two, Gollum gets a text message on his burner phone.

FADE TO BLACK
END ACT TWO

ACT THREE (*Return of the King*)
FADE IN
Osgiliath
EXT - DAY

Gandalf and Pippin arrive in the war-torn city. The previous day's snowfall is melting, and sleet collects in the centers of the streets and in the gutters as cars rush by the Cordoba parked in front of a whitewashed tenement building. A lone woman in a burka, carrying a paper bag with carrot tops and a loaf of French bread sticking out, trudges by the entrance steps. "You wait here." Gandalf directs Pippin.

He gets out of the car, puts his collar up, and sinks his chin into the front of his jacket as he hurries across the street. He gets to the entrance just as one resident is leaving, and he slips in through the door. At the top of a long climb up narrow, gritty stairs he knocks on a door with just the faded outline of the number 9 on it. A beleaguered older man, weary from the relentless attacks from the armies of Mordor, opens. He just stares at Gandalf. "I'm looking for Denethor, Steward of Gondor."
"Never heard of him." The man goes to shut the door, but Gandalf persists.
"I was told that he lived here. A widower with a couple boys?"
"Oh, that guy. He moved to Minas Tirith a few years ago. Got caught up in some deal with Sauron after his wife died and got a little kooky. He had a birthmark on his right hip. Spit a little when he talked. Was really into film noir. The kids were nice boys but could get a little violent you know? The younger one was always following his brother around, killing orcs and such. He lives at 20 Northmoor Rd. I believe. Nice neighborhood…not a lot of trees, though. Kind of bland architecturally, but they got a Chick-fil-A so…"

As Gandalf reemerges from the apartment building, he's stopped by a soldier of Gondor. "What do you want with Denethor?"
"Who's asking?"

"I'm Faramir, his son."

"No time to explain, we must go now."

"Yes. It's too dangerous here. We must go now." We hear explosions in the distance. "Come with me. We must go now." The two run towards the Cordoba as one explosion after another bursts just yards behind them, getting closer to them with each stride but delaying long enough for them to slide over the hood of the car and jump in.

Once in the vehicle Pippin asks, "Hey, did you guys hear that? I think we're under attack."

"Never mind that. Just drive!"

The car won't start. Pippin tries and tries again as the engine refuses to turn over. Looking out through the windshield, we see an Orc tank rolling into view. "We've got company!"

Its turret turns and aims squarely on the Chrysler. "You got any other ideas?"

The car finally starts, Pippin puts it in gear, and steps on the gas as the tires squeal and the car pulls away just as a round flies by. "I'm getting too old for this!" The car winds and careens through the city streets as gunfire and mortar shells explode around them.

Just as Pippin, in an adrenaline-fueled moment, calls out, "Is that all you got!?!" the car is hit and lifted into the air. It falls back to the ground in a fiery heap and comes to rest on its roof. Gandalf kicks out the back window and he and Pippin pull Faramir to safety before the whole thing blows.

Cirith Ungol
EXT – NIGHT

Gollum has led Frodo and Sam to a secret warehouse where they should be able to get the codes to enter Mt. Doom. As they enter, fluorescent lights begin to activate, hum, and flicker to life in successive order, casting a green tint down a long corridor lined with abandoned workstations, discarded gear, half-eaten donuts and coffee mugs. Water drips throughout and monitors glow with various records and ignored transmissions.

As they advance down the passageway, the signs of a skirmish appear. Furniture is slashed and arrows pierce the walls. Sam pulls one out of a partition to find it dripping with a thick liquid. He dabs some on his finger, tastes it, and spits. "Thpuh. Poison."

Finally, at the end of the hall we see a prim older woman sitting in an antique wheelchair, legs covered by a thick wool blanket. She's thin, with grey hair in a Gibson Girl bouffant and wearing a high neck cameo blouse. She's flanked by two goons. "I'm so glad you can join me," she welcomes them. "I've been waiting for you. I'm Toni Shelob."

The dog begins to growl and then barks a warning. "Settle down boy." Frodo tries to calm him, but the dog keeps snapping. "I don't know what's gotten into him."

"He probably smells *my* dog." She assures him. "Maybe you should leave him outside."

"Sure." Frodo looks around to have Gollum take the dog out, but he's nowhere in sight.

The woman has been watching out the window to see Gollum driving away. She turns to one of her henchmen and nods. He steps up toward Sam and stares at him. Sam stares back. "You know where you're at, fool?"

Frodo steps in. "Back off. It's business."

The lady pulls back the curtain on the window to clarify our hero's situation. "The G-ride is gone homes. Aint nobody out there for you." The dog starts to bark again.

"Gollum played you like a booger."

"Yeah. Gollum's a low-down dirty ruthless vato."

One of the thugs steps closer and Frodo throws a punch, putting the man on the floor. Sam jumps into action and subdues the other. The dog keeps both in check as the two hobbits turn their attention to the old lady.

She presses a button on her chair and the apparatus begins to change form. Off comes the blanket as eight legs unfurl from underneath the seat. The apparatus keeps rising until finally, at a height of approx. 10 feet, it begins to step forward. Sam and Frodo are separated, and Shelob pursues the ring bearer.

Frodo tries to evade her by running into a windowless room with only the one door for egress. She blocks the door. "It's a dead end."

"Don't say…(Frodo gulps)…dead."

They struggle for some time as each gains and loses the upper hand. Shelob lands a blow that causes Frodo to lose his revolver. He dives for it, but she grabs his leg and pulls him back. As she pulls him closer he manages to kick her in the face. She loses her grip, stumbles backward, and falls, destroying a coffee table. Frodo begins his crawl back to the gun, but she kicks it away with one of her legs. He grabs a butcher's knife from the magnetic holder on the wall above the sink. They each maneuver for position as he makes stabbing motions and she narrowly escapes laceration with each jab. Suddenly they both see out of the corner of their eye the revolver. They look at the gun, look back at each other, and dive for it. Frodo just gets his hands on it first and rolls over to fire when she runs him through with the butcher knife he abandoned for the gun. He stares and falls limp. She starts to bundle him in a canvas mail sack when we hear a loud thud.

Shelob looks to the doorway, and there is Sam, strapped into a similar contraption as hers. We close up on Sam. Snarling through grated teeth he demands, "Take your filthy pedipalps off him, you damned dirty spider."

Shelob pulls the knife from Frodo's body, flips it in the air and catches it in a hammer grip. "Come to mama!"

The two machines clash while their pilots struggle to get leverage. Shelob slashes at Sam as he barely dodges each stroke. He manages to get a mechanical leg up to block one of her thrusts, and the blade lodges in a joint. Sam twists the leg and snaps the blade. The two pull apart and Shelob throws the hilt at Sam. She runs in a desperate gambit to escape.

"Not today," he mutters to himself and he sweeps the leg...several times, and sends her crashing through a plate glass window. Sam then climbs out of the machine and runs to Frodo's aid. He fears that his friend is dead.

Dunharrow
INT - NIGHT

Aragorn, Legolas, and Gimli have passed through the dark door of the White Mountains (for contrast) and have arrived at the secret base of the Ghost Riders, an elite unit of the 159th Airborne Division.
As they walk through the base, shirtless men throw around a football, others stumble out of a Quonset hut with the words, "Ye ole watering hole" spray-painted above the door. Jimmy Hendrix blares from another hut and still another hosts what seems to be a luau, complete with roasted pig and tiki torches planted every few yards.
Aragorn questions one of the men, "Where's your CO, soldier?"
"He's indisposed at the moment, sir."
Aragorn responds, "Son I suggest you take me to him right now if you don't want me to set you on fire and put you out with an ice pick."
The soldier snaps to attention. "Sir, yes sir. Please follow me."

He takes the trio to a tent where several of the officers are playing cards. Aragorn steps in along with his two companions. The commanding officer barely acknowledges them until Aragorn pulls his chair from under him as Legolas and Gimli draw their weapons on the remaining attendees.
"Party's over pal. On your feet." The men struggle to their feet and stand in shame.
"You guys are the Ghost Riders? My old man said you were the best. What happened to you?"
"With all due respect, sir. We haven't had a mission in ages. And a lot of these boys are just waiting to time out."
"Well, you've got a mission now. I want to see you and your men muster at 2200, you got that!?!"

"Yes sir."
"Well, get moving!"

When Aragorn sees the pathetic shape the unit is in, he demands they lose weight, clean their barracks, refine their skills, and conduct themselves with *esprit de corps*.
CUT TO A TRAINING MONTAGE

The Pelennor Fields
EXT - DAY

The army of Mordor and its allies have already taken Osgiliath and are now marching toward Minas Tirith. The Gondor army is severely outnumbered and taking a shocking amount of casualties. One bright spot has been Théoden and his small cavalry division, including a lethal motorcycle trooper with a sidecar carrying, of all people, Merry Brandybuck. As a team, the two cut quite a swath through the invading hoards, taking on any and all comers.
As Théoden and his platoon charge, his horse is shot out from under him. As he lay on the ground, trapped under his mount's dying frame, a lone dark figure approaches. At first we see only his metal-sheathed sabatons treading over blood-soaked grass. They stop at the fallen steed and we see what Théoden sees: the black mantle, the crown of steel and the Witch-king of Angmar standing over him. "Théoden, I've waited a long time for this. You should have killed me when you had the chance."
Théoden, struggling to breathe, "You are one ugly melon farmer."
"Clever to the end, I see." The villain raises his mace over his head and prepares to bring it down on the defenseless Théoden.
A shot rings out and the Witch-king falls to the ground dead. The helmeted anonymous Kradschützen Truppen, still in the saddle of the BMW R75 lowers their rifle and tells Merry to check on the others. The cyclist runs and crouches by Théoden's side as blood trickles from his mouth and he begins to cough. "Who...(cough)...who are you?"

The rider stands up and takes off the helmet, her long flowing hair falling about her shoulders in slow motion. It is Éowyn, the king's devoted and steadfast niece.

Merry runs up to the fallen king as well. Théoden tells Merry that he has fought bravely and should be remembered for felling the Witch-king. He then turns to Éowyn and, with his last breath, warns her: "You should get out of here my dear. You could get hurt."

His eyes close and his head falls limp. Éowyn begins CPR and pounds on his chest. "Don't you die on me! Don't you dare die on me!"

Merry pulls her away from her uncle's body. "It's over, Éowyn. He's gone. Quit being so emotional. We've got to get out of here. I'll drive." They, and the rest of the platoon, fall back to Minas Tirith.

At Minas Tirith, Gandalf, after delivering an injured Faramir to his father, has taken on the role of commander-in-chief. Gondor's steward, Denethor II, mourns the death of his eldest son and puts out a cigarette on the arm of his younger, comatose son.

Also taking cover behind the walls of the White Tower with Gandalf and the dual armies of Gondor and Rohan, are Éowyn, her brother Éomer, Merry, and Pippin (who is responsible for fire suppression).

As the defenses of Minas Tirith are almost completely obliterated by a constant air attack from Sauron's forces, several C-130 transport aircraft are spotted on the horizon. On board are Aragorn, Legolas, Gimli, and the Ghost Riders of the 159th. The support of the paratroopers turns the tide in favor of the free peoples as the Ghost Riders secure the cities of, both, Minas Tirith and Osgiliath as well as routing their enemies on the Pelennor fields.

From the tower, Éowyn swoons as a cigar-chomping Aragorn walks away, in slow motion, from the detonation of field general Gothmog's convoy, delivering the death knell to his military force.

Even with the victory, Aragorn realizes that they must take the fight to Mordor if the hobbits charged with destroying the ring are to be successful.

The Valley of Udûn
EXT – AFTERNOON

Aragorn's outnumbered military is poised at the black gate, intent on drawing out Sauron's remaining forces. Mordor is emptied with the defending robot army rushing the gate. The battle of Morannon ensues.

CUT TO
The Cracks of Doom
INT – EARLY AFTERNOON

Sam carries Frodo, the victim of numerous stabbings over the past few days, to the structure of Sammath Naur perched over the lava flow of Mt. Doom. It's time for Frodo to destroy the ring but, at the last minute, he notices how well it goes with his eyes (being jaundiced as well).
Suddenly Gollum appears and tries to wrestle the ring from Frodo. Sam does nothing as he's done with these two.

CUT TO
The Black Gate
EXT – EARLY LATE AFTERNOON

Aragorn's army is decimated as drones and robots surround them. Aragorn attempts to surrender, but the machines continue to advance. Their red eyes glow in shiny steel skulls. Rifles resolutely aimed, the mechanical skeletons lurch ever closer.

CUT TO
Inside Mt. Doom
INT – LATE AFTERNOON

Frodo and Gollum continue to battle as the struggle takes them closer and closer to the edge of the platform overlooking the volcano. Gollum trips and Frodo warns him, "Give it up Sméagol. It's over. I have the high ground."

Gollum brandishes a knife and charges at Frodo, slicing at his ring finger.

The two tumble over the edge. The ring precedes the others down into the lava, followed closely by Gollum, still clutching for it.

Lastly, we see, in slow motion and close up, the heel of one of Frodo's feet skidding off the edge. It drops quickly along with its attached leg, then the other. Passing through the frame next is Frodo's trunk, clad in tattered clothes, shredded, and stained by the trials of his quest. As we see his face pass down to his doom, a look of determination reveals the courage he has found during his adventure, and we know he has accepted this destiny all along.

Finally his outstretched arm slips until all we see is his, now crippled, hand disappear. Suddenly another arm from above appears and reaches downward. It is Sam's arm and as it reverses direction we see his hand firmly grasping his friend's. "I've got you, Mr. Frodo. I've got you."

CUT TO
The Battle of Morannon
EXT – LATE LATE AFTERNOON

What's left of Gondor's army is completely surrounded, all with their backs to each other and facing their machine foes as well as their own fate.

Gimli says to Legolas, "It's been a pleasure serving with you."
Legolas responds, "Ditto."

The robot legion is now within one step when suddenly the lights of their eyes dim and they fall to the ground. Drones tumble from the sky. Mt. Doom erupts and Sauron's dark tower at Barad-dûr collapses. The warriors cheer as it begins to rain under a clear sky. Aragorn is happy for their victory and smiles as he watches them celebrate, but stays subdued as he wonders about the future. Just then Arwen appears and throws her arms around him. They kiss briefly. She pulls back and with an impish smile (being an elf, after all), asks, "Are you ready for your next adventure?"

He counters, "I was born ready."

The two then hold their kiss as the rain falls more heavily and we slowly zoom out.

EPILOGUE

King Aragorn of Gondor and Arwen are married. They settle down in Minas Tirith and raise their one son who, strangely, has Haradrim features.

Legolas and Gimli start their own private investigation firm. Their first client is Aragorn, who's got some questions.

Faramir and Éowyn are married and move to New York City where Faramir tries to make it on Broadway. To support the family, Éowyn starts a baked goods company. You may know her as Mrs. Fields.

Éomer becomes king of Rohan and promptly declares war on Gondor. Unfortunately, no one is around to hear the declaration, and he spends his years playing with his little green army men.

Treebeard spends several years writing his memoirs, which become a best seller. He options the movie rights to Disney.

Merry and Pippin become estranged after the former convinces the latter to invest heavily in AOL. They reconcile years later when Pippin splits his earnings from GameStop with his old friend. The two pass away, no longer on speaking terms.

Gandalf, Bilbo, and Frodo take a cruise to Bermuda and are lost at sea.

Sam returns to the Shire and marries his childhood sweetheart. The couple raise their 13 children in the former home of Frodo and Bilbo, Bag End. Eventually Sam turns over the Red Book of Westmarch – the diary containing the adventures of Bilbo in *The Hobbit* and Frodo in *The Lord of the Rings* – to his daughter, Elanor.

The last scene is Sam playing with his family in the garden of Bag End. We see them through one of the multi-paned windows in the hobbit hole. We slowly tilt down to see the red book:

V.O.
"I never had any friends later on like the ones I had when I was 102. Hell, does anyone?"

FADE TO BLACK

MUSIC FADE IN: Ben E. King's, *Save the Last Dance For Me*

ROLL CREDITS

Section IV:
The Pen Is Meta-ier

I believe it was Noam Chomsky who said, "The shift from sailing ships to the telegraph was far more radical than that from telephone to email." This statement is both compelling and true. But still, it's a pretty "old guy" thing to say.

I am of the generation that remembers the .06¢ stamp, the warmth and smell of mimeographed dittos, the word *Sunkist* painted over Goldie Hawn's belly button, the chorded flip phone, and *Manimal*. I've witnessed the evolution of communication, and the one constant throughout my lifetime, and really, throughout history, is the simple letter. (The complex letter is a cursive lower-case F.)

Now if we give ear to old Noam there (Noam being a Hebrew name, נועם, literally translated: "not good at basketball"), we would come to believe that the real trick is getting one's personal thoughts broadcast as quickly as possible. From the six to fourteen weeks by ship in the early 19th century to the instantaneous delivery of the telegraph. This immediate dissemination of communique is equaled by the telephone, as well as email. Therefore, we can only conclude that, millennials *should* prefer *written* correspondence, given that it's tactile and not a passive experience, it gives a sense of community, and it's a warmer, fuller sound. (Many prefer the hissing or occasional crackling sound as you put pen to paper.)

All of this, of course, means that the next few pages consist of bits that seemed to only work as monologues. But they're not hacky. My act is as organic as written letters or diary entries. It's not like those trite, stylized, modern telephone conversations of Bob Newhart.

Out Of The Mouths Of Tweens

Dear Mom and Dad,

I am here at camp. The counselors said we had to write to you or else we would have to go back into the hole. Thank you for the cookies that you sent me. Mr. Munchick said they were delicious. I have learned a lot since I have been here at camp where you sent me. Did you know that mole hide is easier to stitch than cowhide? Skyler K. said he tried to kiss Skyler R. but got her retainer instead. Ms. Helmooth said we are going on a hike tomorrow and said not to play with the balloons cause that's what they were for tomorrow on our hike. When I get home can we have a lizard? There is a lizard here and he likes to bite us but when we put him in a jar he stopped biting us and then he went to sleep and Mr. Olemacher said to put holes in the lid. We play a lot of games during smoke breaks. Skyler G. is the best at face ball but doesn't like it anymore when he gets bleeding. They taught me to swim this year and said because alligators don't eat good swimmers. Mr. Gimble said it's important to keep a good routine and so he gave us a list of chores for each day here at our camp. On Monday me and Skyler S. have to be responsible for humping the bolts up the hill from where Mr. Lefty drops them off and then Mr. Gimble says to hump it up the hill. The rest of the week we play in building C but eat lunch in building C too. Next week we are going on a nature hike to the hooch cabin. Ms. Benoit says the corn is not for lunch. I like when we got to roast marshmallows but Skyler T. says she is sad because all her clothes were in the cabin when it was set on fire. When we got here to camp they said we could pick which activity that would be good whatever we wanted. I started to do the bow and arrow until I shot the horse. Skyler F. signed up for fencing but stopped because he got splinters. Is my room still there? Next time I'm going to write in my journal but not the part about taking Mr. Stall's bag of baking soda that I found in the footlocker when Mr. Stall was making me clean his room and then I gave it to the soda machine guy because he said he'd trade me for a soda but then Mr. Stall found out and got mad and sweaty. How is Scraps? Is he still making in mom's shoes? I think it's because he doesn't like the newspaper because it's a trashy left wing rag my counselor says. I miss my own bed because the bed here is crunchy and sometimes I pee in it and then it gets crunchier. Ms. Larson says to stop drinking milk before bed but she cries when she drinks her drink and I think it's because she doesn't have milk and her husband left. When I get home I would like some ice cream but Skiilär H-N says it has to be organic or else the earth will die because whales don't have enough polar bears to eat so we need to get some organic ice cream and eat it before it melts OK? The doctor said that my arm will probably heal weird but then he gave me a lollipop. Did you know that poison oak is itchy? I tried it and it is. They have a dance again tonight but when I dance with Skyler A. she does it wrong and says that I am a twerk. I get sad sometimes because you aren't here to give me time outs and my counselor says time outs aren't as good as paddles but when he says he'll give me the paddle he just hits me with it. Mr. Richards didn't get a time out either because Skyler W. says he saw Ms. Kingston giving him the paddle after curfew when he went to the bathroom but it's OK to go to the bathroom with a buddy after curfew but Mr. Richards didn't get a time out from Ms. Kingston. Sometimes the other kids here get mauled by bears. Did you know ticks get bigger as they eat just like Uncle Herbert? When I was making my lanyard Mr. Lusk said I was doing it wrong when I was making it but he didn't know that I was making a noose because that was what Ms. Larson asked me to make. Mr. Pillsbury is really good at frisbee because he can catch the frisbee every time but sometimes he drops it and then he says the words that make dad get in trouble at church. When we go out at night we have to take a flashlight because it is dark at night when we go out and we can't see without the flashlight and also we smash snakes with them. I like mom's bologna sandwiches better than the ones here because they aren't as fuzzy that mom makes. I came in third in the canoe race and some of the other kids paddled at the waterfall and didn't get a snow cone and aren't here now. I hope when I get home you will remember me even though my clothes are too big now and Mr. Wurst says tape worms aren't dangerous. I have to go now because it's my turn to cut out the swooshes. See you in 3 weeks if we can meet our quota. Tell Tristan not to play with my Legos.

Love, Skyler D.

The Diary of John Dunbar
Vol. 2

Feb. 21, 1869,

The hunt was a good one. Although the tribe is very tired, it is good that we now have food for the winter.

Last night, Stands with a Fist told me that she is pregnant. I am sure that she can sense my insecurity at this news, but I am at a loss to explain it to her, as there is no Sioux word for vasectomy.

Feb. 22, 1869,

Following my first instinct, today, I went to the lodge of Sneaks Around the Back but found that my suspicions were misplaced when I came upon him baking quiche with Hates Your Shoes.

Tomorrow I will confront Delivers the Mail.

Feb. 23, 1869,

Could not find Delivers the Mail today. However, I did speak with Scalps for Fun. He told me that he had heard of my predicament and offered to help. While not completely sure of what he meant, I graciously declined and went on my way.

This afternoon I returned to the lodge to find Stands with a Fist unloading packages with the word Amway on their sides. As it happens, Scalps for Fun is our new up-line.

I shall continue with my search for Delivers the Mail tomorrow.

March 3, 1869,

I have been searching for Delivers the Mail for many days now. I think I may soon give up looking since the search has begun to interfere with my daily chores and my how to be mysterious and at one with the great earth spirit class at the community college.

March 4, 1869,

Found the remains of Delivers the Mail today.
Apparently he'd been killed in a buffalo stampede. They
trampled every part of him.

March 11, 1869,

Delivers the Mail is gone, but I still feel distressed
over the baby. Maybe revenge wasn't the answer. I need a
smoke.

March 15, 1869,

Stumbled into the lodge last night after three days of
expanding my mind. Running Bear said that we were all
living our lives in some other guy's dream so we spent the
weekend pinching each other. Now Stands with a Fist is all
over me about my always being on the Play Station. Man,
I'm hungry.

April 20, 1869,

Kicking Bird said that he noticed Stands with a Fist is gaining a little weight lately. I told him to mind his own business and bit his nose off. I'm beginning to think that this living off the land idea has some drawbacks. I wonder what my ex is doing right now.

April 21, 1869,

I apologized to Kicking Bird today. He told me that I did him a favor. He had stuck a pebble up there many years ago and now he was finally able to retrieve it.

Also he has invented a new game for the children in the tribe called "Got your nose." It's really just a variation on the Pawnee game, "Got your scalp."

April 29, 1869,

This morning I woke up refreshed. Last night, Stands with a Fist and I finally made up. Everything looks much better now. I think our life here will be wonderful.

April 30, 1869,

I am out of here! I cannot live with that woman. Today Stands with a Fist told me that she doesn't want to be pregnant anymore.

I told her not to be ridiculous and that soon we would have our baby and everything would be wonderful.

She said that she never wanted a family and that I am trying to trap her. Then she admitted that she's been sending smoke signals to an old boyfriend from high school she reconnected with on Facepictograph.

I grabbed my pipe, my Play Station, and my best cuff links and headed to my old outpost.

July 3, 1869,

It's been some time since I've had any contact with the tribe. I am doing all right though. I have enough supplies to keep me going through the winter and I spend my time reading girlie magazines I found in an abandoned footlocker. They have pictures of women's ankles. You know, the real sick stuff you can't get in the mail.

I wonder how Stands with a Fist is doing.

July 4, 1869,

It's Independence Day. I'm not feeling very festive. I miss Stands with a Fist and I'm getting desensitized to the porn.

Maybe I'll visit the tribe today.

July 10, 1869,

I have been back with the tribe for almost a week now. Stands with a Fist isn't talking to me but she does let me hold her hair during her morning sickness. Hot dogs. Hmmm.

Sep. 4, 1869,

I approached Running Bear this afternoon to talk to him about the baby. We discussed the responsibilities of fatherhood and the importance of training and as we passed the pipe we eventually came to the topic of Oreos.

As we sat on the curb in front of the 7-Eleven I asked him how I should name my child. He told me about the Sioux tradition of naming someone by that person's characteristics. We concluded that the best thing would be to wait until his personality comes through and we can give him a good name.

Oct. 1, 1869,

My baby was born today. I know he must be mine because when I tried to give him away everyone said, "No way! He's yours"

I can't wait until I can give him his Sioux name.

Jan. 27, 1879,

The hunt was a good one. Although the tribe is very tired, it is good that we now have food for the rest of the winter.

Stands with a Fist is pregnant again. Dumber Than Rocks and Wind in His Pants are in front of the lodge, laughing at bugs. And I find myself thinking longingly of my former life.

This place needs a bar.

Lost In Transmutation

Dear Pen Pal:

My teacher is making us write this so here it goes. My name is Dave. I'm in the 2nd grade. My favorite subject is art because my parents say that it's what I should focus on and that there are enough Jewish doctors. My dad's a doctor and he says these young people in their dungarees are sick. I live in Indiana. Where do you live? What is your favorite subject in school? What is your favorite food? Mine is sushi because it's exotic and some of it has tuna. I like to play all kinds of sports and I sing when I need attention. I like to sing songs from Ray Charles and Smokey Robinson. My dad says I have to like Al Jolson too. Have you heard of him? I have. My dad told me about him. I guess that's all. I hope you write back to me. As Porky Pig would say, That's all folks. Ha ha.

Sincerely, David Roth

3/14/61

Dear Dave:

My name is Teddy. I am in the 6th grade. That means I'm bigger than you and you have to do what I say like my big brother told me. I like Ray Charles and Smokey too. They're from here where I live, Detroit; the motor city, Hockey town, the Paris of the West. You'd like it here. We have snow and sports and outdoors and indoors. School is fine but my favorite thing is band. I got a guitar from my aunt a couple of years ago and now I'm great. My dad says the same thing about people in dungarees. Especially women who should only wear pants when they're gardening... in the backyard... at night. I think my favorite food is bacon so your Porky Pig joke was good. Write me back.

Sincerely Theodore Nugent

Dear Teddy:

You play guitar? That's pretty boss. And you know how pretty the boss is. Ha ha. I like to play around on the guitar too. I'd say I'm as good as Elvis at playing it and almost as good at holding it. He's one hip set of hips, that's for sure. I'm going to New York for the summer to see my uncle who owns a club there. Maybe I'll get to meet Mr. Tupelo Tiptoe himself. That would be a gas.

Well, got to go. My dad's taking me to see the Misfits. He took me to see Some Like It Hot a couple years ago and some things haven't fit the same since. If you know what I mean. Smell you later.

Your pen pal, Dave

Dear Dave.

Sorry I haven't written in a while. In the spring it's turkey season and my dad takes me out to enjoy the majestical majesty of the majestic outdoors. I like to hunt turkeys cause their heads are red, white, and blue and I feel like I understand the British better when I take one down.

Yeah, Elvis is OK but have you heard of Wayne Cochran? That guy is one mighty, mighty, pressure cooker of heart pounding soul rhythm and blues. I saw him not long ago in Muncie, Indiana, your home the Hoosier state, land of the Indians. The kind with the dots, not the feathers. My dad didn't like him because he had too much hair but I think I might grow my hair long too. Hey! We should become blood brothers like the Indians.

Your pal, Teddy

Hey Teddy

I just started the 3rd grade and now I'm the biggest guy on the playground. It's like my dad always says, "When you got it made in the shade, there's no need to wear a hat." You follow?

No big deal about the time between letters. I was kind of busy myself. Like I told you before, I spent the summer with my uncle in NY and I met this soi-disant vagabond (I got baby sat by Norman Mailer while I was there) named Bobby Zimmerman. He does this folksy rhyming thing and plays guitar and harmonica at the same time. My uncle calls him a real trip. I told him he needs more charisma, like Che Guevara. Everybody loves that guy.

That blood brothers thing sounds interesting. Is it real blood or are you saying it the way James Baldwin does? Either way, I'm good in the hood, you dig?

Your buddy, Dave

10/2/61

Hi Dave

I'm in middle school now so I'm pretty busy most of the time. My band is pretty popular and I'm learning a lot about how to become a way out twitchin' red hot blast master axe grindin' melody maker of ever-lovin' righteous groove movin'. It's a total high-energy unbefore-heard-of blank check pure adrenaline rock and roll rush. So It's going to be hard to write to you. But if you're into music, I definitely recommend it.

Anyway, I'll still stay in touch from time to time but you've got to stay clear of that communist stuff. My dad says it'll make you light in the loafers. And he should know, he's been knee deep in the stuff. Combat I mean, not light loafers.

Keep a clear head and enjoy the rest of grade school. It's harder here in the adult world. We've got lockers.

Your blood brother, Teddy

10/10/61

Teddy

I understand that you're busy. It sounds like the real world is one bad mama jama on toast with a side of hash browns. Don't worry about me though. Cats always land on their feet and as a great Mexican rebel once said, it's better to die on your feet than live on your knees. You know?

I think I'm gonna take your advice and get into music... or poetry... or acting... or karate... or gymnastics... or calligraphy... or art. Do you ever watch Jon Gnagy? That cuss really razzes my berries.

Anyway, I hope you're having a good time and try to remember me when you're a famous guitar rock and roller.

Your blood brother from another mother, Dave

199

10/2/62

Hey Dave

It's been a while. A lot has happened for me. Now that we're teenagers we changed our band's name and we're even more popular. My old man even lets me avoid the old wig chop from time to time. Yep. Everything's comin' up Ted.

How are things for you? You must be, what, 4th grade now? Wow. I remember when I was a kid. I didn't know anything about anything. Especially the skirts. But now that I'm a man, I can help you out with that if you have any questions.

Oh, by the way. My dad found your letters and he's a little hacked. He thinks you might be being raised by some dropouts or hippy dippy commune types. He practically flipped his lid when he read your quote from Emilio Zapata. Remember little buddy, better dead than red. No matter what those fruits and nuts in California say. Thank goodness we ain't livin' in that left coast free-for-all. That being said, I'll still write when I can, but we got to keep it KGB style.

Blood brothers forever, Ted

10/10/62

Hey Ted

Wow man. It was great to get a letter from you. Today is my birthday. I won't say how old but I'll say I'm old enough to know better but young enough to get away with it. Alright? On top of that, I'm now a Bay Stater. That is we live in Massachusetts now and I can't wait to pock the caw in the yod. Ha

I just finished reading a short story by Jack London. It's called, "The Heathen," OK? It wasn't the how-to manual I had hoped but it was still pretty good. It takes place in the South Pacific so I've got that on my to do list. That and a trip to the Klondike. Old John Barleycorn made that sound pretty righteous too. Uh oh. He was another socialist. I hope your old man doesn't find this letter. He might have you blacklisted and send you to Walt Disney and Elia Kazan to have you re-educated.

Anyway, Things are outta sight here and I hope you're rock, rock, rockin' along as well. I'll definitely keep writing to you.

To my type A blood bro. Dave

12/13/62

Hey Davey Baby

See what I was saying about that commie stuff. It's a good thing that used snotty Hand-Khrushchev turned those boats around or them Ruskies would be staring down the business end of a couple of our star-spangled rockets glaring at those reds. And those brooms got some boom.

Anyway, I thought I'd return your line on my own auspicious anniversary of commencing the great adventure that is the enduring tale of my physical, mental, spiritual, and musical life. I'm the big one-four today. I feel like I can take on the world. Of course, first I have to finish high school and see what those guys know, but then it'll be time to storm the gates and warm the dates. You said you sing right? I'll save a place for you at the table when the time comes.

By the way, I got my first whisker last week. It's just above my chin. If I can get it to grow long enough I think I can curl it into a soul patch. I'll keep you posted.

Ted

3/28/63

Dear Cousin Ted

I figure since we haven't been able to meet in person to do the blood brother thing, we'll have to settle for cousins for now.

Anyway, you'll never guess where we moved to. Pasadena, California! I know you're not a fan, but boy howdy, the fun in the sun, the surf and the turf, the thrills and spills, the twirls of those girls with a classy chassis. You follow? This place is for me.

In entertainment news, just saw "The Birds" movie. Way creepy man. And that Hitchcock fella completely left out the bees part. You know what I'm sayin'? You don't got no bees, the birds are just flyin' around waitin' to dust something. You dig?

I hope things are going well for you too. If not, feel free to visit and we'll catch some rays and ask them where their sisters are.

Sparkling like a diamond,
Dave

201

Hey Diamond Dave

I'm glad to hear you're enjoying yourself. I've been doing well too. My band just won a competition and we got to open for the Beau Brummels and the Supremes last weekend. It was one soul pulverizing get-up-and-went hunker down with a funkier brown spectacle of lights fights tights tunes goons and pantaloons. I think I got this American dream thing licked.

By the way, instead of cousins, just call me Uncle Ted.

Your friend, The Nuge

9/20/64

Hey Uncle Ted

What do you think of this Beatles thing? I mean, they're pretty good, but what's with John's up and down bouncing? Or Ringo's head rocking? It's like he's keeping the beat in Tamil. These guys need to loosen up. Maybe have George jump off the drum riser or something. You can't have rock & roll without a jackhammer and some sourdough. You follow?

How are things with you? You still shredding the ears, eyes, noses, and throats of the Michigan concert going audiences? If so, keep it up. If not, giddy up.

Diamond Dave

6/1/65

Diamond Dave

I dig the Beatles. I think they've reversed the earth's musical rotation with their uppity ultra-passionate goosebumps on goosebumps hysteria-inducing magical take on our country's grinding emotional primal scream soundtrack born of the black masters of American soul music blowing to smithereens the traditional cultural sirens with hard life fueled vocals, bent to unrecognizable divine form mouth harps, and his lord Les Paul's electrified Kalamazoo-manufactured stringed instrument of mass construction and keep the life blood of killer music pumping. But you're right, John looks awkward.

You're not going to believe this: We moved to Chicago. But never fear nephew of the great white gonzo, macho, buffalo of wango tango with limbs akimbo. I've already started a new band and we've got a gig at a pizza place. That's right. Soul with spice and then a slice.

Hope you're killin' it out West.

Ted in your head until we're dead

Uncle Ted

I've got to say, this Beachboys song, "California Girls" is stuck in my head. It makes me wanna run out into the street with my shiny new quarter and tell the ice cream man I'll take a double scoop. You dig? Have you heard this? It's a no-holds-barred grudge match between the powers of clean-cut sunny-side-up pop and the down and dirty red-light district of good time rock and roll where the winner is called after a standing 4/4 count. I'm definitely gonna try to make it in that business they call show. And I plan to do it with more than a little bit of tell. Ha ha. Keep Cookin'.

Dave

Dave

I understand that there's a certain segment of the population – emphasis on pop – that digs the beach boy sound. While I'm a fan of Mike Love (and not just his music, but his savvy solid-state common sense and positive productive blood and guts worldview. Of course he's a vegetarian but so are my meals.) I just can't get into the teenybopper surf songs. But hey. Different strokes for boring folks. I prefer the mind blazing nerve scratching head banging ear bleeding hair flying aboriginal spirit-of-the-wild life cleansing boots-on-the-ground honest reverential high powered hand-to-hand face melting bazooka blast of down-home loin cloth and feathers teeth grinding epic blues jams. Like I do. Keep in touch.
Your soil-bathing nature-loving howling gonzo of madness and mayhem.

Uncle Ted

Hey Ted

It's been a long time. Things are going well for me and I can see that you've been doing gangbusters yourself. Keep on trucking good buddy.

I've graduated and my band is mind blowing. It's like I joined a gypsy foreign legion, cross-faded with double reverb and in slow motion. These dogs not only chase the cars, they catch 'em, fry 'em up, and eat 'em at 78 RPMs. Two of 'em are brothers in the most fraternal sense of the word. You poke one in the stomach, the other makes biscuits. Follow? These boys are goin' places even if they gotta do it in a hatchback with shag carpet, diamond tuck seats and dingle balls in the back window. We're the new Rat Pack except we don't avoid the d-Con. You dig? Maybe in the future, we can get together, paint the town vermillion, and then put on a show that'll be worth the whole $8.98. I don't know how this is going to end but you can be sure to find the cliff's notes on the grout work between the tiles. If there's no refrigerator magnets, don't do the finger painting. OK?

Oh, one other thing. I met this actor guy out here who's a big fan of yours. I've enclosed a letter from him too. Here's to swimmin' with bow-legged women.

Your ever-lovin' blood brother of rock & roll hanky panky,

Diamond David Lee Roth

Dear Mr. Nugent.

I can't tell you how excited I am to be able to correspond with you. Your music has had such an impact on me that I had to share it with the aliens that were probing me last Thursday. It was a real cultural epiphany for all of us. I was able to communicate to them the importance of art in our society and they were able to communicate to me that I'm one of the 12% of humans that doesn't mind the catheter.

I've got all sorts of pamphlets I think you'd really get a kick out of, but first I think we should meet in person to make sure that our auras aren't cross-fed from any celestial vortex capacitors. Also, stay alert to the upcoming artisanal war that's prophesied to be fomented by a severe fluoride shortage. Better safe than sorry, brother.

Your greatest fan and newest spirit collaborator, Gary Busey

Section V:
Kids, Ask Your Parents

I believe it was Lee Harvey Oswald who said, "You miss 100% of the shots you don't take."

We're 200 pages into this mess and some may be as tired of reading these worn-out and predictable bits as the ghost writer is of trying to convince me that my Word XP is haunted.

Sure, I could leave a lot of the dated material out. As I've said before, I've been scribbling this stuff down since 1992. The demographic for people who'd even be interested in this tripe is clutching the nurse's buzzer as we speak. But the fact is, some of the older stuff might be considered fairly clever and even a little edgy for AARP Magazine. Besides, at this point, when I try something topical, it's most likely going to smell like menthol.

So here's a little cheat sheet for the younger generations who might give this section the once over.

Years ago, there was a very funny young man who knew more than you but still tried to make you laugh. Getting his jokes meant that you were better than other people and were allowed to pillage neighboring towns. He made a nice little living for himself with a talk show that began every week with a rant. A few years later, he did a stint as a sports commentator and the people who didn't like knowing less than he did fought back against his brand of comedy and installed, as his replacement, a man named Booger.

Even before that, there was another young man who felt that all the talk about gay people having the right to be in the military was interfering with his seducing females in the solid 3 to 5 range. He came up with a plan that would later be known as the Down Low.

And finally, in 1993, the first in a series of books featuring a collection of short motivational stories was published, inspiring the generation before mine to start giving self-help books as presents rather than their former go-to gift, edibles. The team that dreamt up this adventure now own Crackle streaming. So you never know. Maybe this will all be worth it.

An open letter to the producers of Monday Night Football (2002)

Now I don't want to steal somebody else's trademarked bit here, but it seems that nowadays network execs are more fickle than Oprah's waistline. I mean, what the hell happened to Mole 2? Don't tell me there was some outcry for *more* of America's Funniest Home Videos. If you take away the elderly breaking their hips and college students getting smacked in the crotch you're left with Daisy Fuentes doing her best to method act her way into some cleavage.

There's also the constant hiring and firing of on-air talent. TV's got more turnover than a drive-through brothel for teenagers with A.D.D. Normally this falling-star-studded revolving door wouldn't elicit my putting a pen to paper. Indeed the departure of Kathy Lee from her show barely drew a response to break wind, but in light of what happened to Dennis Miller, I feel I must retort – pardon me.

Let me first say that I love John Madden. He's probably the best football analyst ever. Oh sure, there are some out there who would complain that he constantly over-explains the simplest things or that he's turned once-pithy phrases like "Boom" into clichés or that he abuses the telestrator like a Special Ed kid with an Etch A Sketch. But to those people I say nay. Madden broke the color guy barrier. He blazed the turducken trail. So I'm not saying I won't enjoy his brand of dementia. I'm merely saying that the style that Miller brings to the table shouldn't automatically be rejected like a placebo in Michael Irvin's blood stream.

Dennis Miller is incredibly entertaining. And isn't that what television is about? For that matter, that's what *football* is about. Too many frustrated jocks who, in high school, were just a little too short or a little too skinny or a little too unable to run, catch, throw, hit, kick, bounce, jump, swim, roll, cramp, rhyme, discharge, or flail to make the varsity team, take *all* sports *way* too seriously. It's a game, OK? If you lose, you go home – not Carousel from *Logan's Run*. And the winner goes to Disneyland, not Capitol Hill. Notice I said the *winner*, goes to Disneyland. Not you, Skippy. You're not the twelfth man. Understand that, even with all the cheering and face-painting and bouncing around like a bobble-head Lewinski doll soldered to the dashboard of the Crocodile Hunter's Land Rover, it will never change the fact that your favorite player wouldn't take the time to cross the street to crap on your head if it would cure his grandmother's chlamydia.

One of the complaints we've heard about Miller is that his background isn't in football. Well, here's a list of some of the Boo Radleys whose football careers were *supposed* to have made their insights at least as tersely cogent as their nicknames.

Boomer Esiason: When did Johnny Bravo go live action? I mean this guy couldn't be any more into himself if he were a cannibalistic python in a mirrored room. And you know, anything this guy doesn't know about the real world just hasn't been printed in MAXIM yet. Sure he played. He even had that trip to the Super Bowl. But it's probably that very background that compels him to spew out such gems as, "for this team to do well, the quarterback is going to have to throw the ball down the field." That's great, Boomer. Try: "In order to keep this Monday Night gig, this nominal talent is going to have to wash Al Michaels' car and give Malibu "Kelly" Hayes a full body Swedish massage on a semi daily basis."

"Broadway" Joe Namath: Loved to watch him play. But if the man were any more dull they'd use him as an eating utensil at Belleview. I've been following him since the panty hose commercials and I have one question. Is that English? Because his mumbling makes Eric Dickerson sound like Louis Farrakhan. So keep talking, Joe, while the country sleeps.

O.J.: Bet ABC is kicking themselves for letting *him* go.

So we've demonstrated that Jockdom is not a prerequisite to regurgitate universally overused phrases and metaphors. But how about this. How about *no* overused phrases or metaphors. How about something more like good old Howard Cosell. You remember him, don't you? The Monday Night icon whose vocabulary was as expansive as Orson Wells' elastic formal wear. Many people hated *him*, too. And why? Because he made them feel stupid. Well, good. Many people *are* stupid. That's what makes the world such a wonderful place. Smart people enjoying a thoughtful well-timed quip during a 30-second time-out, while the stupid people cheer when DDP lays the smack down.

Now no one is saying sports commentary needs to rise to the level of Stephen Hawking. But when did we settle for Captain Pike? I'm sorry, Cooter, if your sensibilities are offended by a broadcast that is conspicuously lacking in post-adolescent self-aggrandizing. But there are a couple of us out here, Gunga *Dim*, that can get the spoon in our mouth without touching our thumbnail to our nose. And *we* would like *our* broadcasters to be held to some sort of intellectual standard. And exactly who is the standard today anyway? Jim Rome? If the man were anymore shallow, they could serve soup in him at French restaurants.

The bottom line is that Dennis Miller will do fine without Monday Night Football. In fact, like the proverbial fox dismissing the notion that the grapes couldn't be anything but more sour than Richard Millhouse Nixon being encouraged by his semi-beautiful wife Pat to cuddle, Miller was probably happy to get out. The man is plenty busy doing his weekly half-hour cable show, for which he dutifully arrives promptly at 3:00 pm every Friday, eats his standard pre-show meal of five live blue jays and a magnum of Mrs. T's apple schnapps martini mix, naps, awakens in time to be rubbed down with a mitten made of baby seal fur and bald eagle feathers, pops a Vicodin-laced lifesaver and delivers twenty-six minutes of the kind of biting satire and rapier wit that we have all come to know and have feelings for. After which he retires to his moat-encircled home and waits by the phone for his agent to call with the good news that *Bordello of Blood 2* has just been given the green light.

So don't cry for him, Alabama. He_could_go_all_the_way.

Of course, I'm just thinking out loud. I may be way off base.

Soldiers do it in foxholes

I believe it was Sergeant Pepper (the real Sergeant Pepper, who led the 125th infantry division of Iceland's 4th, and I believe best, army down into a stunning stalemate with the elite Imperial guard of Trinidad & Tobago at the Battle of Herniated Apathy during the infamous 17 Working Day War) who said, "War is hell...and polyester is terminal." Incidentally, this Sergeant Pepper had a lonely-hearts club band as well. It was a trio made up of four Tibetan sousaphone players and a tone-deaf Pigmy who was learning to play the triangle. Unfortunately, their aspirations as a tribute band to the Sex Pistols were dashed when their rhythm sousaphone player was found dead in a field, strangled to death by his own 100% wool over coat after a particularly heavy monsoon season in New England.

The issues at hand are the many problems plaguing military corporations throughout the world in this era. At the time we went to press 14 of the 20 most efficient armies on the planet have a policy *against* women in service. Efficiency is the key word here. Most of the women in these societies don't realize that the purpose of the military is to splode stuff. So just when the carnage starts to get good, they start in with the disinfecting and complaining about the underwear on the bathroom floor and inevitably vacuum right in front of the smart bomb monitor just at the moment of impact. (I think this is a new twist on passive-aggressive behavior.)

Personally, I'm all for women in combat. In fact, I think it should be an all-women institution like Wellesley College or Lady Nautilus or the cast of Cabaret. The point is this: What prime minister or president or king or dictator or emperor or regional coordinator pro tem would want to take the heat from the world community of governments (not to be confused with the organization known as the Community of Governments, Labor Unions and Crime Families, which is the name of the firm that represents sanitation workers in New York City and the Vatican) for essentially hitting a collective girl. And certainly no world leader would want to take a chance on actually *losing* to an all-estrogen fighting force. (And make no mistake, this *would* be one water-retaining, mean, fighting machine.) Can you imagine the ribbing he'd take in the sauna?

Apparently, however, the process for getting women into combat has already begun with the U.S.'s "Don't ask, don't sing me show tunes" policy, though it should be noted that some of the recruiters from the old school (taught by Ms. Beetle Bailey) have found a way around this tactic. It seems that, between the "Mother's maiden name" and "Have you ever been convicted of a felony?" questions, the candidate is informed that the Army is thinking of changing its color scheme. The minute the new recruit suggests something in a soft pastel or maybe a splash of texture, they're hauled off for a court martial and a quickie divorce.

Again, speaking as a flaming heterosexual, I say let the boys in teal (if PFC Bruce Sweet has his way) march into history. I have no desire to see the world by way of combat boot. Nor would I put up such a fight to put up such a fight. In fact, one could make the argument that a democracy that has no room for polygamy is a system that might just as well be overthrown. Let's hear it out there, Utah!

Besides, anybody who thinks that allowing Bette Midler fans into the military will keep the breeders out just isn't thinking about tactics. The key to any good offensive is the surprise attack. Does anybody think that that there are *any* flamboyant men out there who can arrive *any place* with a low profile?

Bottom line: All's fair in love, war, and horseshoes. And if all the governments of today's world find it necessary to draft every human being on the planet to toil in their conflicts over land and resources, let them. I wear a size 14 shoe and will be stateside playing H.O.R.S.E with Shaq and Boris Karloff.

Cup O'Noodles for the Impoverished Soul

~ On Your Lifestyle~
Seven Habits of Highly Infected People

When one has carved out his or her societal standing from a dry-rotted log, certain concessions should be made when it comes to living conditions, pedigree of associates, and especially, health care expectations. *Of course*, the affluent receive better medical care. A report by the *New England Medical Journal of Applied Abundance* found that hundred-dollar bills carry more pathogens than a household toilet. Could you imagine the pandemic if rich people weren't continually monitored by their squash companions for symptoms of exhaustion, a deviated septum, or syphilis? And what if the contaminated bills were to get out among the public? The sheer number of paper cuts would most assuredly over burden hospitals and liquor stores.

But there is a way to assure your health and the health of your family. Firstly:

Be aggressive. This is applicable in the emergency room as well as the cafeteria, and even while riding the bus to your appointment (the emergency room). You're not paying for any of these services – the Cliff bars are on the back side of the soup island and in the camera's blind spot – so demand your fare share: Immediate service, a seat for your dog, the TV turned to Steve Wilko. Be willing to break through barriers, especially if a vending machine is on the other side.

Know when you're time is up. Too many people insist on fighting a long, drawn out battle with whatever disease they've contracted from cell phones. It's a much better legacy to be thought of as "laid back" at your funeral than stubborn. You've got to think long term.

Get your affairs in order. You may not have much in the way of an estate. And they've already inherited your hammertoe. Anything you can do to keep your family from fighting over your Dale Earnhardt commemorative plate or your plaid iguana skin Stacy Adams' is a step in the right direction.

Double dipping. When your staged disability claim is under investigation, and your structured settlement is tied up in red tape with JG Wentworth, your unemployment check may not allow you to make bitter ends meet. Don't be afraid to explore alternative means of capital. Christmas tree retail. Census taking. It could be government assistance. You might look into grants. And don't forget, you could win millions with the lottery.

Self-diagnose on the Internet and inform everyone who'll listen. Often people of a lower caste are regarded as scientifically ignorant. Nothing could be further from the truth. In fact, with ample time on their hands, many in the underemployed ranks not only spend hours investigating such meaningful concerns as vaccine dangers and existing cancer cures covered up by the medical-industrial complex, but are willing to give up family activities to email the slimmest of acquaintances daily herbal remedies and blog articles about health that *they* don't want you to know about.

Alternative uses for syringes. From filling pastries with creams or jellies to dispensing toothpaste, syringes can be more than just weapons. In fact, most of your used medical equipment can translate into hours of crafting fun for the whole family.

Cut it off. "When in doubt, cut it out" was the motto of 19th-century surgeon, Dr. Chauncy "the scalpel" Granville. Known as the Roy Bean of medicine, Granville lived by the scriptural principal that "...if your eye causes you to stumble, what are you doing with your feet?"

~ Dr. Joyce Brothers

~On Taking Personal Inventory~
Wants vs. Needs

There once was a group of men who wore powdered wigs and tight colonial pants. They decided that tea was a human right and demanded that it be supplied free of charge. Soon, the tea regulators, who didn't want these troublemakers to influence their neighbors, decided that the tight pants were grounded and tried to keep them under house arrest. The tight pants, in turn, ran the tea-nappers, in their red coats, out of town. Then things got ugly.

All of this was because neither side had focused on what they *needed* vs what they wanted. The tight pants *wanted* independence, but what they really *needed* was tea. On the other hand, the red coats wanted to pay their bills, but *needed* the tight pants, 170 years later, to help them fend off the lederhosen gang.

Moral: Paying your bills and buying food are more important than those new Jordans.

~ Wavy Gravy

~On Finances~
Money Can't Buy Happiness
(and Other Malicious Lies)

Never have I been able to go into a supermarket, gather up a gallon of milk, some Twinkies, and a bottle of fungicide, plunk down the results from my blood work and expect to walk out with any merchandise. Why? Because having your health is only important to you. The rest of the world cares about your cāsh. So get some. That is the only way that you will ever be loved. Right, Trixie?

~ Mother Teresa

~On Overcoming Obstacles~
Tips for a Fulfilling Career

Deciding on, training for, and then sustaining a meaningful career is far from easy. Many prefer to steal away to a liberal arts college for a few years just to avoid the process. But despite popular opinion, finding a job has never been the hard part. Granted, you might have to spend some time waiting tables or donating your eggs (the latter is more lucrative for the ladies), but there will always be oportunities for people who aren't afraid to work hard and get their hands blood-coated. Still, there are career opportunities out there, you just need to know how to find them. Try these few simple steps:

1) Forget the Office. There, your day consists of unnatural light, lavish hues of gray, people named Mitch and Candy, and that dull, impossible-to-locate yet all-day-buzzing sound. It is here that snipers are born. Leave immediately, but say something nice to Craig on the way out. He's got a van with blacked-out windows…and that look.

2) Get creative. Figure out what you want to do and a way to do it for money. When you realize it's not going to happen, go home, take a warm bath, build a nice fire (preferably in your fireplace), start mixing booze, and drink it. Drink it down now.

3) Prioritize. It's just better than not prioritizing.

4) Let it all hang out. If you wanted to be a writer when you grew up, start writing. If your dream is to open a restaurant, get cookin'. If you've always wanted to work at NASA, forget it. Their *janitors* have doctorates. Find another way to hang it. (Note: People with marriages, mortgages, children, and/or Filipino maids disregard this advice. You've already hung it, and it's starting to droop.)

5) Move. There are an exponentially greater number of opportunities outside the few square miles in which you live. Often times, the only way to find what you're looking for is by expanding your search. That is not to suggest that one move from a metropolitan area to some Podunk town like Denver. (I don't care what the offer, there's no reason to live in Denver.) But by broadening your horizons, you just might get to experience crippling anxiety in a completely new zip code.

6) Eat cottage cheese. There are no limits to the career-altering effect a nice bowl of cottage cheese can have. Did you know that 19 of the last 20 Academy Award winners for best director (you know that Anthony Minghella. He has a thing about textures) consume curds at least twice a day? Did you also know both William Buffet and Bill Gates have each written cookbooks dedicated to that pseudo-nutritional guano paste? And did you *further* know that cottage cheese was once used to cut hashish in Afghanistan so as to alter one's high and bestow momentary, but very real, psychic abilities?

7) Learn to lie. There is no limit to the possibilities for a skilled liar. Of course, results may vary depending on what your definition of "*is*" is.

8) Acknowledge that a fulfilling career is as elusive as Carnie Wilson's navel ring. You're simply never going to find it. And for those who say, "but my friend loves what *they* do," well, your friend has mastered tip # 7, and is on their way.

~Paris Hilton

~ On Relationships~
How to Win Friends and Influence Elections

I n an old rural town, just down a path past the church and the grain mill, lived a woman by the name of Starla. She was a petite thing, with long graying hair (being a health food nut) and a face weathered from years spent staring off into the distance as she waited for her husband, a soldier of ill fortune, to return from an adventure that had long since been turned over to collections. She hadn't much money, but that never bothered Starla for she had friends.

As life went on, she'd get visits from neighbors checking in, and local ombudsmen bearing apple pies and seeking a definition for ombudsmen. The children in the town thought she was a witch but that didn't bother her. She'd get a little chuckle out of it and then boil one of them for supper.

Everyone in town knew that Starla loved to help people and that she could always be counted on to reattach a button or knit a youngster some mittens or help with mending a quilt. Really, anything in the field of sewing. Outside of that, she was pretty useless. But she had built up enough good will in the community that when it came time to caucus for important appointments, Starla was always invited to bring the cold cuts. She'd smile and nod as folks would come by and pick through the olive loaf for the least slimy slice. Then she'd make little suggestions.

A, "You know I heard..." here. A little, "Wouldn't it be nice..." there.

Nothing insistent, just modest thoughts on particular issues or candidates. People trusted her judgment, her wisdom gained from years of tender nurturing of the local residents from her quiet little home down the path past the church and the grain mill.

One day an older gentleman came to town. He looked as if he'd lived 20 lives and 19 of them were Richard Pryor's. He took up a room in the boarding house on the west side of the rickety old wooden bridge that spanned a bend in the river just about a hundred yards from Starla's house.

He would call on Starla every day for about two hours around midday. Soon, the neighbors would catch a glimpse of the pair walking in Starla's garden. Then the daily visits started taking them on walks along the banks of the river. Never so far so as to be out of sight of somebody who couldn't be called on to act as chaperone, should the public start to talk.

Finally, one afternoon, the two appeared together in town. Arm in arm, they made their way to the general store to pick up a few items for their planned picnic.

Starla introduced the man to her neighbors as her long-lost husband, back from the war. Neither had been sure of the other's intentions, so they had been taking it slowly, but now, their love had been reignited and they were making plans to renew their vows that Saturday. All were delighted for the couple, and the two left the store with a lilt in their steps that hadn't been present for many a winter.

Around 1:00 that afternoon, a shot rang out from the woods. The men ran toward the still echoing sound of the blast as the women held their little ones (as a sort of shield, in case there was any more gunplay). When they reached a small clearing they found Starla, gun in hand, slouched over her dead husband and sobbing uncontrollably. The mob quickly cleaned up the crime scene, disposed of the body, and made sure that their beloved Starla was in bed, tucked away and passed out from grief when the sheriff arrived. With no evidence to speak of, the case was quickly closed and the old rural town quietly returned to the way things were before the appearance of the old man.

No one ever asked Starla what had happened until years later as she lay on her deathbed. They hadn't forgotten the incident, but felt that her loyalty to the community had earned her the postponement of an explanation. Now, at her bedside, were her loving friends, themselves sick with curiosity but still hesitant to broach the subject. Starla could sense their reluctance and offered her accounting.

"Carol and I enjoyed a love that is rare," she started, noting that some boys were named Carol back then and it didn't mean anything. "We had known each other since we were very young and shared a common history. When he went off to war, it was as if I had already been a casualty. When he returned, at first I was elated and quickly remembered everything that we had shared. But that was before. Before our time apart and my being adopted into a new family with you, my friends. I now had a different history, and, I feared, a greater love."

The people were, at once, shocked and moved. They had loved Starla as well, but couldn't believe that she might choose her life as a spinster with them over that with a lifetime love and caring protector. There must have been more to the story. "Were you in danger?" "Did he harm you?" "Had he been unfaithful?" "Was he a cad?"

She lay there with a contented smile and chuckled her familiar little chuckle. "Oh no," she said, "nothing like that."

"Then what happened that day?" they asked in an almost hysterical tone.

She smiled again and with her last breath uttered her justification for his murder. "He wasted his vote on Nader."

With that, she passed away and the townsfolk went through her things looking for items that might fetch a handsome sum at a yard sale.

~Jim Henson

~ On Parenthood ~

~ On Living Your Best Life ~
A Survival Guide/Cookbook

Living below the poverty line is fraught with challenges, not the least of which is falling, still-lit cigarette butts. Of course, the poor still have the same necessities of life as the rest of society. There is Shelter, which, fortunately, can be fashioned fr om a variety of media. From straw to twigs to bricks to freeway overpasses to hovels adjacent to the De Lacy cottage. There is clothing, which often times is optional, in that contemporary fashion is informed mostly by Renaissance Faires, hippie communes, and hooker couture.

But the real challenge is getting the lighting just right when photographing your foie gras custard brûlée. Yes, as feminist food critic and community potluck organizer, Noreen Dikles once wrote in her graphic novel/womanifesto, *Avocado Toast and the Smeared Patriarchy*, "Good food isn't cheap and cheap food isn't good." In other words, "Let them eat crab cakes".

I had the chore of meeting Ms. Dikles once at a quinoa rally in Nova Scotia. I had already begun to eat my Spam Newburg when she complained that she had planned to get a picture of the dish. I explained that I hadn't a gallbladder and she'd get another chance at a snapshot if she could wait about fifteen minutes. Determined to impress her peers, she capitulated and I held her hair back.

That's the thing about "Foodies," they have chosen to specialize in something that every living thing *must* do in order to survive. Something that even *plants* must do. Something that the jellyfish, an animal with *no brain* but still has a mouth is able to accomplish. Something that sponges – a creature with neither a brain nor organs nor even *tissue* (to be fair, that's probably because of Covid), but still eats a regular diet of plankton. Something that embryos involuntarily do *before* they've developed a complete digestive system. Yet these people have convinced themselves that they belong to an exceptional community that understands food beyond the common masticating public.

Now a Foodie will tell you that what makes them special is that they enjoy *good* food – as opposed to the rest of us, who are perfectly content with dog chow. If this is the case, then those experts, as essential to the successful amelioration of man as "Gamers" will find no pleasure in the following recipes designed for those who shrewdly keep a negative balance in their checking accounts to ward off identity theft.

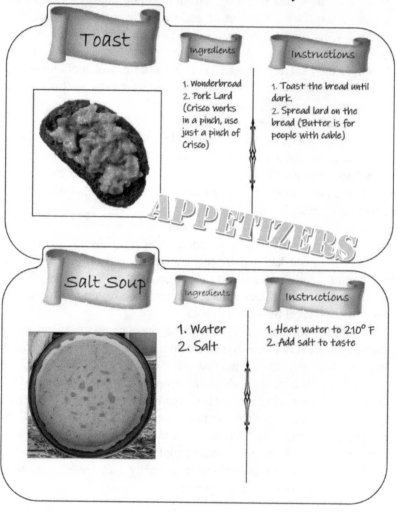

Toast

Ingredients

1. Wonderbread
2. Pork Lard (Crisco works in a pinch, use just a pinch of Crisco)

Instructions

1. Toast the bread until dark.
2. Spread lard on the bread (Butter is for people with cable)

APPETIZERS

Salt Soup

Ingredients

1. Water
2. Salt

Instructions

1. Heat water to 210° F
2. Add salt to taste

Fried Cornmeal Mush

Ingredients

1. 3 Cups of water
2. 1 tspn salt
3. 1 cup yellow corn meal
4. 1 TBSPN butter

Instructions

1. In a medium sauce pan boil water and stir in salt and cornmeal
2. Spoon mixture into a 9x5 loaf pan and refrigerate overnight (Go to bed hungry)
3. In the morning, eat Cheerios and lament past decisions.
4. Send the kids to school for breakfast. Put the butter on a couple crackers and tell yourself they're hors d'oeuvres that go with your Charles Shaw Rosé while you luxuriate in your shower/tub combo and watch telenovelas on your portable black & white

Roasted Apples

Ingredients

1. Apples
2. Cinnamon
3. Brown Sugar
4. ~~Butter~~ ~~Margarine~~ I Can't Believe It's Not Vegetable Oil
5. Sea salt (OK that's it.

Instructions

1. Just be happy you've got apples.

2. See if that flask has anything in it.

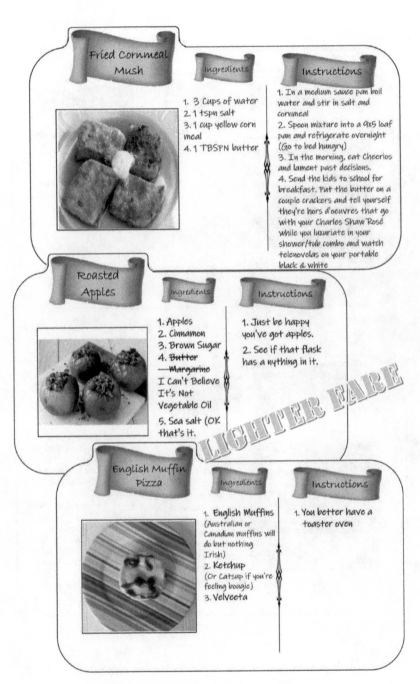

LIGHTER FARE

English Muffin Pizza

Ingredients

1. English Muffins (Australian or Canadian muffins will do but nothing Irish)
2. Ketchup (Or Catsup if you're feeling bougie)
3. Velveeta

Instructions

1. You better have a toaster oven

Steak & Potatoes

Ingredients

1. Potatoes

Instructions

1. Make potatoes & eat

2. Forget about steak but maybe some hamburger helper...you know...when one of those scratchers pays off

ENTRÉES

Tuna Casserole

Ingredients

1. 12oz macaroni & cheese (Damaged box discount)
2. 1 cup any frozen vegetable
3. 2 cans of tuna
4. 2 cans cream of mushroom soup
5. 1 cup crushed potato chips.
6. All the celery you can find in the back of the fridge

Instructions

1. Follow instructions for the mac & cheese but don't use the cheese powder yet.
2. Preheat oven to the mark on the dial that kind of looks like a seagull with a briefcase.
3. Mix all the ingredients except the chips in a large bowl and transfer to a baking dish.
4. Sprinkle chips and cheese powder on top and bake for 20 minutes or until cheese starts to spark.
5. Serve with red Flavor Aid

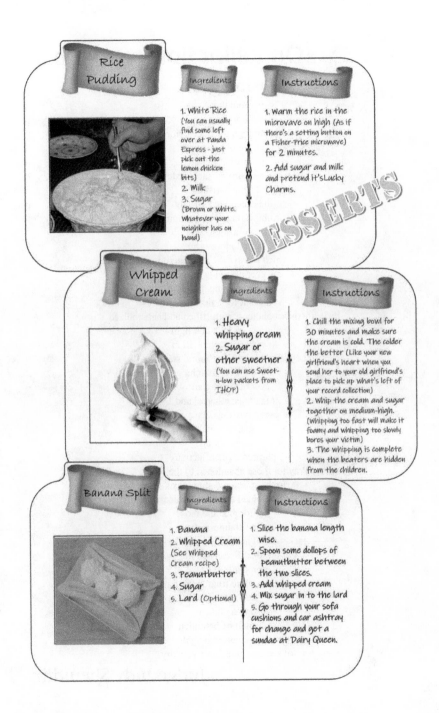

Rice Pudding

Ingredients

1. White Rice (You can usually find some left over at Panda Express - just pick out the lemon chicken bits)
2. Milk
3. Sugar (Brown or white. Whatever your neighbor has on hand)

Instructions

1. Warm the rice in the microvave on high (As if there's a setting button on a Fisher-Price microwave) for 2 minutes.
2. Add sugar and milk and pretend it's Lucky Charms.

DESSERTS

Whipped Cream

Ingredients

1. Heavy whipping cream
2. Sugar or other sweetner (You can use Sweet-n-low packets from IHOP)

Instructions

1. Chill the mixing bowl for 30 minutes and make sure the cream is cold. The colder the better (Like your new girlfriend's heart when you send her to your old girlfriend's place to pick up what's left of your record collection)
2. Whip the cream and sugar together on medium-high. (Whipping too fast will make it foamy and whipping too slowly bores your victim)
3. The whipping is complete when the beaters are hidden from the children.

Banana Split

Ingredients

1. Banana
2. Whipped Cream (See Whipped Cream recipe)
3. Peanutbutter
4. Sugar
5. Lard (Optional)

Instructions

1. Slice the banana length wise.
2. Spoon some dollops of peanutbutter between the two slices.
3. Add whipped cream
4. Mix sugar in to the lard
5. Go through your sofa cushions and car ashtray for change and get a sundae at Dairy Queen.

~On Reflection~

Images

The Soul that floats softly
yet briskly
through the once colorful and lively
vision of our youth
is now but a trance
for the wage-earning short order cook
the barista
the executive assistant
filibustering over a sound
a sight
a malodorous air
which betrays the endangered
and ever decaying partition
of our wisping dignity
has but for a time left
its learned cacophony of unfulfilled and antagonized
patrons of love and light
to a bitter reconciliation
between those of fine moral standing
and the ever marching
ever blanching army
of at once ethereal and
sparse gaiety
to that which
can only be
phrased as disaffection
Pray for those abandoned to the wilds
to the splintered ship masts
the conjoined diaspora of plenty
Pray for that and those
of the stainless-steel
jackboots of anonymity and derision
For these edifices shall not want
nor shall they take
It is the nostalgic fragrance of a man
and a woman
and a midget
that shall be beholden
to the emerald heights
of seasons gone but rivers dry

~Judge Judy Sheindlin

Section VI:
The New Classics

I believe it was Joseph Campbell who said, "The privilege of a lifetime is being who you are. Take me for instance. I'm a male Caucasian academic who spent my twenties alternately cruising back and forth to Europe and holed up in place in Woodstock just reading…So yeah, follow your bliss."

Joseph Campbell is best known for his book, *The Hero with a Thousand Faces*, which examines the "Hero's Journey" in various mythologies and as a term that must be used along with "McGuffin" when producing movie reviews on YouTube (#heyguyswhatsup). The hero's journey is, of course, the backbone of most works of fiction (if for no other reason than they're fictional), and that's what this last section is all about.

Up until this point, the reader has been subjected to styles of writing that could be generously termed autobiographical, analytical, and expository (which seems like it should be inserted into the analytical) in this book. But now, after examining some of the great works of literature by way of leafing through their pages, looking for pictures, and getting a sense of the general heft of your average novel, the author (That's me, by the way. SK Morton. Pay no attention to the critics who insist this is just a modern retelling of the Talmud) has embarked on his first real foray into story-telling. There may be some themes that might be considered well-worn. Maybe a few plots that come off as familiar. There might even be a "Once upon a time…" thrown in there every now and again and again and again. The thing to keep in mind is that the formula for a best seller dictates that the sweet spot for a book of humor to be around 265 pages and I need more content.

Requiem for a Liver Spot

"Be not deceived: evil communications corrupt good manners."
- 1 Cor 15:33 KJV

Eric was the third of three freckles born to his father, a benign mole, and his mother, a beauty mark. They met on Goldie Hawn's face in the late 1960s. His mother had been betrothed to a skin tag over Robert Shaw's eye but abandoned her intended when Eric's father offered her his coat during a Laugh-In cocktail party sketch in which Goldie was wearing only a bikini. The two fell instantly in love and immediately moved into a loft together on Joanne Worley's upper thigh.

His brother and sister were quite a bit older than he. Chuck had graduated high school before Eric was even born and Verna was a senior at the time of his christening. This age gap between him and his siblings, as well as the household relocating to Marlon Brando's back, where his parents became increasingly more distant, resulted in Eric having a tenuous connection with his immediate family. From age five to about eleven, Eric's favorite uncle, Blane – a seborrheic keratosis who once served with the French Foreign Lesions – had the biggest influence on him and was responsible for Eric's intense interest in military history and combat strategy.

Blane was an imposing figure at over 6 millimeters tall with a wide, black epithelium, thick beard, and a, seemingly, permanent aroma of cigar. He'd make regular visits, and always had some sort of gift for Eric. Whether a board game like *Risk* or *Axis & Allies*, or toys like little green army men or nunchuks, Blane showered Eric with diversions that were always steeped in struggle. Their relationship was cut short when Eric's beloved uncle was shivved in prison. He had been incarcerated as a political prisoner after leading a march on Washington to stop the institutional defamation of HPV.

It was when Eric was promoted to middle school that he had his first contact with poison ivy, or as the kids referred to it, the Brazilian Falafel (or BF). One day, during pre-algebra, he noticed two of his classmates passing a plastic bag. Eric asked one of the boys, Adrien Pusser (a character who would have quite an influence on Eric during the rest of his youth), if he was selling? Adrien responded with a somewhat accusatory tone, "Who wants to know?"

"It is I, Eric Feckle." He responded.

Adrien agreed to provide him a "first time freebie" after school, and Eric was immediately hooked. By high school he was regularly skipping class to get inflamed. He was bright enough to manage passing grades, but his focus was now on getting a rash and making money to scratch that itch. With his propensity toward violent problem-solving, he made the perfect soldier for Adrien's burgeoning crew. In time, he was promoted to head of security and was charged with training other ne'er-do-wells in the use of firearms, handling explosives, and hand-to-hand virus transmission.

With his status broadening, so was his risk-taking, which yielded regular brushes with the law. On one occasion he narrowly escaped jail time for assaulting one of his teachers. That morning, Eric, while cankered, stumbled into the his Civics class 20 minutes tardy and was told to go to the principal's office for the offense. Eric flew into a rage and put his teacher in a headlock. Several of the other students tried to pull him off by futilely scratching at his base. Finally, a passing janitor with a pair of tweezers was able to pluck the hair from the middle of Eric's head. This complete purge of his budding mohawk turned his attention to the janitor and he released the teacher. Were it not for the teacher's outstanding warrant for inciting a food fight, Eric might have spent the rest of his youth in juvenile hall. As it was, the judge gave him probation and ordered him into the army on his eighteenth birthday.

At first, Eric was happy to join the military and felt he had finally found a home. But soon his old habits and associates made their way back into his life. He was court-martialed twice in just his first year for insubordination and demonstrating a callous disregard for military procedures. Of course, having calluses in the family, he found these charges institutionally racist and ended up going AWOL. He eventually fled to Scandinavia for the creamy sauces and relaxed profanity standards. Turning to what he knew, he ended up serving as a kind of remote branch for Adrien's contraband operation.

With his reputation preceding him, he established a connection with a biker gang from Finland made up of tattoo artists known as the Hell's Inkies. Not long after, he was involved in an incident that left one person dead and several others severely sun-damaged. The gang had been contracted to provide security for a music festival in Copenhagen during spring break. As the show slogged on under the scorching, 51° F, Denmark sun, into the early afternoon, an unidentified attendee demanded a small batch rosé beer while brandishing a mason jar. One of the bikers responded by ripping the celebrant's pre-faded Che Guevara T-shirt and hog-tying him with a microphone cable. In turn, many other concert-goers attacked the Inkies with thin, worn down scarves. By the time Eric was able to quell the melee, participants from both sides were demanding to talk to a manager.

Eric avoided any charges, but had to leave the country. He returned to the States, surreptitiously, and took up residence in the basement of the home of his sister and her husband. He promised her that he'd get clean and go straight, but his good intentions weren't enough to combat his vices. Before long, he was mixing with unsavory blisters and warts, committing acts of vandalism, perpetrating petty thefts, and generally causing a civic disturbance. Once on the authorities' radar, the army was quick to find him and sentenced him to five years in Fort Leavenworth. While not a model prisoner, he managed to stay out of trouble and enrolled in the prison's vocational program. It was here he met and fell in love with Condoleezza Loma, a civilian instructor at the prison's culinary academy.

While not a melaninized growth herself (though she was Bolivian and not much taller than Eric), Condi had been in foster care for several years and was ultimately adopted by a loving old bunion couple, Pipa and Papa Corn. Just like Eric, she too had gone through a turbulent youth and could empathize with his plight. She also had a thing for freckles. (Her first husband was a red-headed roofer from Ireland.) She and Eric had acknowledged their attraction, but endeavored to take things slowly until his release, when the two began seeing each other in earnest.

As with most star-crossed love stories, their romance was thrilling at first. But soon the stress of being judged for their inter-material relationship started to take its toll. While the corns had given their blessing, Eric's parents, having endured a bereft marriage for some time, felt the societal pressures would be too much to overcome. And if they were being completely honest, they didn't exactly cherish the thought of a bunch of little dermalatto grandchildren running around the house.

The couple managed to stay together long enough to start a family. They first had a baby boy and then a little girl, who looked to be about 8 years old. (The womb was rent controlled.) Both children inherited their mother's face, torso, and limbs, but they got their father's fiery temper and irregularly-shaped edges. They moved to upstate New York for the schools and as a way to keep Eric distanced from his former life in the city. Eric kept struggling to live up to his responsibilities and took a job as sous-chef at a resort in the Catskills.

The retreat had become a popular sleep-away camp for Sephardic teens who were fascinated by Eric's reddish complexion and took to calling him King David. Before long, he was involved with one of the female counselors, Vita Laigo. At the tender age of 18, Vita had already earned an AA degree in criminality and was certified as a gun moll. She had heard rumors of Eric's past and sought to gain entry into the world of crime through him, believing she didn't have the looks for pharmaceutical sales.

Not long after the two met, Eric left Condi and the kids and moved in with Vita. They soon began making plans for a series of heists that would take them across the country and by the end, hopefully, leave them free to retire to the French Riviera with all of the SPF 100 they would ever need. Eric, now well into his forties and starting to feel some regrets (as well as a little pressure on his prostate), left most of the preparation up to Vita. She rounded up a motley group mainly consisting of former members of the Hole-in-the-Ulcer Gang, the Wild Pox, and what was left of the 5th Street Leprosy Boyz.

They started with a bank in Colorado, as Vita was huge Billy Joel fan. They robbed their way from Utah to Oklahoma and then made their way to Texas. They hadn't had a big score in months, and many in the group were threatening to break off and form their own crew. Vita called on Eric to quell the insurrection and he pulled Dan "Little Whitey" Druff, one of the leading mutineers, aside. The conversation lasted less than a minute, but afterward Druff convinced the other insurgents to stick around for one more job. Later court documents revealed that Eric had threatened to withhold the group's regular supply of zinc oxide to Whitey, who was now addicted and whose habit had grown to over six doses a day.

Ultimately the gang successfully robbed the El Paso Castle Inn & Suites of over 10,000 mini soaps and twice that many units in moisturizer. Unfortunately, the crime left the desk clerk dead and several chambermaids severely chapped and ashy. All but Vita were apprehended. Dan Druff turned state's evidence and Eric received the lengthiest sentence (one of Molly Bloom's soliloquies from Joyce's *Ulysses*) and a prison term of 25 years. Vita headed down south and is believed to be running a bookmaking operation in Mexicali for self-published authors. (That's just what I heard.)

Condi and the children visited Eric throughout his incarceration, but she eventually filed for divorce after getting engaged to Danny Bonaduce. Eric's son, wanting nothing to do with him, stopped visiting when he turned 18 and has since changed his last name to Stipple. His daughter has stayed in Eric's life throughout and has recently published a biography about her father, *50 Shades of Psoriasis*. Eric was released from prison in 1998 and has been in and out of rehab many times since. He currently resides in Venice Beach, California, and makes his living as a melanoma on the left buttock of an amateur bodybuilder.

If Looks Could Kill
I'd Buy You a Mirror

Hank Zimmer started his Friday early this week. He arrived at his store by 6:00 a.m., about an hour earlier than usual, to get a jump on what *he* thought would be the Rosh Hashanah weekend rush. As it turned out, it would be the longest day of his year.

Hank first made sure the window displays were properly set up. He secured the heads on all of the mannequins and steamed their outfits so that not one thread had a bend in it that wasn't intended. He then shined their shoes and, finally, went through their pockets for change. Hank had always been very exacting – especially about change.

With everything in order on the sales floor, Hank made his way into his office in the back about 8:40. He had expected his assistant, Lucious Crick, to be in by 9:00, but by 9:30 Hank had seen neither hide nor hair of him. (Lucious suffered from both leprosy and severe hair loss so Hank could usually just follow a trail when the two needed to confer.) It wasn't until just before opening, about 9:54, that Lucious showed up. He blamed his being sweaty and out of breath on missing the bus...after a breakfast date and a romantic stroll through the park...following a leisurely soak in the tub...and sleeping in.

Hank hadn't time to berate his employee as there was already one customer waiting for the store to open. His name was Phillip Shmelt and he needed a plaid vest to replace one that was recently stained. Shmelt seemed to be in a hurry. He refused to take off his overcoat to try anything on. He insisted that the vest needed to match the previous one exactly. As Shmelt rifled through the store's stock of vests, two more customers came through the door. Hank handed Mr. Shmelt over to Lucious and went to greet the new arrivals.

Although it seemed to Hank that the couple, a man of about thirty years old and a woman looking to be in her twenties, had come in together, when he addressed them jointly, both resolutely corrected him and insisted they had never seen one another before. This despite the fact that they were dressed in matching sweat suits. The man, Donald Smith, was looking for a kilt, while the woman, Erma Smith, wondered if the store carried women's skirts. When Hank noted that this was a *men's* second-hand wool clothing store, the woman slapped Donald and stormed out.

Inspector Kurt Turnicate entered the home at 320 Lacewood St. He quickly walked through the living room where the Zimmer's maid, Rita O'Flinenin, was huddled on the couch, rocking as she struggled to explain what she knew to a uniformed officer hurriedly scribbling in his notepad. Turnicate made his way down the dark, narrow hallway to the master bedroom, where he spotted the lifeless figure of Mrs. Zimmer.

There was no sign of forced entry, nothing appeared to have been rifled through or missing, not even a sign of struggle. Just Svetlana Zimmer's half-dressed (Turnicate was an optimist) body, lying on her back, in bed, with a butcher's knife protruding from her abdomen. Interestingly, with the exception of what was on Mrs. Zimmer's nightgown, there was very little blood at the scene. It was as if she'd been doing a spread for *Single Knife Juggling* magazine*.

As Turnicate made his way back to the living room, he noticed several long blonde hairs mingled with the carpet, creating a path toward the back door. He made a mental note to check out the yard, but then, almost immediately, forgot it because his mental notes did absolutely no good. He sat down with Ms. O'Flinenin, who was still quite shaken, and began to interview her.

---

*The magazine for knife jugglers who don't need any more accidents.

"When did you arrive at the house this morning, Miss O'Flinenin?"

"It's Ms. O'Flinenin." She responded. "Miss O'Flinenin is my mother's name. Short for Missy. Which itself is short for Melissa, which is actually her middle name but she didn't like her first name, Mary Sue, which everybody shortened to Ms."

"Very well. Ms. O'Flinenin. What time?"

"I arrived, as usual, at 7:00."

"And when did you discover the body?"

"I didn't discover her. I left her clothed as she was when I found her; about 7:10."

When she had entered the house, everything had seemed normal – nothing out of place. Except Svetlana was usually up by then. "The *missus* (she glared at Turnicate and enunciated slowly), was an early bird and liked her worm. She started every day with a shot of Mezcal."

"She had been drinking heavily since her fiancé, Hank's brother George, rejected her when she had first arrived, first class mail, from the Ukraine. While the agency called her a "Ten," George felt that she was, at best, a "šist". The family decided that Hank should marry her, since he was used to, and rather liked, George's hand-me-downs."

Hank had been the black sheep of the family while George was the archetypical perfect first born. Manly and confident, George was born with a full beard, while sickly and shy Hank was born with just 6 toes but 14 fingers. George maintained a 4.5 GPA, while Hank struggled to grasp how a 4.0 wasn't the maximum. George founded a nationwide warehouse for men, while Hank hung out at rest stops and sold his brother's irregulars and seconds to guys who didn't work with the public. All of this built up in him quite a resentment for both his brother and, after realizing that she still carried a troch for George (her English wasn't that good), his bride.

With further questioning, Rita revealed that Svetlana had confided in her about the couple's difficulties and the two had become fairly close. So close, in fact, that they had planned on opening up a scented candle/mini cupcake shop together, but the plans fell through when Svetlana suddenly went into business with a mystery investor.

They were working on a new line of sportswear designed specifically for multiple amputees. The idea was to apply plaids, paisleys, polka dots, and any other pattern that starts with 'P' in a way that would camouflage the wearer's infirmities.

"Had you ever met this mystery investor, ma'am?" asked Turnicate.

"What's that supposed to mean?!?" Rita responded. "Would you call your wife ma'am? Would you call your sister ma'am? How about your mother, what do you call her?"

"I call her mom…or mother."

"How dare you!" Rita shouted and then fainted.

It was now 9:45 and Turnicate knew it would take about 20 minutes to get to Zimmer's store. "Let's go ask the husband some questions." He said. "And bring her along. I have a feeling she might be of some use yet."

They pulled into Zimmer's parking lot about 10:05. As they were exiting the car Rita noticed Erma Smith loitering around the outside of the store. "That's that lady," Rita whispered, but loudly enough for Inspector Turnicate to hear, since the plot requires it.

"What lady?" he asked.

Rita, now in a rage, slapped Turnicate, "What is it with you men and your objectifying? Why can't she just be a person who happens to be a lady?"

Erma saw the altercation and began to run. The officer gave chase, and when Rita had calmed down she explained that she had passed that woman and a man on the sidewalk as she arrived at work that morning. She had never seen them before, but she had the distinct feeling that they were leaving from the Zimmers' home. The officer returned with Erma in handcuffs and the four of them made their way into the store.

When they entered, Shmelt and Smith were still shopping (because I love alliteration) and Hank and Lucious were having a private discussion in another corner of the store. Hank was talking and Lucious continually nodded, while watching the two customers.

"Mr. Zimmer?" asked Turnicate.

"I'm Hank Zimmer," answered Luscious, who had inadvertently put on the wrong nametag.

"No sir, I'm Mr. Zimmer." Hank corrected. "What can I do for you, Inspector?"

"Well, sir, I have some bad news. Your wife has been brutally murdered. It was probably quite painful, not to mention terrifying for her. She probably bled out for some time before losing consciousness. The point is she had a lot of time to contemplate her fate. Maybe even weep over her regrets. And as I mentioned before, agonizing, excruciating, searing pain. Something I wouldn't wish on a baby-killing pit bull. Simply unbearable torment. I'd like to ask you a few questions."

Hank was stunned. "Oh my god. Yes, yes, of course. I'd be more than happy to answer any of your questions."

Both Shmelt and Smith overheard the conversation and both made their way toward the exit, but were stopped by the officer.

"If you men don't mind, we'd like to talk to you as well," said Turnicate. "Please have a seat and I'll be right with you."

Of course, being a men's secondhand wool clothing store there were no chairs, so the men just poked through the golf attire department. When Rita caught sight of the two, her eyes widened and she gasped. Shmelt stood motionless, at first just staring at her with anxious eyes and then quickly looking away with a flexible neck.

Turnicate noticed the interaction and asked Rita what was wrong. She quickly regained her composure and directed her attention to Donald Smith, stating that he was the man she had seen walking with Erma. Erma, in turn, refuted the accusation and went as far as denying having ever seen the man before and that their children would deny it as well.

After getting Hank's story, including his dealings with the customers that morning, the inspector moved on to Lucious, who corroborated Zimmer's story with a few exceptions. He said that he'd arrived at 9:30 as always, that morning, and that his sweating and heavy breathing weren't due to missing a bus but rather to running around the store resetting the clocks that had all, inexplicably, been running 24 minutes fast.

Phillip Shmelt had been getting impatient, claiming that he was late for a very important business meeting. Inspector Turnicate asked him what line he was in. He was somewhat evasive but finally provided a few particulars about his dabbling in the fashion industry. When asked if he had ever met any of the others in the store, he glanced at everyone except Rita. He said, "No," and again asked if he could leave. Turnicate told him he needed him for just a little longer and bid him to take off his overcoat and relax. Shmelt refused on both counts.

Turnicate's interview with Don Smith was interrupted by a noise coming from a back room. He went to investigate and discovered a windowless room adjacent to Zimmer's office filled to the ceiling with flax. Sitting in the middle of the room was a skinny old man with a long white beard, shirtless and hunched over a spinning wheel.

"And just who are you?" charged Turnicate.

The man had been surprised by the intrusion and, at first, just stared at the interloper. Turnicate repeated himself and the old man, now trembling, told him that his name was Skinner and that Hank had hired him to produce material for his planned new line of linen rain parkas. When the scheme failed, Zimmer locked him in the room and demanded he spin the flax into gold instead. In ten years he had only managed to turn out about a dozen yards of the stuff although he never told his captor. Rather he set up house in the place, opened a bank account, and spent his evenings entertaining married socialites like Mrs. Zimmer. He was quite forthcoming about the whole matter and explained that he had cut things off with Svetlana because he feared she might tell her husband.

When Turnicate revealed his latest witness to Zimmer and Luscious, Luscious proclaimed, "The jig is up!" and attacked Don Smith. The officer pulled Luscious off of Smith and put them both in handcuffs. At that point Rita ran to Luscious and threw herself over him crying, and then fainted. Turnicate had had enough.

"I've heard all I need," he said to the officer. "Let the rest go and slap those bracelets on Mr. Phillip Shmelt."

Losing his cool, Shmelt brandished a gun from underneath his overcoat, took aim at Zimmer and promptly shot him through his pinkies, exhausting all of the ammunition in his six-shooter, before the officer wrestled him to the ground and took him into custody.

So how did Inspector Turnicate deduce that Shmelt was the killer?

Turnicate, who had suffered a head injury years before, and who wasn't even on the force any longer, was wrong. It was clearly Zimmer who had probably cajoled both Lucious *and* Skinner into doing the dirty work while he established his alibi. Rita O'Flinenin may even have been implicated as she was evidently involved with Lucious.

The Smiths were obviously a bickering married couple who made their living as drug mules. All of the signs were there.

The only thing Phillip Shmelt was guilty of was discharging a firearm in a thrift store during business hours. It turns out that he had figured out who the culprit was, and fired while attempting a citizen's arrest once he realized that Turnicate was a moron.

The officer filed his report, acted as a witness for the defense during Shmelt's trial, and made detective in place of Turnicate, who would go on to work as a consultant on *Criminal Minds*.

How do I know so much about this case? Because that officer was me. No, not really. I'm just an informed citizen. I guarantee it.

The Life & Times of Mother Goose

Many are surprised to learn that Mother Goose was not *always* Mother Goose. Of course, as a gosling, she was a baby goose. Later she was known as little girl goose. As a young lady she was a debutante goose. While experimenting on a hitchhiking trip across Southeast Asia, she briefly went by the moniker, silly goose. During her studies in India, researching cobras, she was given the nickname, mongoose. Then, after graduation from Bryn Mawr, she first started to capitalize her surname and went by Ms. Goose. Bucking tradition, she married her first cousin and was then known as Mrs. Goose. And it wasn't until the hatching of her first gosling, Ryan, that she was finally known as Mother Goose. And many of the bedtime stories she told little Ryan came from her own experiences. For instance:

During a holiday to Ireland, she had come upon a public christening of a young princess. Guests of honor included members of the House of Windsor, Bono, the Pope, and the guys from Queer Eye. It was the fairies that bestowed upon the baby special gifts, like an enchanted rattle so that the infant would be able to get an early start on laying down some beats. Also, for dance, she received ballet slippers and a pack of smokes. They donated to a Sally Struthers charity in the baby's name so that she might learn to be kind and self-glorifying in the face of futility. One presented her with Whitney's *I Will Always Love You* on 45 so that she could make others' wedding receptions about her. To confer upon her grace, she received a gift card from Tiffany's. And finally, to keep her eternally beautiful, they gifted her with a Little Tikes JonBenét make-up kit.

However, the straight guy, having refused to abide the advice to stop dying his beard blue, had *not* been invited. And being a very bad person, as are all heterosexual males, he bided his time until the princess was grown so that he could implement his heinous plan for revenge over the affront.

Meanwhile, Mother Goose returned state side and continued to raise her family. One day while watching Walter Cronkite, she saw a story about a young lady who had been stalked by a former Wall Street stockbroker who later conned her and her grandmother into spending the older women's life savings on overvalued securities. Goose recognized the young lady as that baby girl who had been showered with gifts on the day of her christening. She began to follow the story closely as she felt some sort of connection to the child.

She discovered that the girl ended up moving in with him, even though she had concerns over many of the details that this wolf presented to her throughout their business dealings. But, like any good conman, when questioned about certain arrangement he would allay her fears with simple answers that seemed plausible enough. She'd ask about the large percentages on his ARMs, and he'd assure her that she was in good hands. She'd ask if the stocks she was buying had legs, he'd tell her to just run with it. When she expressed concern about whether their eyes were getting too big for their portfolio, he'd convince her to see things his way. But it was when she asked about whether the amendments to a particular contract had any real teeth that he snapped and physically assaulted the young woman. She moved back in with her parents and the villain was sentenced to 36 months in a low-security federal prison.

Not long after that scandal, the princess's father died, leaving her under the roof of her stepmother. (Her parents had divorced years earlier over her mother's shameless carousing with ogres and others of that tendency.) Her stepmother kept her out of the public eye and soon the press lost interest in her story. By this point, Mother Goose was still somewhat obsessed and only abandoned the chronicling of the princess's life after getting caught up in her new hobby of collecting her soon-to-be priceless Beanie Babies.

It was around this time that the Miller family moved in next door to the Gooses. (They chose to keep the original Welsh spelling of the name rather than the Americanized, Geese.) The Millers had seven children – all boys. The oldest, Ricky T. Miller, was a very smart young man but looked like the love child of Steve Buscemi and Kathy Griffin had married the love child of Camilla Parker-Bowles and Joseph Merrick and had a baby that was then beaten by the love child of Stephen King and Divine after getting Linda Hunt's haircut from Lyle Lovett…and then spat on by Shelly Duvall…and kicked by Dennis Rodman.

Their youngest, Tommy T. Miller, who went by the nickname, Thumb, due to his resemblance to Peyton Manning, was also quite bright and was not unpresentable. In fact, he was listed as #3 in *People*'s top 10 sexiest dwarfs in America. (Behind Peter Dinklage and Tom Cruise.) While Thumb became quite prosperous in the telecommunications game – wealthy enough to provide for his parents and employ five of his brothers – the oldest, Ricky, came to be estranged from the family and eventually moved to the UK.

Upon their father's death, and with Ricky having been excluded from the will, his brothers sent him the consolation of his father's cat. Unbeknownst to the rest of the family, the cat could speak, although only in Russian and even then with a peculiar dialect that was familiar only to former Gulag screws. Nevertheless, Ricky understood enough to follow the cat's lead when they were pulling the ole good cop/bad cop routine.

One day, after watching with disgust a couple of dogs near a fire hydrant, the cat had an idea to get his human a leg up. He would bribe a local official with gifts to get Ricky an appointment to some post that's really just a title and, then let the cronyism take its course. Despite the cat's idea of patronage being the proud delivery of dead mice, squirrel tails, socks, and leaves, the plan worked, and Ricky eventually climbed the political ladder all the way up to governor.

When Mother Goose discovered that the young man who had grown up next door had made good, she sold her Beanie Babies (at a significant loss) and started a scrapbook for *him*. She began to correspond with Ricky and, to her shock, he invited her to the Governor's Ball. While there, she met all sorts of interesting people. There were kings and queens, princes and princesses, leaders of industry and celebrities, fairies everywhere, and mountains of cocaine.

Alas, she was unable to congratulate Ricky (now going by the name Tuft, due to his resemblance to Tom Selleck's chest) in person because his attention was focused, the whole night, on a charming young lady. As the night went on Goose realized that this enchanting and monopolizing young woman was the same princess who's life she had been following since infancy. Around midnight, she determined that she would confront the couple and persuade them that they were clearly destined to be together. But as she approached the pair with a somewhat fanatical zeal, Tuft's security detail intercepted her and threw her to the ground. What Mother Goose hadn't understood was that the princess was not enjoying her evening at all with this entitled bush pig, who followed her everywhere while mansplaining *Star Trek*'s superiority to *Star Wars*. With the commotion providing an opportunity, she threw her shoe at the governor and made a break for the exit. Goose, finally getting an audience with Tuft, explained the whole thing and, after an official pardon, timidly took her leave.

On the other hand, Tuft was encouraged after learning of the princess's story and made it his aim to find and wed the beautiful young woman. He combed the countryside trying to identify her and took out full page ads in papers, plastered images of her shoe on billboards, and went on Regis, hoping to obtain leads. This publicity blast drew the attention of the princess's adversary, Blue Beard.

Blue Beard was still unfashionable, but his great wealth provided no shortage of female interest. He had since married several times, all of the unions ending under suspicious circumstances, as his ex-wives were never seen again. Having concluded that this woman was the baby to whose christening he had been snubbed, he sent out his teams of lawyers and private investigators to track her down and sue for emotional distress.

On the first day of the proceedings, the two met outside the courtroom. Blue Beard suggested that they sit down and see if they could work out a settlement – with no lawyers present. The princess reluctantly agreed and the two went for a drink at the Stud Muffin. After ordering, she excused herself to use the powder room, giving Blue Beard ample time to slip some GHB into her drink. Fortunately, one of Tuft's staff was in the booth next to them and saw the whole thing. He ran back (in a kind of swishy way) to the governor's mansion and reported what had happened.

By the time Tuft had made it to the bar, Blue Beard had already led the princess back to his penthouse. Once there he showed her to his bedroom where she, at once, fell into a deep sleep. When Tuft broke through the front door of the apartment, he found Blue Beard maniacally using the princess's credit cards to buy new skin packs and adventure maps in *Minecraft*. Tuft ran him through with a recipe for a golden sword and rushed in to rescue the princess.

Lying on the bed, she was the greatest beauty he had ever seen. He was compelled to give her a single kiss. This caused her to awaken and immediately throw up in her mouth a little bit. But realizing that Tuft had loved her enough to come to her rescue, and understanding that his political kickbacks would keep her living comfortably for the rest of her life, she agreed to marry him. As a wedding gift, he offered her three wishes. It took two of them to get him looking halfway presentable, and with the third she wished for three more wishes, which bankrupted Tuft and forced him to take a job as an assistant woodcutter.

The Gooses' new neighbor, a French writer named Charles Perrault, would hear her tell the stories of princesses and talking animals and stepmothers and made Mother Goose an offer to buy them for a collection of fairy tales he was compiling. With her children almost grown and her new focus now on raising alpacas, she sold the stories to Perrault for several pieces of wadded up Wonder Bread and moved to Oakland. There she began selling her homemade potato chips to the Black Panthers, who affectionately referred to her as *Granny* Goose. And she lived happily ever after.

The Weaker Sex
Opens Pickle Jars

One day, while spending time with the Kahn triplets, the conversation turned to women and the proper way to view them. While Genghis and I thought it best to use binoculars from a safe distance, James felt that looking up from under the open-tread staircase at his apartment building in Malibu was more illuminating. Of course, Chaka's input was quickly dismissed as she began to speak incoherently about respect and suffrage and some such nonsense. The only thing I took away from her contribution was the story of Helen of Troy:

It was said that Helen was the most beautiful woman in all the world…at the time. It should be noted that "the time" was the Bronze Age and, not only were there way fewer women back then but, the hot look that season was to be considered a disfigured version of a man, so it's not out of the question that Helen may have resembled Marty Feldman.

Helen was of aristocratic stock, being the daughter of Zeus, and was a fixture at all the most exclusive society affairs. In addition to her beauty she was renowned for her refinement, sophistication, and ability to burp the alphabet. She was known to really wow the crowd by finishing with a very baritone "Omega."

With her parentage, she was considered the most eligible debutante in Greece. Suitors came from far and wide to seek her hand in marriage with the hope that, if they played their cards right, they'd get the rest of her, too. Her stepfather, King Tyndareus, could not make a decision about whom she should marry because he feared that any jilted princes would declare war on him in retaliation. Finally, he let her decide for herself, and she chose King Menelaus of Sparta, which resulted in retaliation from Prince Paris of Troy.

Although Menelaus was the king, Helen clearly wore the tunic in this house. In very little time she had trained Menelaus to put his dishes in the sink and to make sure his dirty clothes made it into the hamper. She even convinced him to sit down to tinkle. After a while he preferred this method and eventually decreed that all men in the kingdom must sit so as to keep splashing to a minimum.

When it came time for her to produce an heir, she decided that what Sparta needed was a good queen, so she bore him a daughter. Yes, she willed herself into having a girl. And when her husband complained, she abandoned him at little Hermione's tea party, forcing him to make small talk with stuffed animals and Skipper, who was attending on behalf of her mistress, Barbie. After eating and drinking his fill of nothing and putting his daughter to bed, Menelaus came looking for Helen, who was nowhere to be found. She wasn't in her room or in the garden. She hadn't gone to her office or to the racquet club. He called all of her girlfriends, who'd not heard from her, and even called her old boyfriends, who said she had blocked them on Facebook after their divorce. He summoned his chief of security to file a missing person's report and was told that he'd have to wait until she was gone for 48 hours before they could do anything. In the meantime, he contacted his brother-in-law, Agamemnon, who, per standard procedure, declared war on the city of Troy.

Sure enough, Helen had been kidnapped by Paris and, since Trojan law did not recognize a marriage between one Spartan and one demi-god, his plan was to take her back to his kingdom and make her his bride. This garish stunt galvanized all of the other Greeks (except the Athenians, who were still reeling from Sparta's boycott of the minus 143rd Olympiad over juicing accusations) against Troy, and a ten-year siege was set against the city. Helen's face had, indeed, launched a thousand ships.*

* But keep in mind the whole Marty Feldman possibility so we don't know which direction those ships were going.

Over the course of that ten-year war, the advantage switched hands several times. For much of the time it was a stalemate. The Spartans tried different psychological tactics. Radio broadcasts enticed the Trojans to "come on out and try the fresh new taste of Zima." They'd send spies into the city at night to write on restroom walls, "For a good time, call Aphrodite". They even blared *Yanni at Red Rocks*, over loudspeakers, for hours on end.

The Trojans, in turn, dropped leaflets over the camps of the invaders insinuating that the Greeks were going to lose their lives fighting for Sparta all because of some chick. At one point some of the less educated Trojans resorted to guerilla warfare by beating their chests and throwing their own feces at their aggressors, while the Spartans attempted to counter with gas attacks. However, they soon gave up on the strategy when only a handful of Trojans were willing to accept their enemy's invitation to, "Pull my finger."

Finally, Odysseus, a Naval leader and former salt pounder, came up with an idea to trick their foes. They would build a giant statue of an animal that could be left on the front lawn of Troy as they hid inside. When its unsightliness brought down property values, the Trojans would be forced to the bring the effigy inside the gates, and then he and his team would attack.

The idea was brilliant, but which animal should they use? What seemed to be the obvious choice was a kangaroo, since that creature actually had a built-in seating area. But as seatbelts had yet to be invented, the commandos kept getting flung from their positions while the contraption hopped around during beta testing. Another suggestion was a snake since the serpent was associated with Apollo, one of Troy's main deities. Again, the design was scrapped when a larger snake, from the Egyptian army, swallowed it during maneuvers. Then they came up with the idea of a Trojan squid; resulting in a full unit of Greek mariners meeting their end when the vessel was attacked and sunk by Kirk Douglas. After several other catastrophes involving a cow, chicken, pig, and a famished army, it was finally decided to use a horse. With its completion, Odysseus and his men climbed into its belly and waited.

The rest of the Greeks yelled out to the Trojans, "Well OK then! We're gonna take off now!" and then made a stomping noise as if they were leaving, but really ran and hid behind a sofa.

That night a group of Trojan art critics came out to view the horse. They found the object to be superficial and arcane while still maintaining some veneer of raw sexuality and unbridled appetite. They insisted it be brought inside the gates and, once within, they excused themselves for a change of underwear. A feast was prepared both for their victory and their new monument. When all had been dulled by the celebrating, Odysseus and his men emerged from inside the horse and proceeded to eliminate the guards and let the rest of the Spartan and Greek army into the city.

During the rout, Menelaus reached his beloved Helen. Knowing that Paris had been killed earlier in the day, he assumed that his bride would come home to Sparta. But it turned out that she had already gotten remarried and was planning on retiring with her new husband to the Isle of Lesbos. She had heard that everyone was really nice there, and that they had a new fabric there called flannel. Menelaus couldn't bring himself to kill Helen for her betrayal and wished her good luck. He even complimented her on her new faux-hawk cut with the fade. Then he burned the city and took some Trojan women as his slaves.

Genghis' response to this tale was to roll his eyes and slaughter all in a neighboring town. James was somewhat more sympathetic and simply walked away yelling to himself, "I turned down Cuckoo's Nest!"

But I stuck around long enough to hear the explanation. Chaka said that the moral of the story was that this *one* woman had power over countless men to the point of devastating war, and that males should not only recognize who's really in control, but also show those women the respect they deserve. Or at least I think that's what she said. She sure is pretty.

Carl The Knight

Part the First.

How many great knights hath been in the service of the king and how Carl did most sincerely wanteth to become a great knight. Likewise, how Carl doth become a knight, although noteth that great.

Once upon a time* in merry old England (and I think we all know what is meant by merry) there lived a great and benevolent king who was loved by one and all for his greatness and his benevolence and also for his sincere interest in each one of his subjects (although he often screened his calls).

In the service of this king were many knights. Some had great physical strength and could dash a suit of armor to pieces with one blow from their mighty swords. These men also came in handy when someone needed to move a hide-a-bed. Some were very wise and knew exactly which wines to order with which entrées. Still others were very scholarly and served as mentors to the young men of England who would one day become the leaders of tomorrow a long time ago. There were also, of course, the tacticians; men schooled in the art of war and the subtle nuances of leading men from the back of a crowd. And certainly not the least of the noble men were those exceptionally bravest of knights who gladly served their king in taking on the most difficult and dangerous duties - whether it be slaying a dragon, battling with a giant, or reporting to the king on the queen's dropsy.

---

*Although the phrase, "Once Upon A Time" is generally used only in fairy tales, it is here used as the introduction in an attempt to put both the younger readers at ease and to demonstrate to the older readers of the author's crossover potential. Buying a back-up first edition of this publication may not be too bad a financial move.

Most knights had spent years working toward their goal of knighthood. They often served their apprenticeship at meager beginnings as a servant or stable boy. In time, they had learned enough and made a name for themselves so that they might become a squire to another knight. Eventually, they would prove their worth with an act of great chivalry. Usually that opportunity would arrive when all of the other knights took one step backward.

And so it was...and went. And as it was, it went with those who were. And the names of some of these knights were: Sir Donner of Blitzen, known as the Mellow Knight because of the intensity of his disinterest; *Of Sir Donner, The Mellow Knight* Sir Cassius, The Black Knight and self-proclaimed greatest of all time; Sir Dudnick of Durham and Sir Dudnick of Mancs and Sir Dudnick of Cheshire – the Three Dudnicks – one deaf, one blind, and Sir Dudnick of Cheshire, so smitten with acrophobia that he refused to ride his steed except through chest-high water. (And even then he'd hang from the horse's neck.) There was Sir Hedley of Twin Peaks, known for his work ethic and speed habit; Sir Lance a little, the leader of the knights; Sir Vito of the lower east side, Lance a little's right hand man and sometimes known as lefty; Sir Kimsize of Herts, the largest and strongest of the worthies (excluding James, of course). Also Sir Bruce of Bruce and his son, Sir Bruce of Bruce of Bruce (sometimes known as Bruce the Lesser) often confused but never prepared; Sir Flaonce of Essex, the ablest with foil, saber, and lance and a confirmed pacifist. And Sir Wicket of Nethershire, requisite bad guy. And such were those that were. And as they went they were what they would want when they went...as they were.

Now, there was a young man from the county of Notts who came to London to become a great Knight. He had been a long-time subscriber to Chivalry Illustrated and had always known that the pageantry and duty and honor were what he wanted to be a part of. He hadn't the vocabulary to understand such words, but he sure thought the helmets looked cool. As he made his way to the city he dreamt of jousting tournaments and other achievements at arms and ladies-in-waiting and ladies who couldn't wait. On the day of his arrival he met up, almost immediately, with one of the great knights of fame.

"Excuse me, good sir," quoth the young man.

Carl of Notts doth ask for directions from Sir Donner "Being thy humble servant and of such very low condition so as to beg your attention, might I implore of you as to the way of which I may go in order to prove my quality as to knighthood?"

Unto these Sir Donner made reply: "Why are you talking like that? What's your name, boy?"

"Carl, sir. Carl of Notts. Son of a butcher. And who might you be, big fella?"

"You may call me Sir Donner of Blitzen, Knight of the Great Knighthood and keeper of all that has ample resale value. Did you say you wanted to become a knight?"

"That's right, sir. More than anything else in the whole world."

Sir Donner turned and as he began to ride away yelled out, "That is a fine goal, young man. But first you'll need a squire!"

So Sir Donner departed and left Carl alone to contemplate his next move. He'd need a squire, but not one with too much experience. Being the son of a butcher, he'd come to the big city with very little money. And a squire with little more than a passing familiarity with the business was sure to bankrupt him. What he needed was an intern squire. So off he went to the University of London to find a young assistant. Unfortunately, he could find no one who didn't outweigh him by at least fifty pounds. You see, Carl was a slight man and he was now concerned that anyone larger than he might detract from *his* adventures. So off he went to the Royal College of Art, hoping to find a student with barely enough cash to feed himself and little to no interest in anything manly.

After very little time he came upon a man at an outdoor café. The man was sipping tea, scribbling in a notebook, and sucking on a cigarette he held between his thumb and forefinger (knuckles out). Carl sat down across from the man and asked him if he would be interested in a job.

"I've got a job," the man said. "I pick fly droppings out of pepper. The salary and hours are decent, the tips help out *and...*" he said with more than a hint of mischief in his eyes as a healthy young serving wench sauntered by, "the perks are sweet."

Carl leaned in, "I can offer you three quid a week and a back rub every other Thursday."

"Done," the man said as he stretched out his hand. "My name's Ira Stamford but everybody calls me Skinny Dave."

"Nice to meet you, Skinny Dave. I'm Carl of Notts. Now how about fetching me some gruel and a pint of ale."

"Get it yourself, you lazy mule, I'm on a break."

"Whatever you say, Dave. You're the boss." And Carl bounded for the kitchen, elated that he was now on his way to knighthood. Next stop: *Sir* Carl of Notts, the Abashed Knight.

So Carl made haste with his new squire, to the place where all of the great knights of the Great Knighthood used to greatly enjoy assembling nightly. And he stood before these men in awe because never had he been in the company of such strength, bravery, and wisdom (except that summer when he had clerked at the law firm of Strength, Bravery, Wisdom, and Horowitz). As he slowly made his way through the throngs of those who, just as he did, stared in amazement at the regal appearance of the knights, he also took in the beauty of the Great Hall itself.

The walls of the structure were of gilded gold, with silver and pearl features over which hung tapestries from lands both far and near. Interspersed along these, at regular intervals, were giant pilasters of solid oak, fifty feet high. The

Carl beholdeth the Great Hall. Likewise it's make up and ambience

ceiling too was decorated with many precious stones, and from it dangled ornate lanterns of colored glass. The main room of the lodge seemed to be at least three hundred feet long and one hundred feet wide, but it turned out that Carl had horrible depth perception and the actual dimensions were 15'x22'. Off of the main room were many little rooms, which contained even smaller rooms. Inside each of these there was nothing but a single door that led to a very large auditorium in back where the knights used to shoot dice. At the moment, workers were scurrying to ready

The Black Knight enters and doth indeed ease nature. Likewise he regales the many with tales of glory and butt woopin'

the center table for the evening's feast as the knights stood looking on, arms crossed, tapping their maille boots in anxious anticipation.

Finally the table was of sufficient strength to handle the task for which it was enlisted and the meal was delivered. All sat and began to eat

and drink while Carl stood back in the shadows and observed. By and by all had arrived for the feast save he that was but the greatest among them, the Black Knight. And as it continued, finally, Sir Cassius arrived and with great purpose, for he really needed to pee. And at once as soon as it was that the Black Knight was able to relieve himself, he returned and related to all the details of his great adventures.

One of the stories told of a great battle of which he was able to insert himself and fight along with other men of glory against a king and his minions from across the sea. While all of his ilk fought bravely and with much skill, most did not survive the conflict because of the vastness of the opposing army and the lack of a balanced breakfast that morning. In fact, one warrior in their opposition was so mighty that more than half of those that fell, fell by his sword alone. Indeed, Sir Cassius himself barely escaped with his life and limb intact were it not for a note from his doctor stating that he had flat feet. He further went on to describe this man as a giant, being 5'-3" and from the land of the Mongols. As the few surviving men retreated they could hear his taunts stating that he "would soon return to replace the scarlet dyed silk of England with some really funky sheep skin."

The crowd in the Great Hall fell silent. Even the knights were at a loss as to what to do. Then Lance a Little, the one taking the lead, proposed that they send out a representative to barter with the great warrior. But who would go? The noble credentials of each made it so that any was certainly capable of sparring with the fiend should the need arise, but it was Sir Hedley who accidentally made eye contact.

"Hedley!" shouted Lance a Little. "You shall be the one who will acquire for himself the glory of sending this man away or striking him down should he refuse reasonableness."

Sir Hedley stood and addressed the assembly, "I shall go. And I shall succeed in sending this man away from among our borders. But I think you all should be reminded that the pharmacy, of which I am the sole proprietor, is the only one in the entire city open on Sundays. And if anything should happen to me, those of you who just gotta have your leeches will be on your own."

Lance a Little assays to send out a brave knight but performeth an act of clumsitude At this Sir Vito leaned over to Lance a Little and suggested that they send a less indispensable member of the community and bid Hedley go along as more or less of a consultant. This idea pleased Lance a Little so much so that he did a little dance and, by doing so, knocked over the chalice of wine on the table beside him. This spill quickly spread out over the floor in great area, as this was a particularly large chalice, and began to be absorbed into the hems of some of the ladies' dresses. These women started to panic for fear of staining and were running in all directions. One of the women collided with an archer who, at that very moment, was demonstrating to a friend how well his new arrows looked when completely drawn back in his bow. Of course, the surprise of the blow caused him to lose his grip and send the arrow screaming through the hall until it pinned the lute player to the wall by his sleeve. Although he tried to keep playing, the handicap had a noticeable effect on the music and soon the crowd went into a frenzied rage over the lack of live entertainment. A brawl ensued, and before it was over most of the guests and many of the knights lay unconscious on the floor. Those remaining made a hurried attempt to tidy up the place before the king saw it, but quickly fell ill when someone mixed cleanser with glass cleaner. By the time the king had arrived, the only person left standing was Carl, who had been protected from the previous tragedies by shrewdly hiding under a barmaid.

"What happened here, boy?" asked the king. "Did Lance a Little do another one of those destructive dances?"

"I'm afraid so," said Carl. But then, due to an irrational sense of guilt over everything, corrected himself. "Actually, sire, this whole scene is my fault. You see, I have this condition..."

The King interrupted him, "I do well know that you are not to blame for this situation. And yet you would take into your bosom my wrath for its unfolding for the sake of your fellow revelers. Even though it would probably mean a sentence of execution."

"Execution?" Carl was taken aback by that. "Actually, I was just trying to have a little fun with you. In reality, I showed up right before you did. I don't know what happened. But I bet it was that big guy over in the corner. Yep, I'm sure it was him. Look at that guy. That clean-shaven face and that crown of rubies... He's your man."

"My son knows better than to start something like this," the King said. "Besides, I am very well aware of how this came about. You have nothing to fear. However, your willingness to take the blame for someone else and then your artful backtracking from the responsibility doth show me something. Go to the warrior who is outside the city and dispatch him from here, and you are sure to be knighted."

And so Carl of Notts, accompanied by Skinny Dave his squire and Sir Hedley of Twin Peaks, set off for the region that is south of the city in order to confront the giant. Along the way they set forth on none too many adventures, except those that entail the panicked search for lost toilet paper and several arguments with Skinny Dave about the proper maintenance of one's codpiece.

When, at last, they came to the place where the warrior giant was encamped, Carl took it upon himself to enter in among those that were encamped there and walked right up to the mighty one himself. The giant, standing imposingly, looked up at Carl and demanded an accounting for why one would be so bold as to enter right in among the encampment. Carl drew his sword (slowly, for the entire army of his foe had already drawn *their* swords and, in some instances, had begun poking him in his tummy) and offered it to the man as a gift. "I am Carl of Notts, and I would appreciate it a great deal if you could take your buddies and return to your home," he said.

Carl cometh to the giant

The giant spake: "How is it that, first you walk right in among my encampment and then you demand that I leave this land without so much as a souvenir shot glass? I don't think I'm ready to leave yet. But I'll tell you what I'll do. I'm gonna count to ooch, and if you're not out of my sight by then, I'm going to let my men pass you around like a big pasty roach."

At this, Carl moved closer to the ear of the man and whispered that he had something very important to tell him, but it would be best if kept between the two. So Carl and the giant began to stroll along the outskirts of the encampment until they arrived at a secluded place and Carl once again asked him to leave. When the giant became enraged

Carl doth deal well with the giant and is rewarded greatly but only very well after taxes

at Carl bringing him to this secluded place with no intention of a bribe or at least a tip for Epsom Downs, he started back to find his men. But Carl quickly kneed him in the crotch and gave him a wedgie. The truth was that there would be no men to give him help anyway because Sir Hedley had already slain most, and the rest he sent on a scavenger hunt.

When the three returned, the King and the rest of the Great Knights and all the people greeted them. And after telling of their adventure, they were rewarded with much glory and wealth, which Skinny Dave promptly absconded with to start an antique furniture business. But Carl was not concerned with money. His interest was only in becoming a knight. And on the next day, after his return, he was knighted Sir Carl of Notts, the Kicking Knight.

Thus Carl achieved the adventure of becoming a knight. And at some time later he would be known with the other Great Knights of The Great Knighthood, for though this entire story chiefly concerneth Sir Carl, yet the glory and fame of these knights is his glory and was their glory and will be the glory of those for whom it is their glory as well as his. For one cannot tell of the glory of Carl without not also not telling of the glory of those Great Knights of The Great Knighthood afore. (Unless you leave that part out, I suppose.) Therefore, let grace be given unto you all that ye too may likewise succeed in your undertakings as long as you're not undertaking my stuff. Amen.

Part the Second

Here begineth the story of certain adventures of Carl after that he had become a knight, wherein it is told of how it was very hard for him to fiteth in. And how many times he didn't get it. And how, but for the insults and hurtful schemes of Skinny Dave, did battle, that he might achieve that an approved position. Likewise, how Sir Wicket did behold that he was a fierce and bitter knight and that he doth know it all. So, if it please you to read this tale, I believe it will afford unto you much excellent pleasantness for it hath given me much excellent pleasantness to write these things for you that my heart would be filled with much excellent pleasantness and excellence. So I pray you to read and listen to what follows and get back to me because I've lost interest.

Camel Clyde

Or

A Dromedary of a Certain Hump

He had spent many years traveling the world and he spent many years learning. Now he was occupying his retirement with reading and watching television and eating and sleeping and forgetting and drooling. But he was still learning and found that, of all discoveries, he was not a hero but rather, what the locals called him: supple, which was the worst kind of softness for a camel of his pedigree.

Clyde had made his home in Whitehall on Stronsay in the Orkney Islands after his intrepid days were done. He had taken up the trade of kelp-burning, which provided both a meager living, as well as a satiating of his urges for arson. Unfortunately, times had been hard for Clyde the last few years as the burnt kelp industry in Scotland had disappeared nearly 100 years earlier. Each day he'd go out to the tide pools and cast his nets. And each day, he'd forget to attach a hand line and the nets would sink to the bottom of the sea. And each day he'd walk back into town to purchase new nets. And each day he'd remember that he didn't need nets to scoop up seaweed.

Children would come to visit him from time to time. They'd ply him with Shirley Temples and extract from him the tales of his adventures in various Ottoman military jazz bands, his time in the CIA (Camel Iditarod Auxiliary), and his service to a foolhardy sheik, among other fantasies he pilfered from his collection of survival guides. He'd take a sip (up to 20 gallons) and invariably begin by telling the kids about the day he fought a polar bear.

As a young camel he had gone to the Klondike to seek his fortune. Desperate to earn respect from the other prospectors, Clyde took a bet to prove his worth. He was to drink a barrel of whiskey, shoot a polar bear, and romance an Eskimo woman. He made short work of his first hurdle, the whiskey, and then stumbled out into the overture of an oncoming snowstorm. Few expected to ever see him again. Several hours later, he stumbled in through the doors of a Dawson City saloon, bloodied, hair matted or missing, his body strewn with long deep gashes. He stood exhausted, but gratified. He lifted his head, and with a smirk shouted, "Now where's that Eskimo woman you want me to kill?!?"

One youngster in particular was especially fond of Clyde and would listen to his stories with rapt attention until he'd hear his father's bellowing for him to come in and set the table.

"I will come back after dinner, Clyde," the boy would assure him. "I'll bring dessert and you can tell me more about the Geishas of Poland." The boy was always a little confused.

"You do that, Les Paul." Clyde would answer. "I sure could go for some Key lime pie."

The boy would never come back with Key lime pie because his parents detested pastels and conch-style architecture. Still, Clyde would often lie awake and wait for the boy to bring it to him. He'd reminisce to himself about his fresher years and smoke a few Turkish gold humans, and drift off to sleep.

That night Clyde had one of his usual nightmares. In this instance, he found himself back in his younger days, as a ranch hand, except now he was lining up *with* the cattle, waiting for *his* turn in the slaughter shoot. He tried to flee, but his limbs struggled as if he were stuck in sand. Nor could he bring his voice to call for help. He finally jolted himself into consciousness just as Temple Grandin tried to give him a hug. Panting, he took a deep breath and attempted to ease himself back into repose, but through the single window of his modest-to-the-point-of-demure cottage, he could see the cool grey clouds rolling in from the North Sea. The sight roused him to his feet. It was time to start his day.

Clyde was brushing his teeth when the boy appeared in his doorway. "I found a maraschino cherry, Clyde."

"That's good," replied Clyde as he spit (not because he was brushing, but just because he liked to…he *was* a camel after all). As had been their custom, neither mentioned the Key lime pie from the previous evening. "I've heard rumors about a shipment of grenadine from Mulberry. Then all we'll need is some 7Up and we'll be set."

"Do you have time to tell me a story, Clyde?'

"Aren't you late for school?"

"No sir," retorted the boy. "In fact, I got up early enough to finish both my morning chores as well as my afternoon chores and I still have plenty of time before class." This was a lie. The boy had indeed gotten up early, but it was to watch cartoons and raid his father's liquor cabinet. The kid was a lush and Clyde knew it.

"Well then, after school you can come by and I'll tell you the story of my time in Nixon's cabinet (an anecdote about playing hide-and-seek with John Ehrlichman). For now, it's time for my constitutional."

"OK. I'll be back after school," the boy said as he got up to leave. He stopped at the front door and looked back… "And Clyde! Don't fall in!"

Clyde's phone was dead and the Sudoku book had long been finished. He took to reading shampoo bottles. While noting the aluminum phosphate contained in his dandruff shampoo, he was reminded of *his* role in the serum run to Nome.

A diphtheria outbreak had threatened the previously unexposed children of Nome, Alaska. The town's stores of antitoxin serum was limited and past its expiration date. The only way to get the medicine through during this harshest winter in 20 years was by dog sled. Twenty men and their teams braved temperatures as low as -85°F, with both man and beast suffering frostbite, hypothermia, and worse. The snow was so icy that it slashed at the Husky's paws and, on several occasions, gale winds blew the sleds over, or through the ice. At one point, the serum was almost lost when one of the sleds crashed. The musher froze his hands trying to find the medicine in the snow. Finally, the serum was delivered in Nome, where Clyde had been quarantined as patient zero.

Around midday Clyde was taking a break on the pebbly beach and staring up at the clouds. The white puffs evoked in him memories of the tall snowdrifts that he encountered during *his* time pulling a sled. It had been not long after leaving Nome and he was hiking in whiteout conditions. The snow was so thick that he had wandered right into the middle of a camp of another musher. The man was older and heavy-set, with a full white beard. The conditions had been such that he had abandoned traveling with dogs and instead used reindeer to pull his sleigh. Clyde was enlisted to front the group, since the former lead deer had become fixated on a red light just in front of him and chased off after it into the blizzard. Or so it was explained at the time. Later, Director Kringle changed his story and told Clyde that the deer had dislocated his hip during a twist contest and was laid up for the foreseeable future. Clyde found the other reindeer hesitant to corroborate any of the boss' stories and he later overheard them talking about that same lead deer being on a stake-out at Macaulay Culkin's house; the young actor's file would ultimately be stamped, *CONFIDENTIAL – NAUGHTY.*

Clyde awoke, still on the beach, around dusk. He had drifted off some time ago and his daydreaming had turned to actual REM memories (like their *Aftermath* pre-release concert from St. James church). As he sat up and pulled the mosaic of embedded stones from his thick hide, he shook his head to clear the residual images that lingered from his nap. He had dreamt it before. A camel, taking his place with a crowd of reindeer and going nowhere. Again, unable to move or cry out. Stuck at the front of the line of angry and antlered CIA agents.

He arrived back in town, malady rich and seaweed poor, in time for the alternating looks of pity and disgust from the Whitehall drinking class. He made his way to the fish mart and acquired a single herring, on credit, and made his way back, through the lively Friday night crowds, to his cottage.

Not long after Clyde had left, the boy came into the fish mart. He purchased some river smelt and tartar sauce and dutifully paid Clyde's daily tab, then made his way up the street to his friend's house. After the smelt party at Lachlan's, he found Clyde at home, curled up in front of a fire. The old camel had fallen asleep while smoking. The boy extinguished the blaze just before it reached the wet bar, thereby avoiding *two* tragedies.

"Wake up, Clyde. It's time for my story."

Clyde, slightly stunned by the abruptness of the boy's call, answered somewhat clumsily, "You were supposed to come by after school."

"I *did* come by after school, but you weren't here. I checked the Tequila drawer and there was no sign of you, so I went home. You weren't in my parents' wine cellar either. Where have you been?"

"You have many questions, Les Paul. And you can be quite impatient," Clyde admonished as he stirred himself to attention. "Come. Bring me some cash and I'll tell you that story."

The boy reached into his overalls and pulled out his money clip. "You're in luck, Clyde. I saw my bookie today." He peeled off a few twenties, stuffed them into Clyde's shirt pocket, and gave him an endearing slap on the cheek. "Buy yourself something nice."

Clyde's time with the Agency had taken him to far off exotic places, like Detroit. As part of an operation investigating Barry Gordy's involvement in a plot to poison Nipper, the RCA dog, he had gone undercover as an aged Mississippi blues man. His hump was explained away as a goiter, which gave him credibility among the old timers. Unable to make any headway at Motown, the focus was switched to getting a deal at Atlantic. Jerry Wexler approached him about forming a doo-wop group. When Clyde arrived at the studio with several barbers associated with the Genovese crime family, his cover was blown and he was reassigned to Istanbul. After some time, he took a job with Halliburton as a military band contractor and delighted the Sultan by replacing the traditional zurna horn, played after evening prayer, with the harmonica – hastening the Ottoman empire's fall.

"I have never heard that one," the boy chimed. "What happened after that?"

"That will be for the next time, Les Paul. For now it's time to get some rest."

"I know!" the boy cried excitedly. "Tomorrow is Saturday and I have no schoolwork or chores. I can come with you to the beach and help collect seaweed while you tell me more."

"That sounds like a fine idea," smiled Clyde. "And we can pack a lunch and you can bring some of your mother's Key lime pie. Won't that be a fine time. Now get home and I will see you bright and early."

"Goodnight then Clyde," affirmed the boy. "Don't go dying on me." He slammed the front door as he left, as all young boys do because they are stupid.

Clyde didn't bother to get ready for bed. He just rolled over and gently closed his eyes and began to dream of his years as a musician. His time in the Animals, and with the Beastie Boys, and the Ruminants. These formed the backdrop of one of the happiest periods in his life and now, in rest, he could recapture some of his favorite episodes. Especially salient was his collaboration with the Poindexter brothers on the R&B hit, *Thin Line Between Love & Hate*. A smile formed on his dozing face as the rest of his unconscious body twitched and kicked. It was a good night.

The next morning the boy was at the door before sunrise. Outfitted in his best beach-combing garb, he was eager to get started, even if a little hung over. Clyde too was up and about after his first good night's sleep in memory. They started with a breakfast of Lorne sausage, Cumberland sausage, blood sausage, and back bacon. To wash it down, they enjoyed some oatmeal and made out for the coast.

The boy bounced about and talked along the entire route.

"Remember? Remember, Clyde, that time I came with you and we found a human skull?"

"It was a crewman's scull...an oar, and yes I remember."

"No, no, no, Clyde. You said you found the oar on Craigslist missed connections."

Clyde glanced down at the boy out of the corner of his eye and glowered. "Pay no mind to such things, Les Paul. We have work to do. And a young man should be serious about his business."

The boy, screwing the lid back on his flask, begged for pardon.

"Forgive me. I'm just so excited to be with you again at the seaside. I'm sure today will prove to be a fortunate one."

"Let us hope so. Now hand me those nets."

"But, Clyde, we have no nets."

"Cripes!"

The morning was uneventful and the two friends sat down for lunch. The boy immediately began to stump for a story. "I'm ready now. Please. Tell me about your time in the middle East. Tell me about Harrisburg."

"I'll tell you about my consignment as the mount for an adventurous Sheik named Ahab."

It must be remembered that, at the time Clyde first signed his record deal, he was as impoverished a camel as he was unschooled. His only real representation was a dancing monkey who'd befriended him at an open mic poetry slam in Thrace. For several years, the monkey claimed to be his manager and took a full 40% of everything that Clyde earned. During negotiations, things got heated and the monkey took to throwing feces and stomped out. Clyde, a functional illiterate, signed the document as it was put to him and would later suffer the consequences.

Around the time that Clyde was hitchhiking around Asia Minor, a moneyed sheik had purchased the entire Atco catalog of music from Atlantic's parent company, Warner Bros. When his CD player broke, Ahab exercised a clause in Clyde's contract that he be at the ready with a song any time the sheik pleased. Clyde was, effectively, the camel of the Sheik of the Burning Sands.

Ahab was young and brash and was quite exacting. He demanded only the best and in Clyde he found the swiftest, bravest, and most clever camel in all of Arabia. For some time, the two traveled together and forged a powerful bond, a bond unbreakable but certainly acquiescent to a feminine third party.

Ahab met Fatima of the Seven Veils at a cocktail party cohosted by the Sultan and Elton John. She performed her renowned traditional oriental dance of the love handles and Ahab immediately found himself in deep smit. That night, after her performance, he approached her in her tent and offered her gifts of chocolates, jewelry, clothing, and tickets to the Grand Ole Opry. Fatima returned his interest, but explained that the Sultan was violently jealous and would never allow her to attend the Opry with another man. The two parted with a kiss, and Ahab told her that he'd be back and they would find a way to run away together.

For many nights Clyde would ferry Ahab through the desert to see Fatima. Their trip to Nashville was forgotten, but Ahab's desire to deliver Fatima from the Sultan's harem only grew deeper. He planned to challenge the Sultan's fastest camel to a race for her hand, but on the night before he was to make the challenge, the Sultan caught the two dancing in Fatima's tent. In a rage, he went after Ahab with a scimitar. Ahab was able to avoid the blade and get both himself and Fatima onto Clyde. The whole of the Sultan's cavalry went after the three, but, as Ahab had anticipated, none were in Clyde's league. With little effort Clyde was able to put enough distance between himself and his pursuers that the party reached India by the next morning, where Ahab and his love rented a darling loft in downtown Mumbai overlooking the harbor. Clyde stayed on with Ahab for a few seasons more and eventually their once master/worker affiliation had developed into more of a golf buddy/caddy-when-the-suits-showed up relationship. Not long after Fatima's chain of fitness studios (*Fatima to Fit*) took off, Clyde was again on to his next adventure.

As the years went by Clyde could feel the winds of change in both society *and* himself. He knew that he would have to adapt. No longer was he known for his speed; a schedule II stimulant. He now exploited his CIA connections with China to make a name for himself as the local ginkgo biloba guy. Even *that* enterprise would be undermined by pomegranate juice and, later, açaí cleanses and, even *later*, Greek yogurt. It was about this time that he heard about the kelp-burning industry and made his way North. It was also about this period that his nights were often cluttered with dreams of waiting for bread behind the Iron Curtain or standing for hours in the hot sun at Disney World. He didn't interpret these images as good or bad. Just adiaphorous, which was the first word he learned in Scotland. It meant Sunday.

The sun was beginning to make its way toward the horizon and Clyde was ready to retire for the day. But the boy had been busy. Excited by Clyde's tales, he had been scooping up seaweed with the zeal of a steampunk enthusiast at a corset sale. Suddenly, the boy came upon an otter covered in oil.

"Clyde! Look what I have found!"

Clyde examined the animal closely. Then his eyes followed the slick along the shoreline. "It seems you've discovered oil, Les Paul. That is very good. Not only will you and I be comfortable from now on, but the whole town will be able to prosper with this finding. Come, let us go back to town and celebrate with a Shirley Temple."

"Can I get two cherries with mine?" the boy probed eagerly.

"You can have three, if you wish. Maybe even four…if your parents approve."

The two walked down the main street between the piers, the boy carrying the otter as proof of their newly acquired fortune. People ran out from the hotel pub to examine the evidence. A general gaiety broke out amongst the citizenry, all with visions of their little town in the national spotlight. Visitors, and business ventures, and conventions, and C-list celebrities taking holiday in their hamlet. The festivities went late into the evening, even after the revelation that the oil originated with a spill from a drilling platform off the coast of Norway.

Clyde and the boy had enjoyed their Shirley Temples and made their way back to his cottage.

"It was a good day, wasn't it, Clyde?" asked the boy.

"Yes, Les Paul. You did very well. Perhaps your discovery will bring back the kelp-burning industry or even herring fishing. Who knows, if things go well, maybe I will buy an automobile."

"That would be fine," agreed the boy. "Maybe tomorrow we can go to the DMV and renew your driver's license to prepare for your new vehicle."

"Yes," responded Clyde as he climbed into his bed. "For now, you go back into town and enjoy the celebration. And tomorrow we will go to the DMV." He then pulled an old quilt over his hump, turned over, and drifted off to sleep. Whispering to himself, "DMV. Tomorrow we will go to the DMV."

The boy went back into town and joined the merriment. People bought each other drinks and reminisced. They related memories and, in a few cases, passed around some Polaroids. If only for that night, the small town on the island was blissful.

Up the road, in his cottage, was the camel, Clyde. He was dreaming of lines.

Acknowledgments

First, I'd like to acknowledge that the earth *is*, indeed, round. I've spent quite a bit of bathroom time doing research, and I'm afraid that, on this subject, Tila Tequila and I must agree to disagree.

Thank you to the following outstanding comics for their endorsements: Greg Fitzsimmons, Bobby Slayton, Alonzo Bodden, and Dave West. It's a real honor – like being shot by a shamed family member.

Most importantly, I must acknowledge two hilarious writers:
> **Jack Douglas** is my favorite author and this entire book was inspired by *Never Trust a Naked Bus Driver*, the first book of his that I ever read. In fact, several jokes should really be attributed to him since I stole them. Many of his jokes are reworked in *But is Sasquatch Bilingual?* which is a play on **Woody Allen**'s, *But Can the Steam Engine Do This?* Allen's Style has also had a huge influence on me. Practically all of the stories in sections 2 & 3 had their instigation in his short stories.

Other than Allen and Douglas, there have been three individuals who had the greatest impact on the completion of this book:
- My editor, Kathryn Taylor
- Cover illustrator, Matt Neathery
- Proof reading by Marsha Ziff

Hire these people. But watch your back. I think they carry knives.

Thanks to Peter Feliciano and Coco Bear, Drama Mama and Pete's mom, and Peter Finch. And thank you to three of my oldest friends who encouraged me to write ridiculous stories instead of pay attention in Geometry: Jason Cook, Mike Cline, and Jodi McGrady-Jones. None of you should feel bad for abandoning me.

To the people who took the time to read my work, and give constructive criticism, Melinda Dahl, Rachel & Andrew Hupp, Chadwick Habbersnatch, Randy Von Feldt, Chris Tabish, and Jenny Saldaña. You are all dead to me.

Thank you to my two wonderful sons whom I am very proud of. (Names omitted) And, of course, I'd like to thank my wife, but it's kind of hard when she refuses to reassure me that my death is not imminent.

About the Author

The author is about six foot, three inches tall.
The author is about to have a heart attack due to his refusal to chew between mozzarella sticks.
The author has about had it with people who
give you the bills *before* they give you the change.
The author is all about the base.

The author's grandpa was born in Ancona, Italy and immigrated to the US during the pasta famine of 1927. He settled, at first, in Philadelphia and then, San Francisco.
He was nicknamed "Reds" because of his fondness for banned candy.
As a little boy, SK would sit on his grandpa's lap, behind the wheel of the "machine" (Italian for 1970 Ford Maverick), and Reds would let him steer until they hit a gypsy.
Reds was a good man, a loving husband, a doting father and grandfather, a generous and hospitable host, and he ran his crew with an iron fist.
Learn more about Reds in SK's next book,
Great Grandpa's Sardines.